MERCAT CROSS
AND TOLBOOTH

MERCAT CROSS AND TOLBOOTH

Understanding Scotland's old burghs

CRAIG MAIR

JOHN DONALD PUBLISHERS LTD
EDINBURGH

For George

ISBN 0 85976 196 7

The publisher acknowledges subsidy from the Scottish Arts Council towards the publication of this volume.

Photoset by Pioneer Associates (Graphic) Ltd., Perthshire. Printed in Great Britain by Bell & Bain Ltd., Glasgow.

Preface

This is a book for general readers, so there are no footnotes or references which might distract from the text. Nevertheless, I must acknowledge the use of Professor G. S. Pryde's excellent book *The burghs of Scotland: a critical list* (revised by Professor A. A. M. Duncan) in compiling the lists for Appendix 2. Extracts from burgh records have also been sufficiently anglicised to make them more easily understood, though I do regret that in doing so, some of their wonderful flavour has undoubtedly been lost.

Inevitably, in a work of this variety, I owe much to the knowledge and expert advice of others. First I must thank Central Region archivist George Dixon for his exceptional help and for the use of his own copies of the Elgin, Banff and Nairn burgh records. Thanks also to Chris Walker, librarian at Wallace High School, Stirling, who allowed me to carry off an excessive number of reference books, and to Virginia Wills from whom I obtained the Stirling, Lanark, Ayr and Peebles records at a bargain price. I am also grateful to Craig Smith and Andrew Jennings for the use of their Honours dissertations on the development of Perth and Stirling respectively, and to Geoff Stell for a copy of his paper on tolbooths. Further, thanks to Bill Wolsey and Betty Wilsher for their help and advice on gravestones, and to the Kincardine Local History Group to whom I gave the original slide talk which is now this book.

As must be obvious from the use of borrowed photographs, I am very grateful to several museum authorities around Scotland. Many, such as those at Elgin, Aberdeen, Huntly, Dumbarton, Irvine, Selkirk, Hawick, Dumfries, Kirkcudbright, Forfar and Brechin have helped with information or have allowed me to stay on after closing time. I particularly thank the curator at Inverkeithing and the staff at Stirling and Montrose. If this book encourages more people to visit local burgh museums, then I will be well satisfied.

Finally, sincere thanks to Lynda Walton for the beautiful illustrations and to John McKinlay who drew the maps. May their pens and talents never run dry.

Craig Mair

Contents

Preface		v
Introduction		1
1	The Beginnings of Burghs	5
2	A Typical Burgh in 1650: the Street Layout	29
3	A Typical Burgh in 1650: the Main Features	45
4	The Social Classes in a Burgh	69
5	Town Councils	82
6	Burgh Courts and Punishments	95.
7	Merchants, Shops and Markets	104
8	Crafts and Trades	126
9	Burghs and the Reformation	136
10	The Kirk's Role in Burgh Life	144
11	Military Matters	156
12	Housing in Burghs	169
13	Public Health	193
14	Games and Recreation	201
15	Recognising Newer Towns	209
Appendix 1: Is your town here? A list of burghs and dates		218
Appendix 2: Reference tables: coinage, weights, liquid measures, grain measures, measures of length, kings and queens		221
Appendix 3: How to find out more		224
Index		227

Introduction

Today, more than ever before, interest is growing in local history and the roots from which we have grown. Local history groups are springing up in many towns, preserving and often discovering many features of past life, from buildings and graveyards to the re-enactment of ancient ceremonies or traditions; this book itself began originally as a slide lecture to the members of one such local group, for all over Scotland there seem to be people eager to know more of their local area's background. Guidebooks to historical walks through Scotland's older burghs have also become increasingly popular, and many are linked to a growing number of useful information plaques now to be found in many places. Heritage centres have similarly been opened in many towns and offer a wide variety of ways to understand the past, from a wealth of books and leaflets to slide shows and exhibitions. Local museums are also enjoying a happy growth in popularity; more and more seem to appear every year, and are much used by hordes of earnest youngsters armed with worksheets and pencils. Even archive centres are now being used more than ever, as people search out the histories of their houses or clubs or schools, or pore over old newspapers and maps.

19th and 20th century history is relatively easy to find out about. Photographs and documents abound, and objects from the past can often still be found in granny's attic. This is a period within living memory for some, and certainly well within the period of accessible, easily read, records. Those who set out on that interesting journey down the family tree usually find little difficulty in tracing their ancestors back to around 1830, perhaps even earlier — but then it gets harder as the records become thinner and surviving evidence grows more vague. There are fewer older buildings, even farms or churches, to tie in with other details. There are no birth certificates any more, and even records or marriage or death may be difficult to find. There are no photographs of people or places, few records of what people looked like or said or did, few maps even of exactly where people once lived.

This book tries to paint in the picture of burgh life in that more

1

vague period before the industrial revolution. It covers the 17th century, from the Union of the Crowns in 1603 when Scotland's King James VI also became king of England, to the Union of the Parliaments in 1707 when the two separate countries were finally joined together as Great Britain. Occasionally it wanders back a little further into the 16th century, or ventures forward to around 1730, but only to include an interesting story or example of burgh life. The idea is to show that this earlier period of history need not be so vague. There is much to discover — and it's quite painless!

Most Scottish towns with a history going back to before the industrial revolution still have surviving signs of that early past. There may still be a 'mercat croce' standing in the town centre, or a 'tolbuith' perhaps now called the town hall or district council offices, or converted now to an information office or local museum. Possibly there is still an 'auld brig', even if it has been much changed over the years, and there will very likely be an old kirk, even if it now stands lost among modern shops and its steeple no longer dominates the skyline as it once did.

But if your old burgh has none of these more obvious pointers to its history, don't worry yet! There may still be little cottages, perhaps with pan-tiled roofs or crow-stepped gables, and even one or two larger 'town houses', with the stone-carved coats of arms of their former owners perhaps sculpted into a lintel or above an ornate doorway at the foot of some spiral stair tower. On the other hand there may be an old graveyard, perhaps vandalised or neglected, but with the 17th century carved headstones of traders and craftsmen from the past — fascinating evidence to help paint a picture of the people who once lived and worked in your town before the days of industry and big business.

And even if none of these things survive either, still don't despair! There may yet be 17th century life all around you, even in a town seemingly full of nothing more than modern shops or Victorian tenements. The very layout of the streets may be original. The closes and vennels, with names like Baxter's Wynd or Gallowhill, can still tell a lot about your old town, now apparently gone. For it's *not* all gone — it's all around you, if you just know how to look.

Some old burghs such as Stirling or Edinburgh, or smaller places like Crail or Culross, still retain enough very obvious evidence of their 17th century appearance to give anyone with some imagination a fair idea of how they used to look. But most towns are not so lucky; they have only a scattering of old remains and it is more difficult to visualise how they must once have been. Because the signs are more scattered and less obvious, most people tend to look but see only what's there now, not what used to be there. And yet it is not so difficult.

Most 17th century Scottish towns were fairly similar in layout and appearance and a general 'photofit' description tends to match most old burghs. Your town may no longer have a town wall, for example, but in this book you find details of what it used to look like and a photograph of the one at Stirling. There are also details of burgh gates and a photograph of the only surviving example, at St. Andrews. You may never have seen the public stocks in a burgh, but here you'll find several examples including those in the main street at Crieff. And if vandals have smashed the old carved stones in your local kirkyard, or they have weathered away like a bar of soap, don't worry — there are others elsewhere which still look sharp. In fact, somewhere in this book you'll find surviving examples of almost every aspect of old burghs you can think of, for they still exist *somewhere*!

And what of the folk who once lived in your town? Buildings or town walls may survive but surely the people have all gone — wrong again! Who were the men with strange occupations like cordiner or webster? Who were the town councillors, the thieves, shopkeepers, town guards, packmen or poachers, maltsters or ministers? They're all in here! Or perhaps you wonder, did they play football or golf in those days? Did pubs have closing hours? Was there cheating in the market place? How were people punished? Who cleaned the streets, or ran the postal service, or checked the town's weights and measures? How long could people expect to live? What happened to the girl with an illegitimate baby, or the beggar found wandering the streets? What sort of rates did people pay in those days? What did they teach in the school? You'll find them all in this book.

How do we *know* about the people? After all, they're dead and gone now. Fortunately most burgh records still survive today — that means the town council minutes, the law court proceedings, the burgh accounts, the kirk session records — the charters and documents of three hundred years ago, still bursting at the seams with ordinary life. Like George Wilson who, in 1662, 'for stealing some bridles and stirrups, is ordained to be publictlie scurgit (whipped) throue the haill streittis' of Banff, and then was banished from the town, to be 'hangit without mercie' if he ever returned. Or the six unfortunate women who were burnt as witches at Paisley in 1697. Or the tailor who was ordered by Edinburgh's burgh council in 1659 to remove the billiard table at his house because too many students were going there instead of studying.

So if you live in a town with only a few remains of its history, read on! Use this as a guide to its past and its people, and discover more on your doorstep than you realised. Or if you enjoy visiting Scotland's historic places but wish you could imagine better how they once looked, keep this reference handy in the car. There's no need for you to worry about scribbly, dusty old records, or know much about architecture, or even the history of 17th century Scotland — it's all been done for you. All you need is this book, some imagination, and a curiosity for living history. Then you're on your own!

CHAPTER 1

The Beginnings of Burghs

What is, or was, a burgh? A town, certainly, but in Scotland not just any town. It was a place with privileges, mostly for trade, and a particular form of government generally granted by the king. It was a place with the right to have gates and walls, and in the High Street, a mercat cross and tolbooth. It was often small, often with a population of less than a thousand, but it was a special place, and proud of it.

Many communities which today would be called towns never gained recognition as a burgh, or did so only for a few years. Others developed only during the industrial revolution and so missed the heyday of burghs by a century or more. That's why even now, in this age of Regional and District Councils, defunct burghs still proudly retain old customs, or use their coats of arms and call themselves by the title *burgh.* The signposts are there outside many Scottish towns — the Royal Burgh of Linlithgow, the Royal Burgh of Auchtermuchty and so on — linking with the past to remind us of a once-special status.

It would be nice to imagine that Scotland's old burghs have a history stretching far back into the mists of time, but sadly this is not so. Unlike parts of Europe and the Middle East, where towns and even huge cities were flourishing back in biblical times, Scottish burghs certainly did not appear until at least AD 1000, probably nearer AD 1200. Some *towns* may well have existed before then but the legends are fanciful and the proof is vague.

Take Forres, for example. The 16th century historian Hector Boece, at one time Principal of Aberdeen University but a gullible man for all that, mentions that in 535 the merchants of Forres were murdered by Toncet, King Coranus's chancellor, in order to obtain their 'great wealth and substance', so an established trading place must already have existed. Boece goes on to report that by the 9th century, Scottish kings would often stay at Forres, even to hold court or execute robbers seized over the whole north-eastern part of Scotland. We are told that in the 10th century three kings even died there — Donald, son of Constantine, poisoned at Forres Castle in 908, Malcolm I murdered by nobles in 959, and Duff murdered in 965. It all sounds very authentic, but his dates do not tally with other scholars, which must cast doubt on everything else.

More promising are the finds now being unearthed at Whithorn, which seem to show that this was a trading place at least in Viking times, and perhaps a religious centre much earlier still. Time, and more digging, will tell. Frequent references in Norse sagas suggest that Thurso and Kirkwall perhaps also existed during Viking times.

Nevertheless it is a sobering experience to stand outside the huge, domed church of St. Sophia in Istanbul, built in the 6th century by the Emperor Justinian, and to realise that it served a vast city four centuries before the first few wooden huts ever appeared in Edinburgh or Glasgow. And what of Rome, Jerusalem or Athens — even older? Scotland's burghs cannot compare.

Perhaps this fairly late development is not surprising. Until at least the 12th century Scotland was a wild and divided land of Angles, Picts, Scots, Britons and Vikings, with as many tongues and cultures, versions of Christianity and claimants to the throne. Indeed, few Scottish kings were lucky enough to die in bed. Most, or their potential successors, were murdered or perished in battle as Shakespeare's *Macbeth* illustrates.

Nor was Scotland the same size as it is today. Until the 11th century Scotia, or the land of the Scots and Picts, extended only north of the River Forth, and even then Caithness and Sutherland were controlled by the powerful Viking Earls of Orkney. King Duncan I was actually defeated by Earl Thorfinn when he tried to capture this northern area.

Even Lothian was not acquired until Malcolm II's victory over the Angles at the Battle of Carham in AD 1018. At about the same time the future Duncan I inherited the kingdom of Strathclyde and the south-west, an area of Britons. When he later succeeded his grandfather Malcolm II to the Scottish throne in AD 1034, he united the two areas and something more like the modern Scotland began to appear. Even then, the power of the Viking 'Lords of the Isles' in the Hebrides was not broken until the Battle of Largs in 1263. Last of all, Orkney and Shetland were added in 1472 in lieu of a debt owed by Norway to Scotland.

Meanwhile, Duncan I did not live long to enjoy his new, enlarged Scotland. He was murdered by Macbeth in 1040 and upheavals resumed. Still no burghs appeared in Scotland — indeed any settlement must have had a precarious existence in these troubled times.

Eventually Malcolm III or Canmore achieved some stability during the later 11th century, mainly because he realised that he could not afford to anger his new and powerful neighbour, William the Conqueror. Malcolm's wife, the English princess Margaret, founded Dunfermline Abbey and is remembered today by St. Margaret's Chapel at Edinburgh Castle, the oldest surviving building in the capital.

Then in 1124, after a period of more upheavals, came Malcolm's youngest son, David I. Like his father, he had a healthy respect for England's fearsome army of Norman knights but he also saw much to admire in the way Anglo-Saxon England had been transformed by Norman ideas. He married a Norman-English heiress, became Earl of Huntingdon (as well as King of Scotland) and learned for himself how England's King Henry I governed through his nobles in the shires by the feudal system. It was an arrangement which could suit him too.

David offered Henry's nobles additional lands in Scotland, and before long a procession of Norman lords was heading north to settle in the lowlands and border valleys. Among them was Bobert de Brus who became Lord of Annandale and whose descendant was to become Scotland's famous king. Other Normans also brought names now often thought to be just as Scottish as Bruce — including Sinclair, Fraser, Barclay, Crichton, Grant, Maxwell, Beaton, Lindsay and so on. These lords brought organisational skills and military power to help King David subdue most of his kingdom. Strong stone castles appeared everywhere. Sheriffs were appointed to establish law and order in most accessible areas. Monasteries and abbeys were built, for example at Jedburgh, Melrose, Selkirk, Kelso, St. Andrews and Holyrood, and the monks brought farming knowledge and trade. Contact with England, France and the Low Countries improved. And now the first burghs also appeared.

The first places recorded as burghs were Roxburgh and Berwick-upon-Tweed (then still Scottish), somewhere around AD 1120. Within a year of David I's accession to the throne in 1124, however, nine more burghs were created, almost certainly verbally by the king but then later confirmed by charter. These towns reflect the areas where Norman lords were settling, and were Dunfermline, Aberdeen, Perth, Stirling, Edinburgh, Renfrew, Rutherglen,

Peebles and Hamilton. By the time of David's death in 1153 still more burghs had been established, to form the backbone of Scottish urban life for centuries to come. These additional burghs were Forres, Elgin, Linlithgow, Montrose, Crail, Jedburgh, Lanark, Inverkeithing and Inverness. Some others created before, say, 1250 include Dumfries, Nairn, Banff, Dundee, Ayr and Dumbarton. In all nearly forty royal burghs appeared before the coronation of Robert the Bruce in 1306.

The difficult question is, how did burghs develop? Did they grow out of existing villages, or appear suddenly round castles and monasteries? One thing is clear — they did not have Roman origins, for the Romans built no towns in Scotland and their forts decayed when they left. It is also very unlikely that burghs sprang from the brochs and hillforts of the Celtic peoples. Dumbarton was capital of the kingdom of Strathclyde well before the 10th century but it was more a fort on the rock than a town. The exception is perhaps the influence of the Norsemen. As archaeological discoveries at Whithorn indicate, the Vikings may have encouraged trading settlements in Scotland. The remarkable Jorvik museum at York certainly indicates the size and bustle of a Viking town in England. But it does not explain why so many Scottish burghs should suddenly have appeared in the 12th and 13th centuries.

It used to be said that towns developed around some focus — a castle, or bridge, or where roads met, but that suggests that these things were there first and so encouraged people to come and settle. The fact is, however, that in Scotland most monasteries or stone-built castles appeared only with Malcolm III and David I, in other words simultaneously with the first references to burghs in historical records. Most bridges, markets, crossroads and the like came even later. For example the earliest bridges at Dumfries, Stirling, Inverness or Ayr date only from the 13th century while the first recorded at Perth, Glasgow, Berwick, Haddington and other crossing points are even more recent. Berwick's 'old' bridge, for example, dates only from 1611.

What of monasteries or abbeys? While it is true that some burghs, such as Canongate (now part of Edinburgh) appeared at the same time as a local abbey, the fact is that most monks, especially Cistercians such as those at Melrose, wanted to avoid contact with people. They often prohibited the erection of villages nearby and sometimes even had them pulled down. Many monastic centres

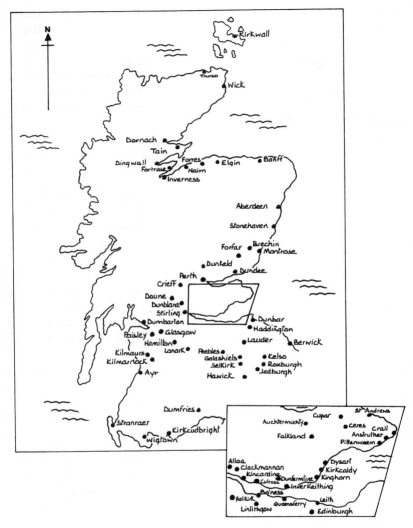

Some of the more important Scottish burghs of the 17th century. Very few had a population of more than 1500.

such as Inchcolm or Scone never became burghs at all, while even Kelso was only briefly a burgh of barony.

What about castles? Some burghs such as Stirling and Edinburgh

were closely associated with local castles, and the buildings still
stand dominating the town for all to see. However Perth, Lanark,
Elgin and other burghs where the castles have now disappeared
also come into the same category. On the other hand Ayr,
Dumbarton and some other burghs grew quite separately from
nearby castles while some notable towns such as Haddington or
Inverkeithing never had a castle at all. So why *did* burghs appear
where they did?

The answer may lie in their charters. Before a burgh could exist,
it had to receive royal assent, so it was actually *created*. This was
probably first a verbal proclamation before witnesses (since few
people could read or write anyway), but then formalised, sometimes
years later, by a written charter. Many surviving charters actually
use words like, 'know ye that I have given' as if confirming a
previous act, rather than, 'I hereby give'. In other words it seems
that many burghs were created verbally by kings giving their
nobles permission to erect a castle *and town*, or even just a town, for
the trade benefits to be gained. Many burghs were probably founded
from nothing by royal decree, and were then built simultaneously
with a castle, as at Nairn for example, where both appeared together
on previously empty land around 1190. So a burgh did not need to
spring from any previous settlement. It could be constructed from
nothing like a 'new town' today. Later kings often confirmed the
charters granted by previous monarchs, but they could also rescind
them so that some towns were burghs for only a short time.

What was the actual charter, this proof of a king's assent? To look
at one today, let alone hold it, is a tingling experience — the
handwritten, faded parchment so old, and the seal so fragile now,
yet the whole thing little more in size than a piece of A4 paper.
Examples are treasured to this day by many burghs — Stirling's at
the regional archive centre, Irvine's in the Burns Club museum, for
example. But what did they actually mean?

In essence, the charter defined the burgh's rights and privileges,
and the obligations which the king expected in return. Sometimes
these were added to over a series of documents; Dumbarton's
charter, for example, was extended three times between 1222 and
1230. Charters were often lost in fires or wars and had to be
replaced by a later copy, re-confirmed by the king of the day. Most
kings preferred to re-confirm the charters of all their royal burghs
in any case; it gave them the power to withdraw a burgh's charter if

desired, or to amend it in some way. Aberdeen, for example, still has a charter from the time of Robert the Bruce — but four earlier versions as well. Most burgh charters are much more recent; Cromarty's dates from only 1593 even though the town existed as a burgh in Robert the Bruce's reign. In fact, very few original charters for early burghs still survive today, and most are later re-confirmations. The first charter known to have been written, rather than just granted verbally, is that of Ayr, dated from references to it in other documents to between 1203 — 1206 during the reign of King William the Lion.

The terms of most charters varied little from place to place. Indeed one town's charter was often described by reference to another's, though the fine print dealing with particular local factors was sometimes changed. The main features were usually the same, however.

First, the town had the right to be protected by a wall or palisade, with gates which could be guarded and closed at night. Second, the burgh had the right to elect its own town council and magistrates, and to govern itself by making laws for local matters. The king's laws, of course, overrode all burgh regulations. The king could also specify the size of a burgh council if he wished, as at Berwick where there were to be 'twenty four good and trustworthy men'.

More importantly, burghs had an exclusive right to trade, a monopoly of all commerce within a defined surrounding area called the burgh's 'liberty', and which was jealously guarded against any infringement. Anything sold in this area had either to have been made by craftsmen in the burgh and sold there by a merchant, or to have had a duty tax paid on it at the burgh, if it came from elsewhere. Either way, it brought financial advantage to burghs. Travelling packmen were therefore a common cause of friction, since they could often sell goods in a district but have moved out again before the council knew of their business. Another common source of friction was when a king created a second royal burgh near an earlier one, and subdivided the liberty lands to give both towns a share. In the case of Inverness its vast liberties originally included most of Ross, Sutherland and Caithness but this was whittled away by the later creation of Dingwall, Chanonry, Fortrose, Rosemarkie, Cromarty, Dornoch, Wick and Tain. In the end, all of these burghs suffered from having too small a slice of the liberty lands to make them viable.

The Stirling Burgh Seal, with a representation of the castle on one side. The reverse shows Stirling Bridge, emphasising the two key reasons for the burgh's growth. In the same way, Burntisland's seal shows a trading ship. *Photo*: The Collections of the Smith Art Gallery and Museum, Stirling.

As well as the right to liberty lands, only burghs could hold annual fairs or weekly markets. The exact number of fairs was specified by the king and varied from place to place. Clackmannan began with just one annual fair but it could last up to eight days. On the other hand Peebles could hold four fairs, each with a specific purpose such as the Beltane Fair on the second Wednesday in May when stallions were sold, or the Lamb Fair on the last Tuesday in June when lambs and wool were sold. Some burghs had even more fairs — Selkirk had five, for example — whereas others had no more than the right to a weekly market where foodstuffs especially could be bought and sold.

Only royal burghs were allowed to trade overseas, or to sell foreign imports such as fine cloth, wax or French wine. This was a particularly lucrative privilege, for outside traders were also not allowed to sell direct to the public. They could sell only wholesale to burgh merchants — who then made more profit, it is said, from selling foreign luxuries to a few rich customers than from selling the day-to-day necessities to everyone else.

Trade could be regulated because of the burgh walls. Taxes were often levied at the gates where everyone had to pass. Any outsider coming with goods to market could be stopped and made to pay a charge according to a fixed scale depending on the kind of merchandise. At Haddington the 'stent stone' still marks where the burgh tax collector sat levying tolls during weekly markets. Stirling Bridge was another convenient place where tolls could be collected from any trader approaching the burgh from the north across the River Forth.

Clearly there were great advantages and profits to be had from being a burgh merchant. On the other hand some burghs never flourished and merchants there must have struggled to make a living. Such burghs included Fyvie in Aberdeenshire, and Auchtermuchty and Falkland in Fife, almost certainly because these places enjoyed no particular economic advantages from their location. Falkland, for example, was centred round a royal residence but this in itself was not enough to ensure prosperity when the privileges which actually made money were to do with trade. Roxburgh actually disappeared altogether and today the few remaining stones are barely noticed by motorists driving from Kelso up the Teviot valley. Nevertheless, for most burghs a royal charter assured the town of at least some modest success.

In return for these benefits the king expected something back. First was the loyalty of the townspeople and local nobility. After all, there was nothing to stop a king stripping a burgh of its status if he felt that its inhabitants had not supported him in some matter. It is remarkable how the canny folk of Scotland's burghs managed to please everybody, especially during the troubled 1640s and '50s, the period of the Covenanters and Oliver Cromwell, when generals from either side could appear at the gates demanding volunteers or supplies or accommodation. Whatever they did, most towns seem to have escaped retribution later and kept their privileges intact.

Even more important than loyalty was money. Between them, the royal burghs were expected to pay about one-sixth of the royal exchequer's needs. The amount to be contributed by each place was fixed the Convention of Royal Burghs, an independent body of representatives from most important towns. This tax or 'cess' was

calculated proportionately to each burgh's income from trade, tolls
and customs. Sometimes the figures were revised to take account of
the rise or fall in a burgh's fortunes. Edinburgh paid the most,
generally around 30% of the total. In 1612 Dundee came next with
10%, followed by Aberdeen on 8%, Perth and Glasgow on 4%, and
several more after that, right down the list to a sizeable number
which paid nothing at all because they were too poor. The changing
situation can be seen by then looking at the list for 1690. Edinburgh
was now followed by Glasgow on 12%, then Aberdeen on 7%,
Dundee on 6%, Perth on 4% and so on. At the lower end of burghs
which did actually pay something, Dysart, Ayr and Dumfries
slipped lower and lower.

In addition, royal burghs were also expected to contribute to the
exceptional cost of specific events. This usually meant military
campaigns against the English, such as the contribution made by
Tain in 1532 for conveying the king's artillery to the border, but
there could be other examples. In 1557 Stirling paid £236 to help
defray the cost of Mary Queen of Scots' wedding to the Dauphin of
France — a contribution recorded almost with pride, in spite of the
hardship it must have caused, for it compared well with Linlithgow's
£151 or Haddington's £147. Once again, of course, Edinburgh paid
the most.

Although a handful of royal burghs dominated the scene (to the
extent that smaller burghs 'knew their place' and normally did not
even send a representative to the Convention), it was a fair system
which for centuries worked well for king and merchants alike. The
problem came with the spread of 'burghs of barony', more correctly
called 'burghs of barony and regality' — a lesser category of town
bound by no royal obligations but enjoying most of the advantages.
Such places included Biggar, Falkirk, Kilmarnock, Leith, Aboyne,
Kirriemuir, Galashiels and scores more all over Scotland.

A burgh of barony was a town established by a charter from the
local feudal lord, one of the king's 'tenants-in-chief' rather than the
king himself. These towns varied in rank according to the status of
the landowner and could even disappear if the local lord lost
favour with the king; some lasted as burghs of barony for only one
or two generations. On the other hand others like Dunbar were
later elevated into royal burghs. Many early burghs of barony,
such as Glasgow, St. Andrews and Dunkeld, were ecclesiastical and

A surviving stone from Glasgow's mercat cross, suggesting the burgh's dependence on trade. *Photo*: Craig Mair, courtesy of the Glasgow Merchants' House.

the superior was an archbishop. A few, including Kirkintilloch, belonged to lay lords.

The rights and privileges of these burghs varied, and sometimes included special concessions or dispensations granted by the king himself. Glasgow, for instance, though created a burgh of barony in 1450, did not receive the right to hold markets until 1490. On the other hand Glasgow was also given the right in 1490 to receive trading ships, which placed it on an equal footing with the nearby royal burghs of Ayr, Irvine and Renfrew. Glasgow was finally made a royal burgh in 1611 but it is clear that it enjoyed the advantages of one long before then.

Most burghs of barony had no right of foreign trade, either in or out — that was an advantage anxiously guarded by royal burghs — but they were usually allowed the privileges of having resident craftsmen, weekly markets and market tolls. Some could also hold fairs, mostly for trading animals. The revenue from trade and tolls usually went to the local landowner, rather than into the burgh's coffers. Bo'ness is an example; created a burgh of barony in 1667 by the Duchess of Hamilton, its charter states that all 'customs, tolls, anchorages, shore dues and others' were to go to the duchess or her heirs. Aberdeen was similarly placed, but on the other hand Fraserburgh was allowed to keep its revenues for the maintenance of the port, while at Abernethy the burgh could keep its income up to a certain figure, with only any surplus going to the superior. Alloa was a more unusual case; it agreed to pay part of the king's cess like a royal burgh in return for the right to trade abroad. It thereafter flourished as a coal-exporting town to the benefit of all concerned.

It might seem surprising that any king would allow the creation of burghs not under his control. After all, they might take business from royal burghs and so reduce the cess which went to the Crown. On the other hand, nobles and landowners also paid heavy contributions to the exchequer and if they grew richer on income from burghs of barony they could be taxed more heavily. It was also a method of distributing royal favours and ensuring loyalty — permission to create a burgh, and to receive its customs, could be given or withheld by the king.

As well as receiving an income from burgh trade, most other arrangements were also dependent upon the local landowner. At Kelso, for example, Lord Roxburghe personally nominated the town's officials. The same happened at Fraserburgh and Aberdeen, whereas the ratepayers of Hawick were allowed by their Douglas superiors to elect their own provost, baillies and other officers.

Friction between royal burghs and burghs of barony began to develop during the 15th and 16th centuries because of a growing encroachment upon the key world of foreign trade. As European trade began to expand, Scotland needed more outlets, and ports such as Leith began to develop. However, as contact with Europe grew, the commerce passing through coastal burghs began to be seen as a national interest rather than just a local concern. More and more burghs of barony found themselves given royal permission to trade overseas.

Doubtless much of this was due to the efforts of local landowners, sensing an income from trade customs and fortunate enough to have the king's ear. But more trade also stimulated more Scottish exports, which could benefit the wider community too. That was not how the royal burghs saw things, however. The king might wish to see the volume of Scottish trade expand, but with the creation of every new burgh of barony the royal burghs saw themselves forced to fight for a smaller slice of the trading cake. From their very localised viewpoint they could not see that the cake was actually growing in size.

Along with more trade came an increase in the number of foreign merchants, and especially craftsmen, allowed into Scotland. King James VI made a particular effort to attract English cloth-makers and leather-tanners, for example, in the hope that Scots would copy their superior products and improve their own skills. Of course this did not please royal burghs either for it highlighted the poor quality of Scottish goods. On the other hand, if Scottish craftsmen did improve, then people might not buy so much from abroad and taxes from imports would fall.

In remote parts of Scotland new burghs of barony were sometimes created in areas where no towns existed at all. Sometimes, as at Gairloch, Thurso or Campbeltown, this was plainly for the convenience of local gentry, who wanted somewhere local to import their needs, but often it was for the ordinary people themselves. The creation of Stornoway in 1607 was especially necessary, for until then the people of the Western Isles had to trade at Inverness, via Glenelg, which forced them to buy a whole year's provisions at one time. Later they traded by ship to Glasgow, but the establishment of a burgh in the islands themselves, to which craftsmen and traders could come, made a great difference to everyday life. Even then, James VI used settlers from the Firth of Forth to found the town, rather as a 'plantation' among the backward, uncivilised folk of Lewis. An unfortunate royal view, perhaps, but at least the town has grown and served as a focus for island needs ever since.

And so the spread of burghs of barony went on, steadily encroaching upon the liberty lands of established royal burghs, sometimes also winning the right to foreign trade. Between 1660 and 1707, for example, only two or three royal burghs were created, but over fifty burghs of barony appeared. It was a trend bitterly resented by royal burghs, as in the case of Dundee and Montrose which for years resisted the creation of a market at Brechin. But it was an unequal struggle and the royal burghs lost. In an increasingly political world, kings needed loyal supporters and lairds wanted more status and wealth from trade. A random glance at some of those who became superiors to burghs of barony shows this. Kincardine-on-Forth became a burgh under Lord Elgin in

Kincardine House, taken in 1945. This was the home of the Earl of Elgin's factor, through whom the earl controlled life and trade in this burgh of barony. *Photo*: Kincardine Local History Group.

1663, Tarbat under the Mackenzies in 1678, Aboyne under the Gordons in 1676 — useful, influential people in their day, and better for King Charles II to have on his side than against him.

Another worry for royal burghs was the creation of annual fairs or weekly markets, or both, in towns which were not burghs of any kind. Examples include Portree, Dalry, Blair Atholl, and Kennoway in Fife. Once again this was primarily for the convenience of the public; Milntoun of Ore was established, for example, because it was 'a place twelve miles distant from any market town or burgh royal'. Between 1660 and 1707 over 130 such towns were given permission to hold markets or fairs, further eroding the dominant position of royal burghs. Indeed by 1707 Scotland had become a land of literally hundreds of burghs of barony and market towns. Today the majority of these have dwindled back into small villages and obscurity — Kilbucho, Minto, Tarland or Inveruchill are hardly household names now — but to royal burghs in the 16th and 17th centuries this worrying proliferation was a serious threat.

Trade was, of course, the main source of income for any burgh. The pattern of foreign trade, from the dawn of burghs in the 12th century to the union with England in 1707, was quite different from today. Most obviously, it was centred on the east coast, where a host of burghs from Dornoch to Berwick traded with Scandinavia, the Low Countries, France and England.

By the 12th century Moray Firth burghs had formed a trading union called the Hanse, which had overseas links. It may even have been established by French or Flemish traders, living in the area and acting like middlemen for merchants back home. Moray towns would certainly have been able to trade overseas, for Inverness was a shipbuilding centre capable of producing seagoing vessels. The new stern-ruddered, wide-bodied ships of the 13th century were also able to carry more cargo, another encouragement to develop some foreign trade. The towns involved in the Hanse were Aberdeen, Banff, Elgin, Forres, Nairn and Inverness (though Aberdeen also had separate interests in salmon exports).

Further south lay Angus and the Firth of Tay, where Perth, Dundee and Montrose were the main trading towns. Documents show the merchants of Perth already trading with Bordeaux in the 13th century, while Dundee ships were often used to trade goods for Arbroath Abbey after its foundation in 1178. Still further south, burghs like Leith, or Crail on the Firth of Forth, though mostly small, were busy. The Forth had the advantage of being closer to most foreign ports, though the scatter of rocky islands in the firth made navigation dangerous.

The greatest trading port by far, however, was Berwick-upon-Tweed. It changed hands often from 1296 onwards, but its dominance as Scotland's main seaport was not ended until it was permanently lost to England in 1482. During the 12th and 13th centuries much more than half of Scotland's trade went through Berwick. Enclaves of Flemish, German and even Italian merchants organised the arrival of an amazing range of goods, from locks, keys and other ironware goods to exotic foodstuffs such as onions, garlic, almonds, rice and especially pepper and cumin (used for seasoning meat, which quickly went off unless it was salted, and who wanted salty meat at every meal?). Another import was grain,

Crail harbour today, largely unchanged since improvements in the early 19th century. This burgh was already an important trading town in the 17th century. *Photo*: Craig Mair.

often bought from the corn-growing English midlands via King's Lynn or Boston. However, this only happened when Scotland's own harvest was poor — in general the country could feed itself. The main buyers of grain were the Scottish monasteries, since they were the focus of the greatest centres of population at that time. Some monasteries and abbeys actually had 'houses' in Berwick, through which they organised grain imports when necessary.

Other common imports were fine cloth and wine. By the 13th century the clothmakers of Flanders (where whole towns sometimes made little else) were renowned for the quality of their materials. High-quality cloth also came from Italy, contrasting with the rough, coarse cloth of Scotland. Most of these cloth imports went to the royal household but before long, nobles and lesser lords began to copy the king's fine dress, which increased the demand for fine foreign materials and boosted Berwick's business. In the same way, the royal household's prodigious import of wines from Normandy, Maine and Bordeaux spread the habit downwards through society. Eventually wine arrived, not just at Berwick, but at Perth, Leith, Aberdeen and Ayr as well. It has even been argued that their developing taste for good living forced Scottish landowners to utilise their ground more, to produce more food to sell, to be able to afford more wine and fine clothes. Certainly the merchants of Berwick did not complain.

Then there was the west coast. The main trade here was with Ireland, and as in the east, some monasteries bought grain during bad years; Cambuskenneth Abbey near Stirling had a house at Ayr, for example. There was also some trade up the Solway Firth, but with only Irish shipping and an occasional vessel from France, there was no comparison with the bustle of the east coast.

Scotland's main exports in the 13th century were mostly raw materials for other countries' industries; wool (particularly from the monasteries) for the Flemish burghs, hides from deer, sheep and cattle, timber and some raw fish were the main cargoes.

By the reign of James VI, three hundred years later, the picture was still much the same, except that Berwick was no longer Scottish. Most trade was still centred on the east coast, where an even longer list of burghs, now including Culross, Pittenweem, Dunbar and Burntisland, made a living from foreign trade. The Kirkcaldy burgh records for 1691, for example, show the loss of a 300-ton ship returning from Ostende. Across the sea a string of ports from Bergen to Bruges did similar business with Scotland's east coast.

Trade was now more organised, however. Scottish merchants sold their goods through a European agent at Campvere (now called Veere) in the Netherlands. This was called the 'staple port' because most of Scotland's staple exports, such as wool or linen, passed through here. At the same time there were also strong links with Norway; the Baltic ports, especially Danzig, from where grain was imported; and France, particularly for wine and brandy from Bordeaux. At least half a million gallons of wine were imported into Scotland each year, mainly through Leith.

The list of imports was long and varied, for Scotland still produced very few finished or manufactured goods. Cargoes now included everything from Turkish rugs and Russian furs to Venetian glass, ivory (known as 'elephants' teeth'), sponges, armour and musical instruments. Baltic imports consisted particularly of Swedish iron bars (for making into other things) and Norwegian ready-cut timber — everything from barrel staves to sawn planks and building joists. In addition there were products needed by the Scottish shipbuilding industry — pitch, tar for caulking, hemp for ropes and flax for canvas. Imported food now included prunes, chestnuts, walnuts and spices, mainly via Holland. Fine cloth was still in great demand too, for the rough 'hodden grey' of Scottish cloth was not much for a grand gentleman to wear. Most cloth also came through Holland.

Exports were now more varied, but still consisted mostly of raw materials, the surplus from Scotland's own very low manufacturing output. As well as wool, hides, timber and fish, however, there was also coal — up to 60,000 tons a year by 1640 — mostly from the Culross-Alloa area. Associated with this was salt manufacturing, the product of hundreds of open coal-burning salt water evaporation pans along the Firth of Forth. The crystals from this rudimentary method produced a dirty brown salt which really only found a foreign market when wars disrupted the usual French supply. A fair amount of lead was also mined, notably at Wanlockhead, and exported to Europe. Finally, in good years there was sometimes a grain surplus to export; in 1618, 320,000 bushels were shipped abroad from Leith alone, which surely suggests that Scottish agriculture was better able to feed the native population than has often been suggested.

Although the bulk of Scottish exports still went to Europe, the Irish trade connection was now also stronger, partly as a result of King James VI's policy of settling Scottish Protestants in Ulster. As Fynes Morrison, a Scottish traveller and diarist, wrote in 1598, 'the inhabitants of the western parts of Scotland carry into Ireland red and pickled herrings, coal and whisky'.

The greatest difference in west-coast trade was just beginning, however, with the gradual development of trans-Atlantic shipping to England's colonies in America. Strictly speaking, England's Navigation Acts of 1661 prohibited any but English ships from trading with the American colonies, and insisted that products such as tobacco and sugar could only be landed at English ports. The idea was to ensure a monopoly of colonial goods for England's traders, but there were plenty of enterprising skippers willing to handle Scottish cargoes en route. By 1707 at least seventy-five documented voyages were recorded between either America or the West Indies and Scotland. One sign of this illegal trade is that Scottish sugar refining began early in the 17th century, long before it became official in 1707 following the Union with England.

King James VI's reign lasted forty years and was a period of peace in Scotland. This encouraged more trade, particularly on the east coast, and as a result new harbours were built at Eyemouth, Dunbar, Leith, Stonehaven, Peterhead, Aberdeen, Ayr and elsewhere. More vessels also came under Scottish owners — a trend which continued through the century. Between 1668 and 1681 the number of Scottish-owned ships doubled and even more harbours were opened, notably at Saltcoats, Methil, Port Seton and Bo'ness.

Though west-coast trade did begin to expand during the 17th century, it was no accident that from the very start, most royal burghs and seaports were in the east. The pattern of trade was one important reason, but just as significant was the distribution of Scotland's own population. Basically, most people lived where the land was most fertile. That meant Ayrshire, the Solway shores, the Moray Firth, the Mearns of Aberdeenshire and Angus, Strathtay, the Firth of Forth, Lothian and the lower Tweed valley — mostly in the east, where it was less rocky and the climate was better for farming.

Even burghs needed to be where agriculture was best, for in the 17th century most town-dwellers were also part-farmers, except in Edinburgh. There is documentary evidence, for example, of a merchant in Montrose with shares in two trading ships and a fishing boat, yet also growing wheat and barley on his land and owning a cow, a calf and a heifer. The fact is that most people depended at least partly on the land.

The population of Scotland in AD 1200, when burghs were still small and new, is difficult to assess. It may have been about 500,000 but then it fell during the 14th century, partly because the climate became colder but also because of the Black Death, which struck Scotland in a series of epidemics from 1350 onwards. In spite of this, by 1560 the population seems to have grown again to around 800,000. It is likely that half of these people lived north of the Tay — indeed this was still so in 1755 when Scotland's first rudimentary national census was made by the Rev. Alexander Webster. Today, four-fifths of Scotland's population lives in the central belt embracing Edinburgh and Glasgow.

Of that total of 800,000 in 1560, about one-fifth lived in burghs; in other words, an urban population of about 160,000 spread over more than forty royal burghs and scores of burghs of barony. Not

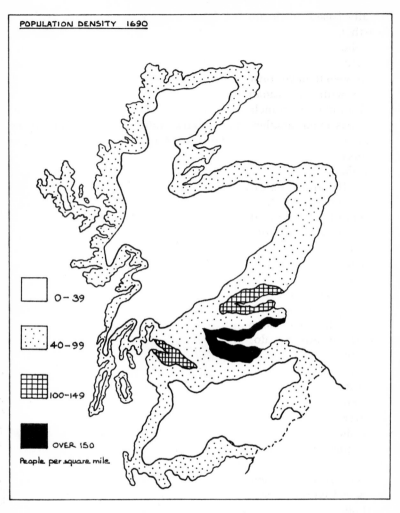

POPULATION DENSITY 1690

0 – 39

40 – 99

100 – 149

OVER 150

People per square mile

Scotland's population distribution in 1690. Most people lived on the eastern side of the country, where the land was more fertile, the climate less wet, and trade existed with the Baltic, the Low Countries, France and England.

surprisingly, most towns had populations in hundreds rather than thousands. Today it is still not easy to calculate accurately the populations of specific 16th or 17th century burghs. Estimates are usually based on documents such as property valuation rolls or hearth tax records, but these list only properties and heads of households and do not take into account the size of families or the mortality rates for children. Nevertheless, from these papers Selkirk can be seen to have consisted in 1714 of a grand total of 187 dwelling houses with an estimated population of about 700. In 1660 the population of Tain included roughly one hundred taxable people, so it was even smaller than Selkirk. Edinburgh was the largest burgh, with a population of about 30,000 in the early 1700s. Glasgow was probably the second largest with about 14,000. Stirling seems to have about 3000 inhabitants. By contrast, Kilmaurs in Ayrshire had barely 100 and even Stranraer had only 279 inhabitants over the age of twelve in 1684.

What of housing in the oldest burghs? With the exception of a few castles and religious buildings, nothing now remains of burgh dwellings from the 12th to the 14th centuries. However, some towns do lend themselves to urban archaeology — these include Perth, Aberdeen, Elgin, St. Andrews and Inverness because their medieval remains have not been disturbed by 19th and 20th century developments, especially cellared tenements and pile-driven office blocks. They also do not stand on rocky ridges as Edinburgh, Lanark or Stirling do, so there is a sub-soil to protect older remains.

Some modern developers have given archaeologists time to excavate building sites before obliterating them for ever with concrete. In 1983, for example, the Central District School site in the Meal Vennal at Perth was dug up prior to the construction of a large shopping mall. By stripping away the topmost layers of soil, down through lower 18th century deposits, substantial medieval finds were made.

Some digs have revealed particular evidence about housing. Work at Inverness has shown that houses were built of wood. One method was to use grooved building frames and then to slot in planks to make walls. Clay was then stuffed into any gaps to make the building windproof. Another style involved sections of woven basketwork 'wattle' walls, fitted into a basic framework of posts. Clay or mud was then pressed into the wattle walls to fill any gaps, then a layer of dung was smeared over the outside to make everything weatherproof. Roofs were made of turf or straw, probably held down against the wind by ropes and heavy stones.

Wattle fences have also been found, forming backyards where animal and craft remains tell more of how people lived. At Perth a 12th or 13th century wattle pathway has even been unearthed, while at Inverkeithing and Inverness cobbled or gravel street surfaces have been excavated.

It is also very likely that the basic layout of modern burgh streets, and even the pattern of individual housing plots, was first established in the 12th or 13th centuries, and in many places has remained more or less unchanged ever since. These original streets may have been widened a little and the house frontages straightened up, or medieval backyards built over, but the underlying plan of many burghs can be shown to have been there for centuries. Burgh high streets, and the lanes running from them, are especially likely to be very old.

The existence of trade and crafts can also be shown to have had very early roots. English medieval pottery fragments have been found at St. Andrews and Perth, and German pieces at Inverness, indicating some pottery trade. Evidence such as kilns and ovens, butchered bones, leather off-cuts, horn-working waste, and fragments of woven cloth have helped to reconstruct a picture of everyday life, craft and even diet in medieval Perth.

Coin discoveries have also added to an understanding of medieval trade and business. There was no Scottish coinage at all before the reign of David I (1124—1153), when silver pennies were minted. However, 13th and 14th century coins have been dug up at Perth, indicating that commerce already existed in the town by then. At St. Andrews an English 12th or 13th century silver penny found at an excavation in Market Street might suggest that the town was already engaged in foreign trade by then.

Sadly these archaeological finds offer only tantalising glimpses into an urban world which must have been just as busy as today. The buildings simply don't survive any more, and to know more historians must use documentary references. This is fine for experts, but not very immediate or visual for others who simply want to imagine how a town might once have looked.

The lack of buildings is not surprising, of course, for if towns were built mostly of wood they were also easily destroyed, generally by enemies or fire. Inverness seems to have been razed to the ground during the 15th century, while in 1706 most of Tain went up in flames. By 1570 Dumfries seems to have been burned down at

Provand's Lordship, a relic of the 15th century in Glasgow. Originally the manse for the Chapel and Hospital of St. Nicholas, it later became a tenement owned by a succession of local merchants and was for a time an alehouse. This view is of the rear, which has more character than the front.

least five times, mostly as a consequence of war. Forres, Elgin and indeed most other towns all have some story of having been devastated either by accidental fire or deliberate destruction. In 1652, for example, about one third of Glasgow was destroyed in a great fire. It is curious how the fire of London thirteen years later is well known, even in Scotland, and yet the fire of Glasgow is not. As recently as 1824 a large part of Edinburgh's Royal Mile around St. Giles Cathedral was consumed by a fire which made hundreds homeless and resulted in the formation of the world's first municipal fire brigade, but it is also largely forgotten today.

Fires did at least force people to rebuild, and gradually they did so with stone or a mixture of stone and wood — Scotland's forests were, in any case, rapidly dwindling. Some surviving examples of early stone buildings are quite old, and date from the 15th century. They include Moubray House in Edinburgh (next to John Knox's house, but even older and dated around 1462), and Provand's Lordship, the oldest surviving house in Glasgow, dated 1471. However, most ordinary people did not begin to live in stone buildings until the later 16th and early 17th centuries. Fortunately, despite several wars, numerous early examples of the stone houses of ordinary citizens can still be seen today. With them also appeared the first stone public buildings — schools, almshouses, tolbooths and so on — and for the first time burghs began to look more as they do today, given a few changes over the years. As a result, it is now quite easy to piece together how a burgh would have looked in, for example, 1650. By then, most important burghs were well established and were largely built of stone. And though it may not seem so to the untrained eye, most still survive today remarkably unchanged.

CHAPTER 2

A Typical Burgh in 1650: the Street Layout

By 1650 it is safe to say that most Scottish royal burghs were well established. In many places their basic features still survive, even if the towns themselves have grown much larger. In most cases the old burgh lies in the centre of the town today, as the Royal Mile lies in the centre of Edinburgh, for example. The trick is in recognising, as you walk outwards from the centre, where the 17th century area ends and the newer town begins.

Fortunately most 17th century towns were small, compact and built to a fairly predictable pattern. Most had a similar street plan, with prominent public buildings usually located in the same place, so that today they are easy to understand and explore. By comparison, modern towns sprawl in a muddled mish-mash of Victorian or later additions. Regular Georgian streets or squares lie poked behind factories. Rows of back-to-back Victorian houses may not jostle with larger Edwardian villas, but they may often have been squeezed in beside canals or railway lines or warehouses. Modern housing estates may lie on the outskirts of town, but may just as easily occupy some reclaimed inner city area, so that today there is no easily understood regularity — no confidence in knowing that the town hall or church in one place will be similarly sited somewhere else. Though they may not seem so at first glance, the 17th century centres of modern towns are much easier to discern.

Let's start from the outside. Any traveller approaching a burgh 300 years ago would have seen a small, huddled cluster of slate, turf or pantile rooftops and smoking chimneys, with only one or two buildings such as the kirk standing taller than the rest. In other words the entire town would have been small enough to take in at one glance.

Our traveller would then have passed through one of the burgh gates. Every burgh was entitled by its charter to a defensive wall, with a number of gates which could be closed at night for security. Not every burgh would actually have had the kind of stone walls often seen in Europe or even at York. Such a wall would have been too expensive for many towns to afford, so they often made do with

Diagram of a typical burgh around 1650.

something simpler, not necessarily able to deter an enemy, but at least marking the limits of the town.

Inverness seems to have been surrounded by a fosse or ditch — an attractively cheaper alternative for the town council and, for the people, a convenient depository for rubbish, sewage and dead cats. Several other burghs were protected in the same way — parts of Stirling's limits were marked by a ditch, for example. Another possibility was an earth rampart, also a cheap alternative. Part of Dumfries was so defended, even if the remains have long since gone, and a five-foot high earth dyke surrounded Selkirk (though it was evidently much neglected). Here again, the importance of the rampart was to mark the town's edge and to force travellers to enter by the gates.

An even more popular option was to use the garden walls of houses which backed onto the outer edge of the town. At Lanark, for example, each householder was responsible for keeping his bottom, outward-facing wall properly maintained to a height of two ells, or six feet two inches. This presented a continuous high wall to outsiders without the town council having to pay anything. Fortunately for Lanark, from the time of Wallace onwards, it was never embroiled in any of Scotland's wars and its walls were not tested. Nevertheless, danger did sometimes threaten, even if it then receded; in 1685 the people of Lanark were ordered to repair their much-neglected walls because of the fear of Covenanter troops — Lanark was staunchly anti-Covenanter.

This use of garden walls was common all over Scotland, as at Falkirk, a burgh of barony, and at Peebles until a more substantial wall was erected in 1569. Contemporary illustrations suggest that many other towns, such as Culross, Linlithgow, St. Andrews, Glasgow and Elgin depended on a similar arrangement of walls for defence. It is unlikely that they could have resisted a proper army, but they were enough to deter thieves and petty raiders. The main purpose was again to force ordinary travellers to enter the burgh by its gates.

Then there were burghs with proper stone walls. These were the more successful, richer towns of the 17th century, such as Edinburgh, Crail, Dundee, Perth or Inverkeithing, which could afford the expense of a proper rubble wall. Sadly, few traces remain of these town defences; a plaque records that Perth's walls were demolished during the 18th century when the need for them was over. Inverkeithing's walls were pulled down at about the same time, for they were last recorded in 1762. At Edinburgh a short

A view of Ayr in the 1690s, by Captain J. Slezer, from across the River Ayr towards the old church of St. John surrounded by the Cromwellian fort of 1652. The bridge of 1491 still stands — one of the oldest in Scotland. The strongest impression is perhaps how small the burgh was — a reminder that all Scottish towns in the 1690s were surprisingly small.

fragment of the Flodden Wall (built between 1513 and 1560 to replace an earlier wall erected around 1450) can still be seen in the Vennel, near George Heriot's School. Another small piece survives inside the National Museum in Chambers Street, but it is not on public display and permission is needed to see it. At St. Andrews an impressive wall still stands round part of the town, but this is actually the wall of the abbey precincts and, though it did help to protect the burgh, it is not quite the same thing as the town's own wall (which was never continuous). Finally, some fragments of town wall still survive at Peebles and Haddington.

The best surviving town walls in Scotland are in Stirling, where they can clearly be followed round almost half of the original burgh. Built in 1547—48 'at this peralus tyme of neid, for resisting oure enemies of England', the walls still stand over ten feet high, running partly along higher ground, so that they would have looked formidable to anyone approaching from the south or east. (The burgh's north side faced the River Forth and was marshy, so a ditch seems to have been considered enough there.)

At corners or bends in the walls there were gun loops or towers which could cover two directions with defensive fire. An excellent

A short section of Stirling's burgh walls, complete with gun loops. Compare with the height of the passers-by. These are the best walls still to be seen in any Scottish burgh. See also the bastion tower on page 158. *Photo*: Craig Mair.

example of a bastion or tower can be seen inside Stirling's modern Thistle shopping centre. Steps lead down into a vaulted guardroom with a bottle dungeon underneath in which criminals were held. From the adjacent underground shop loading and service area access can be obtained to the outside of the bastion and it can clearly be seen protecting with gun loops the right angle of two walls at a corner. It is an impressive and strong-looking tower, fortunately still preserved.

A path known as the 'Back Walk' leads visitors along the lines of Stirling's burgh walls, but in other towns this is not so clear. An easier clue is the location of town gates. It must be emphasised that in old Scots a 'gate' or 'gait' was a *street*, while a 'yett' or a 'port' (from the French *la porte*) was a gateway. Thus a street name proclaiming the Hiegate or the Gallowgate would *not* mean an old entrance to a burgh but a proper street. On the other hand, the Muckle Yett at Elie or Edinburgh's Netherbow Port were gates.

Many modern street names still refer to old burgh gates, even if they no longer exist. There are Port Streets and West Ports in towns all over Scotland, and from these it is possible to figure out what was once inside, or outside, the town's limits. Examples include the East Port in Forfar, the Wellgate Port in Lanark, the South Port in Elgin and so on. Sometimes commemorative plaques can be found — one in Stirling marks the site of the Barras Yett, the main entrance to the burgh.

Although street name references abound, very few town gates still actually stand. To begin with, they were not necessarily very permanent. Those at Inverkeithing were originally made of wood and it was not until 1503 that the supports were built of stone. At Lanark there was much repairing of the gates during the time of Mary Queen of Scots; in 1569 two of the town's entrances were only of timber, but by 1571 the town council had found enough money to replace both with a 'hingand port' and strengthened stone supports. The gates themselves were also reinforced with iron bands.

None of these examples exist today. Like town walls, when the need for them was over, they were pulled down by well-meaning councils anxious to encourage burgh improvements. One town which does still have gates is Berwick-Upon-Tweed, but although its gates are 17th century, the town was by then completely English and should not really be included here. At Dundee there still survives a port known as the Wishart Arch which was once the town's eastern entrance, though it seems now to stand almost in the centre of the city. One stone of Hawick's West Port remains at ground level beside No. 2 The Loan. But the outstanding example of a burgh gate in Scotland is the West Port at St. Andrews. Built in the 16th century, it is remarkably similar to the entrance gates at Linlithgow Palace which were built about 1535.

The original purpose of gates was firstly to regulate the flow of people in and out of town, to know their business and to enable tolls to be collected on market goods. Consequently, surviving gates are all one cart-width and about twelve feet high to allow for bulky loads such as hay or a mounted horseman. Castle entrances of the same period are similarly sized for the same practical reasons. In burghs, pedestrians sometimes passed through a smaller archway on either side of the main entrance, as at Berwick and St. Andrews, and indeed to a pattern unchanged since Roman times. To this day, St. Andrews traffic still has to squeeze through the West Port's narrow central arch just as traffic had to do in towns all over Scotland three hundred years ago.

The West Port at St. Andrews, much restored but the best (almost the only) surviving burgh port in Scotland. Some others were quite different in style, however — see the Netherbow Port on page 66. *Photo*: Craig Mair.

Just as London Bridge (the one which fell down) was a series of small arches with houses built on top, some burgh ports were also part of a larger building. The Muckle Yett at Elie used to be a house, evidently with elaborate ornamentation, to judge from what little survives, with an archway below and living quarters above. The Netherbow Port at Edinburgh, today marked by brass plates set in the street surface, used to have a turreted, almost Disney-like guardhouse built over it.

If burghs did not always have proper walls, they certainly had gates. There was no fixed number of ports — that depended on size and circumstances — but most towns had four. They include Elgin, Stirling, Selkirk, Perth and many other burghs. On the other hand Dumfries had three, St. Andrews had seven or eight and Edinburgh had six gates. Entrances were generally known by some obvious feature such as the Cowgate Port (or gate through which cattle were taken out of the town to graze each day), Friar's Wynd Port (many monasteries or abbeys were situated outside burgh walls), the Seagate Port, Castlegate Port and so on. Most often, gates were simply named by directions such as the West Port at Linlithgow or the East Port at Melrose.

35

Once inside the gates, travellers then had to find their way through the warren of a burgh's streets, pends, wynds, lanes and closes. In fact, this would not have been very difficult because most burghs were not only small, but similarly laid out, unlike today. In 1650 the vast majority of towns consisted of a single important street, usually called the High Street today, but often called the Hiegait or King's Causeway in the 17th century. Examples of High Streets cover the whole of urban Scotland, ranging from Stranraer or Kirkcudbright on the Solway, to Tain, Forres or Elgin on the Moray Firth. And there are any number in between, such as Brechin, Lanark, Culross, Montrose, Peebles, Glasgow, Irvine, Falkirk or Stirling (where the principal thoroughfare was called Broad Street. Hamilton's High Street was demolished around 1700 to make way for the Duke of Hamilton's new palace.

Narrow strips of land, variously called tofts, burgages or tenements, extended from the High Street towards the town walls, and these strips often survive today behind a frontage of shops and offices. This arrangement of strips can most easily be seen in small burghs with low population density such as Whithorn or Lauder, where they remain more or less undisturbed even today. Sometimes

Lanark's High Street, now split by a central chain but once wide enough to hold markets. Similar examples survive at Inverkeithing, Haddington and elsewhere. *Photo*: Craig Mair.

A view of Wigtown from the air. The pattern of burgage strips is very clear, as is the layout of the High Street, beginning at the church, then passing the site of the tolbooth, to the wider market area with its cross. *Photo*: Roland Norris, Wigtown.

a second street formed a cross in the centre of town, providing the burgh with the usual arrangement of four gateways. Most other streets, if there were any, stopped short at the walls and did not continue through them. 17th century Elgin was a good example of this.

Although a single high street was the commonest form in burghs, there were some others where, by 1650, there were two parallel main streets. The most obvious example is Edinburgh, where the Grassmarket and Cowgate run parallel to the Royal Mile. Other easily spotted examples include Stirling, Perth, Arbroath, Dundee, Auchtermuchty, Coldstream, Crail and Pittenweem. Another is at St. Andrews, but here Market Street now lies between the two parallels of North Street and South Street, giving the impression of three main streets. In the case of Haddington, where there appear to be two parallel streets, the houses which lie between the two were not there in 1650 and originally there was just one wide main street.

Finally, there are about a dozen burghs with more unusual street plans. Selkirk's original layout formed a triangle, for example, while the streets at Cumnock converge towards the town centre. Leith has one original main street formed by the Kirkgate, Tolbooth Wynd and the Shore, but it zig-zags with two sharp, right-angled corners, and does not look like an obvious high street.

The most important point, however, is that the vast majority of burghs had, and still have, a clearly identifiable high street running the entire length of the original town. It may sometimes be labelled in two parts, as at Forfar or Linlithgow where it is called West High Street and East High Street, but it should not be difficult to find or follow.

In due course houses were built facing the burgh streets, so then lanes, or more commonly, wynds, vennels and closes, were opened to give access to the land behind these houses. Later still, much of this land was also built over and these wynds became streets themselves, serving a mass of houses built at right-angles to the main street. Some houses still present their gable ends to the high street, and face instead onto a side lane. The extent to which the property strips or tofts were built over depended on local population pressures and a fear of living outside the town walls. For centuries wars were such a threat that no-one dared live outside the security of a burgh. By 1700, however, many busy towns began to see the first few houses spreading beyond their gates. In such places it can be reasoned that, if the land area was already fairly built over, most wynds and closes were therefore already established.

Not surprisingly, the larger, more successful, burghs attracted the most people. Until about 1700 they would have squeezed themselves inside the walls, building on more and more toft land until there was no alternative but to spread beyond the walls. Ayr, Glasgow, Dumfries, Dundee, Arbroath, Stonehaven, Aberdeen, Inverness, and Dunfermline are all examples where there was eventually over 75% building coverage on the original tofts. On the other hand, there are many burghs where the continuing existence of gardens and back yards suggests that the town was never heavily built up.

Another feature of 17th century towns was an arched entrance called a pend, which usually led from the high street to an enclosed lane or courtyard. Most pends had a gate which was closed at night, giving additional protection to any house which faced into the courtyard. (Many closes also had gates, as a walk down Edinburgh's

The use of gates at the entrance to closes still survives in many burghs, such as Haddington or Linlithgow. This example is in the High Street, Edinburgh. *Photo*: Craig Mair.

Royal Mile will quickly confirm.) Pends were often named after the original owner of the land or property, although as with closes, the names often changed over the years, sometimes each generation.

Finally, a lane or path often appeared just inside the town walls, running along the outer limits of the burgh tofts. This usually formed an elliptical shape, mostly parallel to the high street, sometimes joining it at each end. If a burgh became more heavily built over, this sometimes also developed into a back street, serving houses nearer the walls.

What can still be seen of all this today? The high street in most towns is easy to find, and very often something will also mark the original location of the gates at each end — a plaque, a street name, or blocks in the road surface (as at Kirkcudbright). The original side streets are often also easy to find, because many are still called 'gates', such as the Wellgate in Dundee (because it led to a public well). Other obvious examples might include the Kirkgate at Linlithgow, the Marketgate at Crail, the Gallowgate in Glasgow or Sidegate Street in Haddington.

Closes and wynds are not always so easy to spot. Wynds tend to be more substantial and have often become streets, such as the Coal Wynd at Kirkcaldy or the Cow Wynd in Falkirk, but they are nevertheless twisty and usually quite narrow, indicating that they were once little more than footpaths or lanes.

In some burghs, closes are a feature of the main street and have sometimes been restored. Those which run off the Royal Mile in Edinburgh are especially well known, but many other towns can be just as rewarding to explore. They include Haddington, St. Andrews, Lanark, Brechin and Elgin amongst the best. On the other hand, many now seem dark, decaying and probably uninviting, or have been boarded up, or have had doors fitted so that access can no longer be gained. Dunbar, for example, contains several closes which appear to be dingy and run-down, but which are well worth venturing into. In Stirling, Pittenweem, Irvine, Dumfries and many other burghs there are closes which may be full of discarded shop cartons, or dustbins, or restaurant kitchen smells, but which will reward visitors with a sense of adventure.

In the same way, there are pends — sometimes long lanes with arched entrances, sometimes only smaller courtyards. Those at Kirkcudbright, St. Andrews and Elgin are typical of the best. At one time these pends were a considerable aid to burgh defence, for if it came down to street or house-to-house fighting, each pend could be locked and fought over. An enemy in those narrow confines would then have suffered pails of boiling water, showers of stones, clods of dung, or whatever else the local folk could find at hand.

Then there are the back roads — those lanes which once ran just inside the burgh walls. They were often called 'back rows', but nowadays some have new names, such as at Montrose where Mill Street used to be called Back Wynd, or at Anstruther where Cunzieburn Street was once the Backgate, or at Maybole where

A close in Kirkcudbright. The houses beyond face on to the close itself — a typical arrangement in most burghs. See page 188. *Photo*: Craig Mair.

John Knox Street used to be the Back Vennel. But even disguised with modern names, their original purpose is still clear enough to anyone knowing what to look for. Particularly easy examples to spot still exist at Lanark, Forres, Biggar, Lauder, Elgin and so on, conveniently marking today where the original town limits were.

Finally, there are those burghs which can be classed as 'new' or rebuilt, and are therefore not easy to fit into any older street pattern. At Airth in Stirlingshire, for example, the old burgh ran in a typical street layout westwards from Airth castle and kirk, with a modest population and a single high street. In the 1690s, however, the Earl of Dunmore relocated the entire community on a new site nearby and then demolished most of the old burgh. Today the original ruined kirk stands strangely distant from the village.

The same sort of thing happened elsewhere; Grantown-on-Spey used to stand as a burgh of barony clustered round Castle Grant, but the entire community was swept away in 1765 and rebuilt nearby. Fochabers was moved from its original position at Gordon Castle in the 18th century and now only the old mercat cross survives to remind people of an earlier community. Inveraray was similarly moved and rebuilt by the Duke of Argyll in 1742, and most of old Hamilton, known as 'Hietown', was demolished to make way for the Duke of Hamilton's new palace in the 18th century. Even Burghead, perhaps the oldest community in Moray, is now lost beneath 19th century improvements.

These rebuilt towns are exceptions. With some practice it becomes easy to find the layout of most old burghs. Begin at the high street, find the gates at each end, and from there follow the perimeter back streets (with perhaps more side gates on the way). The closes and wynds then become more logical and the burgh quickly takes shape. It is surprising how small many were — Selkirk is estimated to have been no more than three hundred yards long by two hundred and fifty yards wide in 1714, while in 1750 even Glasgow consisted of no more than ten streets and seventeen lanes — so it should not take long to walk round a burgh.

Street names can also help. Anything with George, Anne, Caroline, Charlotte, Victoria, Albert or Regent, for example, will generally be outside the old burgh area. Likewise, streets set in squares, avenues, drives or crescents would post-date the period of old burghs. Names suggesting industries such as mill, foundry, railway, nailer, shuttle, canal or lade are also likely to be more recent. On the west coast, names reflecting trade with the Americas, such as Virginia, Jamaica or Tobago, are similarly too recent.

Finally there is the question of the burgh lands, variously known at Lanark as the Burgh Acres, at Forres as the Greens, at Elgin as the Borough Briggs and Town's Crofts, at Lauder and Selkirk as the Burgess Acres, at Kirriemuir as the Commonty, and so on. At one time most burgh inhabitants were also part-time farmers so there were field strips or 'rigs' all around most towns — still easily seen in illustrations of the period. In addition burgh cattle were pastured on common land outside most towns, though usually further off where the land was rougher or higher.

In burghs which have now grown into larger cities, these lands have been swallowed up by expansion, but clues to their former existence can still easily be found. In Edinburgh the park at Boroughmuir is an obvious example, but between Tolcross and the Grassmarket there also lies a street called the High Riggs, once reached through the town's West Port. At Glasgow the original common land, granted to the town by James II in 1450, is now Glasgow Green. At Falkirk a street known as the Lint Riggs still runs off the High Street in the centre of the town (though there is no record of lint or flax ever having been grown there). Another called the Callender Riggs marks one end of Falkirk's High Street and burgh fairs used to be held there.

Another very striking reminder of the old burgh commons or muirs is the colourful ceremony of riding the marches, an annual event in many Scottish towns. Those in the borders, at Hawick, Jedburgh, Lockerbie and almost every other town, are well known,

The Langholm Common Riding — a spectacular and colourful event typical of many burghs, especially in the Borders. Some have been revived in recent times, having fallen into abeyance during the 18th and 19th centuries. *Photo*: Timothy Neat, Wormit.

but the same scene occurs at Linlithgow, for example, and Lanark, where it is called Lanimer Day. Indeed, Lanark people believe that their burgh is the only Scottish town which has observed the ceremony every year since it was first imposed by the Crown centuries ago.

Burgh boundaries were once very important and were usually marked by streams, trees, crosses or boulders; Steel's Cross and the Ruddy Cross were two markers at Lanark, for example, and a march stone which once defined the parish boundaries between Saltcoats and Ardrossan can be seen in the local museum at Saltcoats. The 'White Stone' at Peebles was a similar marker — in fact, anything clearly visible to people who could not necessarily read was ideal. Eventually maps were made to avoid arguments; one example from 1730 and formerly used when 'perambulating the marches' survives in Tain's local museum.

The modern ceremony of riding the marches once had the more practical function of familiarising everyone with the features used to mark the burgh's boundaries. This was done at least once a year and inhabitants had an obligation to attend. Occasionally it was found that neighbouring landowners had encroached upon burgh land or were using the grazing land, and legal action sometimes followed. Nothing could better convey a sense of burgh history than the traditional scene of riding the marches, still flourishing today. It is something well worth making an effort to watch.

CHAPTER 3

A Typical Burgh in 1650: The Main Features

If the street plan of most burghs was similar, so was the location of the main buildings. Every burgh had a kirk, a tolbooth, a mercat cross, a tron or weighbeam, and usually a school. Most also had some other dominant feature such as a castle, a bridge, an abbey or university or something of that kind.

In most towns this dominant feature is still very obvious. Falkland still gathers round its royal palace; Melrose or Dunfermline round its abbey; St. Andrews round its university; Huntly round its castle, and so on. Very often they stand at one end of the burgh high street — the castles at Edinburgh or Stirling are outstanding examples but there are many more, such as the castles at Forres and Inverness. The high street at Clackmannan has been described as descending 'like a formal avenue from the gates of the baronial castle [Bruce Tower] to which the burgh owed its origin'. In the case of seaports such as Culross, Leith or Aberdeen, the main street often led to the harbour.

In many cases the original castles have virtually disappeared but can still be recalled from local street or port names. Perth, Lanark, Crail or Glasgow are examples. In other towns cathedrals or abbeys have been destroyed or reduced, so that Brechin, a community once heavily influenced by the cathedral and its precincts, now has little more than a splendid parish church, merely *called* a cathedral. Street names and wall plaques do survive to recall better days and remind visitors of how the cathedral once dominated burgh life. The same could be said of Dunblane, Dunkeld, Dingwall, Elgin and numerous other towns whose existence today can also be traced back to the great days of their cathedrals.

It is well worth looking for some clue to a town's history and raison d'être — not 'Mill Lane' or 'Foundry Road' or 'Canal Street' which clearly date from a later period, but something older to help explain the town's origins. It may not always be an immediately obvious ruin such as the Royal Palace at Linlithgow, but with a bit of observation, some clue will generally surface — a reference to 'Castle Wynd' or an 'Abbey Port' perhaps, or possibly just the grassy hill where a castle once stood high on its motte (as at Hawick).

A seaport might seem to be the easiest to spot but even this can sometimes be misleading. At Culross, where vessels simply rode at anchor or were left high and dry on the beach at low tide, the original shoreline has been pushed back by a railway and the beach is now a village green. Today it is difficult to imagine trading ships just a stone's throw from the tolbooth; many visitors mistakenly believe that the 'village green' is traditional, whereas it dates only from late Victorian times. However, the shoreline street is called the Sandhaven, which is a helpful clue.

The local castle or abbey or palace may once have been the most imposing burgh landmark, and even a reason for some prestige, but the most *important* was the tolbooth or town house. This was the predecessor of the more recent town hall, and generally served the burgh's needs in several ways.

First, it was the meeting place of the town council. Here councillors administered the burgh's affairs, stored its records and banners and ancient charters, and kept the burgh's incomes. As the name suggests, it was also a place where various tolls, custom dues, taxes and other moneys were sometimes collected and usually kept (since there were no banks at that time). Strong iron-banded chests with wonderfully complicated locks were often used for this purpose, and some still survive today, as at Inverkeithing Museum.

In addition the tolbooth was often the guard house. Weapons were sometimes stored for public emergencies, but they tended to go rusty and were frequently unserviceable when next examined. By 1650 most tolbooths were also used as courtrooms and prisons, and it is noticeable that many surviving examples have thick walls, barred windows and stout doors — as much for keeping prisoners in as robbers out. If the burgh was also a county town, the courtroom would serve the county sheriff as well as the burgh's own magistrates. By the early 16th century the sheriff of Fife was already holding regular courts at the Cupar tolbooth, for example. Finally, some tolbooths even housed shops, as at Lanark, where the town records show that there were semi-sunken shops in the eight vaults below the main council chamber.

These varied functions meant that, in practice, the tolbooth building was usually subdivided into different sections. The largest and most important room was the council chamber. It was generally the best decorated, quite possibly with a painted wooden ceiling (some remnants of which still survive in the tolbooths at Dunbar

Stirling Bridge, a vital reason for the growth of Stirling as a burgh. Shipping came up the River Forth to this point, and tolls were collected on the bridge from merchants taking goods to market. This bridge is 15th century and does not have any connection with the Battle of Stirling Bridge in 1297. *Photo*: Craig Mair.

and Canongate in Edinburgh). The courtroom was usually a smaller, more functional place.

The greatest problem was in the location of the cells. Prisoners frequently escaped from tolbooth cells all over Scotland. At Lanark a blacksmith jailed in 1695 for debt 'by extraordinary strength wrenched the lock off his cell door, breaking the great nails, and with two other prisoners, broke through the jail wall and escaped'. Lanark's tolbooth cells were on the ground level, but this was quite common. At Dalkeith the council chamber was on the first floor above the crypt-like cells — a similar layout, but it did mean that prisoners could escape more easily, perhaps with outside help, by tunnelling out, or even by undermining the walls so that they collapsed. Because of the embarrassment of escapes some burghs housed their prisoners above the council chamber on a second or even a third floor (though the 'black hole' or condemned cell was still usually tucked away in some windowless corner of the basement).

The cells in many tolbooths continued to be used well into the

19th century. The Prisons Act of 1839 did result in the erection of larger, purpose-built jails in many towns, but even then the cells in some tolbooths were still kept available for petty overnight offenders or prisoners on remand. The solitary cell in the Falkirk tolbooth steeple was only closed in 1984.

Most tolbooths were placed in an important, central position, normally halfway along the High Street, often at an intersection of two streets. In most burghs the main street widened at this point into a market area, so there was (and usually still is) an open space beside most tolbooths where a crowd could gather to hear the town bellman proclaim the town's 'statutes and ordinations'. This was often done from the steps or balcony of a tolbooth.

In Edinburgh crowds could also gather to watch hangings, which were sometimes carried out on a second-floor terrace of the old tolbooth, next to St. Giles Cathedral. A cobblestone heart in the street marks where this much-detested prison stood until its demolition in 1817. To this day Edinburgh citizens, some extremely respectable, still spit into the heart's centre in memory of the stinking rat-infested cells which once stood there. Visitors tend not to notice this feature of Edinburgh's tradition and walk right over it, but local people seem to have a built-in radar which guides them round it. It can be quite amusing to watch from a distance.

Some tolbooths had a tower, often a strong, peel-like structure such as can still be seen at Crail or Dysart, and which might suggest an original defensive purpose — tolbooths were usually among the very first buildings in most burghs to be built or rebuilt of stone, so they may well have acted as a last line of refuge in wars. Tolbooths did also house the burgh's wealth and charters, which alone would have been good reason for strong walls.

This tower sometimes contained the cells, but its most useful additional function was often as the steeple for a bell or clock. The grandest surviving tolbooth steeple is undoubtedly the one at Glasgow, built in the 1620s. It still stands seven storeys high, although the imposing five-storeyed tolbooth once attached to it was regrettably demolished in 1921 — it would have made a notable landmark today. There are other surviving tolbooth steeples, more modest perhaps, but which capture the essence of smaller burghs; examples include those at Clackmannan, Maybole, Musselburgh, South Queensferry, Tain and West Wemyss in Fife.

Most tolbooth towers incorporate clocks today, but these are

Clackmannan tolbooth, mercat cross and the 'Stone of Mannan'. Only the tower and west wall of the tolbooth survive, but the situation halfway down the High Street is typical. *Photo*: Craig Mair.

sometimes fairly new additions, often added in Victorian times. Even in the 17th century, however, some burghs employed a man to keep the town's clock in order. One of the earliest references is in the Aberdeen burgh records, which mention that on May 22nd 1453 John Cruckshank was given 'the service of keeping the orloge for this year'. Many other burghs did the same. The Elgin records for 1658 state that 'the Council has condescended to make John Cowie, tinker, burgess and freeman of this burgh for keeping of the town clock in good order during his lifetime . . .'

Not many really old tolbooths survive, although numerous

Crail tolbooth, also near the burgh's mercat cross and market area. This building survives comparatively unchanged since its construction. It is now a tourist information office. *Photo*: Craig Mair.

Victorian or later town halls stand on ancient tolbooth sites today — Elgin's is an example. One study has suggested that no more than twenty-two surviving Scottish tolbooths actually pre-date 1707. Many of those which are older have been so heavily modified since as to make them hardly recognisable as traditional vernacular buildings. Examples of greatly changed tolbooths include those at Aberdeen, Linlithgow and Dumfries. Of the oldest unspoiled survivors, those at Crail (1590s), Dunbar (c 1620) and Dysart (1576) probably still look much as they would have done back in the 1650s.

The much-photographed tolbooth at Culross is very well known to visitors, but its present appearance, complete with central tower, dates only from 1782 — much later than most of the burgh. Stirling's tolbooth is another fine example and dates from around 1705, but with a dash of civic pride it was designed in an early Classical style and somehow does not convey the homespun feel of a 17th-century burgh. On the other hand, the much simpler but later 18th-century tolbooths at Lauder or Kilmaurs look just as they must have done in their heyday and are very appealing.

Close to every tolbooth stood a mercat cross. Indeed, even if the

The tolbooth at Culross. Inside, the courtroom was to the left while the council chamber was to the right. The prison cells were on the ground floor. The clock tower is an 18th-century addition. *Photo:* Craig Mair.

town was a burgh of barony and there was no tolbooth (the superior would hold a barony court instead), there would probably still be a cross. A great many crosses remain today, some in very small country villages but quite a few in towns. Even in the few miles between Stirling and Culross, mercat crosses still survive at Airth, Alloa, Clackmannan and Kincardine. It is the same in most areas; around Haddington they still remain at Prestonpans, Gifford, Ormiston, Musselburgh, and so on. They are also plentiful along the shores of the Moray Firth, in the Borders, and along the Fife coast from Inverkeithing to Crail.

The form of mercat crosses varied. First, very few were actually like a cross — those at Kinross or Banff are fairly uncommon examples. Most consisted of a stone pillar, usually mounted on steps so that they were more easily visible over a crowd of heads, and with some sort of crowning edifice on top. Royal burghs had a penchant for heraldic beasts such as unicorns or lions, and armorial shields which were sometimes painted or gilded. Good examples of

The 18th-century tolbooth at Kilmaurs. The windows still have iron bars and the jougs still hang near the front steps. *Photo*: Craig Mair.

this type can be seen at Crail, Stirling or Prestonpans. More modest burghs often settled for a stone ball on top, as at Clackmannan, Prestwick or Moniaive, or a sundial as at Melrose or Cumnock. Other variations included urns, square tops, weather vanes and even Celtic crosses.

Some mercat crosses stood on a round tower, with a parapet from where the bellman could proclaim to the people. Excellent examples still stand at Prestonpans and Edinburgh. Selkirk's cross stood on a square tower, but the result was the same — a prominent central place in the burgh.

By being placed in the market area of any high street, the cross became a natural focus for public events. Markets were, of course, held around it, though some towns such as Ayr or Elgin had a separate fish or meal cross. At Thurso the Fish Stone (now in the

The mercat cross at Culross. The steps are original but the top was restored this century. It is nevertheless a fine example in a striking setting of 17th-century houses. *Photo*: Craig Mair.

local museum) marked where fishwives sold their catches, while the Cocky Stane was a similar marker for farm wives. The location of stalls for different crafts or foodstuffs was often defined by reference to the cross, for example that the butchers must not sell their meat below the cross, or the cordiners their shoes above it. Well into this century the fishwives of Forres still sold fish around the steps of the cross.

Public announcements were also made by the bellman from the cross, 'that none may pretend ignorance' of some new proclamation or bye-law. In the same way, public gatherings were often held at the cross. The town guard sometimes mustered 'by the croce', for example. At Dundee the full turnout of provost, bailies, the town council and dean of guild would meet at the cross before riding the

Prestonpans mercat cross, also restored, but an excellent example of its kind. Another stands beside St. Giles Cathedral in Edinburgh. *Photo*: Craig Mair.

marches. Celebrations were also held there; the cross at Edinburgh was specially decorated to honour the arrival of King James V's new wife Mary of Guise in 1538, while at Stirling the cross and tolbooth were decorated with leaves of gold for a visit by King James VI in 1617.

Many punishments were also carried out at the cross. Public humiliation was a common form of punishment and was cheaper than locking someone up in the tolbooth, so miscreants were variously flogged, branded, burned or hanged at the cross. The commonest form of low-grade punishment was to be sentenced to a period in the 'jougs' — an iron collar, often fastened by a chain to the kirk or tolbooth wall, but sometimes to the cross. Elgin's records tell that 'John Stronach, flesher in Elgin, is ordained to stand in the jougs from nine hours in the morning this day to twelve hours

The top of the mercat cross at Airth, built in 1697 when the entire village was relocated by Lord Dunmore. The sundial is typical of many crosses and was necessary at a time when few people or even burghs had clocks. See also page 59.

thereafter, bare-headed, and because he was found in like fault before, he is ordained to be banished from this town or else to pay £20 and to be put in the jougs in case he fall again'.

In addition, the burgh stocks were normally placed near to the cross, again in a prominent public position to increase the punishment for wrongdoers. Most Scottish stocks consisted of a hinged wooden bar with holes through which a prisoner's feet and ankles could be inserted and padlocked. Occasionally there were

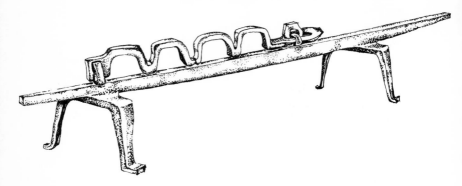

The stocks at Crieff, preserved today behind railings in the High Street. The ankle hoops hinged upwards to open, and could be locked shut.

fetterlocks or iron loops for the ankles, but the principle was the same. The English 'head and hands' type of stocks or pillory does not seem to have been widely used in Scotland.

Sometimes an explanatory paper was pinned to the chest of someone committed to the stocks, as at Peebles in 1665. The burgh council decided that 'Hew Black, for his miscarriage, brawling last Tuesday, breaking several doors, offering injury to several of the inhabitants, and his cursing, swearing and imprecating, to be put in the stocks at the cross next Wednesday, and to lie there the space of one hour, with a paper upon his face written in great letters, and thereafter to be banished this town, and if he be seen or found in the burgh at any time hereafter, without a call or public authority, then to suffer death as an adulterer'. Punishments are explained in Chapter 6.

Although numerous surviving mercat crosses date from the 16th or 17th centuries, many have been heavily repaired and altered over the years. Of the fine cross at Stirling, for example, only the top is original — the shaft is quite new. Likewise, workmen repairing the cross at Doune found that its shaft was also a replacement, with stone even from a different quarry.

In most cases mercat crosses were made of sandstone, but this varied in durability across the country; just as many old gravestones have been weathered smooth with time, so many old crosses have also worn away, and have sometimes been replaced. A good example of a much-worn original survives at Crieff but there are not many now in Scotland.

Some crosses have been pulled down altogether, often because they blocked high street traffic or because they offended the eye of some Victorian improver. In many cases, however, the original location is still marked; a wall plaque indicates the site at Hawick; stone setts have been embedded in the street at Lanark, Montrose, Forres and Brechin; and at Biggar an original fragment has been built into the wall of the Exchange, close to the site of the cross. It is a particular shame, however, that the crosses in major burghs such as Perth, Glasgow and St. Andrews have gone.

On the other hand, some old crosses have been replaced — but with Gothic or Victorian substitutes which look nothing like the originals. Haddington has an example which combines a traditional-looking cross with a Gothic base, but those at Forres, Cullen, Jedburgh or Irvine, for example, are pure Victorian fantasy and must be voted an eyesore. Their only merit is that they do at least preserve the traditional site of the burgh cross. The cross at Aberdeen probably deserves the same verdict; it is actually an old original but one which has been moved, rebuilt and redesigned so much that it is now virtually a Victorian creation.

Finally, there are the crosses which have been moved. Even in the 16th and 17th centuries mercat crosses were sometimes relocated in burghs — when the town became larger, for example. Some crosses originally stood at burgh gateways; in 1669 Grissel Jaffray was burned as a witch at the Seagate Port in Dundee, where a cross had previously stood before being moved to a new site in the High Street. The cross at Inverkeithing has had two previous sites, all three within yards of each other. The Peebles cross likewise stands today a few yards from its correct, original position.

Some other crosses have been moved because the burghs which they served have become extinct. The Rossie mercat cross now stands in the grounds of Rossie Priory in Perthshire, moved there when the burgh dwindled away. Longforgan's cross is now at Castle Huntly, and when Kincardine burgh died out its cross was moved to nearby Fettercairn and became the town cross there instead.

Associated with many mercat crosses was a tron, or public weighbeam, where market goods could be checked before being sold. This was necessary at a time when weights and measures were

The mercat cross at old Airth now stands alone in a field. The entire burgh has disappeared. *Photo:* Craig Mair.

not always accurate. One farmer's pound of cheese was not always another's, so to avoid argument everything was weighed on a common weighbeam. Weights and measures are detailed in Chapter 7.

Like the mercat cross the tron was also a place of public punishment. Most trons had a wooden post to which the jougs could be fastened, or a public notice could be nailed. At Peebles on October 15th 1683 John Lawrie, servant to Archibald Halden, was placed in the 'thieves' hole' until eleven o'clock the next day, at which time he was taken to the tron 'to stand with the jougs about his neck, for stealing malt out of the mill, and the malt to lie beside him from eleven to twelve'. He was then banished from the burgh.

Very few remains of trons survive today, except in street names such as the Trongate in Glasgow. A large stone block outside the Culross tolbooth is said to have been the socket base for a wooden post, and there are the remains of a socket at Kirkcudbright, but little else still survives. At the village of Stenton in East Lothian, the Girl Guide Association reconstructed a wooden-posted tron to commemorate sixty years of Guiding in 1970. Although Stenton was never an old burgh, it seems to have had a parish market where

The mercat cross in the burgh of Airth today, dated 1697. Apart from the 18th-century house behind the cross, little else dates from the period. *Photo*: Craig Mair.

a tron was used; the reconstruction accurately copies old illustrations of trons in Scottish burghs. For want of anything better, it is the best there is to see.

Apart from the tolbooth, the most prominent building on most high streets was the church, or kirk as it was invariably known by the 17th century. In many towns it is by far the most striking feature, despite the changed surroundings in which it now stands. A good example is the church at Falkirk, which is surrounded by shops and offices but still catches the eye for miles around because of its commanding position on the ridge of the High Street.

There were certain favoured or strategic positions for kirks. Many stood facing down the high street as at Pittenweem or Lanark. This had the advantage that it was easily seen by anyone out of doors, but perhaps there was the additional suspicion that the kirk could also see everyone else. At a time when the Kirk and its views held great authority over people's lives, this dominant location was perhaps not accidental.

On the other hand, some kirks were built halfway down the high street beside the tolbooth, as if to portray the twin powers which the

This representation of a weighing scale survives on a house at Ceres in Fife. No tron weighbeams exist now in Scotland, although a reconstruction stands at Stenton in East Lothian, and the stone socket for a post remains at Culross. *Photo*: Craig Mair.

church and town council had in every burgh. The kirk at Lauder, and St. Giles at Edinburgh, are both good examples. Observant visitors will easily find more.

Many burghs conformed to one or other of these patterns but there were exceptions. Sometimes the kirk was so prominent that it needed no further status. The cathedrals at Brechin, Dunblane or Dunkeld towered high above the surrounding houses for all to see. The kirks at Linlithgow, Whithorn or Stirling were sufficiently famous. The kirk at Hawick stood on a hill, looking down the High Street, while the one at Elgin formed an island in the High Street itself, next to the now-demolished tolbooth. The kirk at Tain was a place of pilgrimage to the birthplace of St. Duthac, an early

St. Andrew's church at North Berwick, typical of burgh kirks all over Scotland. As in this case, many occupy a prominent position in the town. *Photo*: Craig Mair.

missionary to the Celts and Picts to whom some miracles are ascribed. And so it goes on — there is hardly a burgh kirk in Scotland which does not make an impression somehow, just from its position.

In pre-Reformation days there were also many abbeys and friaries attached to burghs, often just outside the walls. By the 17th century many of these had been swept away by the Reformation but street names keep alive their former existence. There must be a Black or Greyfriars *something* in dozens of burghs, certainly at Elgin, Perth, St. Andrews, Glasgow, Edinburgh and so on. Friars Vennel in Dumfries and Friars Street in Stirling are similar examples.

There are also street references to the actual kirk in many towns, from the simple Church Street at Inverkeithing to Kirk Close at Dalry, the Kirkstyle in Biggar, or Kirkgate at Irvine. Chanonry Wynd at Brechin is also a religious reminder but refers to the Cathedral in pre-Reformation times. The principle is nevertheless the same and can be seen repeated in the Nungate at Haddington or the Canongate at Jedburgh (which has nothing to do with artillery, of course!).

61

Just as some tolbooths have been replaced by more modern town halls, many churches have similarly been modified or totally replaced. At Inverkeithing, St. Peter's Church tower dates from the 14th century, but the main building was rebuilt in 1826 after a fire. The present kirk at Forres, though on the original site, dates only from 1909. The most important thing is that, whatever the age of the present building, it almost invariably stands on the traditional site of the burgh kirk. There are, as always, exceptions to such generalisations; at Lanark the original kirk was outside the burgh walls, while at Culross it now stands in ruins and the site has not been reused.

None of this should be confused with the welter of new churches which sprang up in many towns after the Disruption of 1843. Unlike many smaller English towns, dominated by a single church spire, it is not unusual to find the spires and towers of Episcopalian, Roman Catholic, and United Free churches in most burghs, plus an assortment of nonconformist churches, perhaps housed in less church-like buildings. They could be misleading, but can generally be identified as later churches from their less prominent positions, or because Kirk Street leads somewhere else, or because they have no graveyard round the church — the kirkyard is almost always associated with the original burgh church. For the purposes of discovering burgh life in the 17th century, these later buildings should therefore be ignored. Details of the kirk's part in burgh life are explored more fully in Chapter 10.

Another feature of most 17th-century burghs was the grammar school (so called because it taught Latin). Few physical traces remain of these grammar schools today, although the institutions sometimes survive. Lanark Grammar School may have been founded as early as 1183, and Ayr's High School in 1233. Aberdeen Grammar School seems to have begun even earlier, in 1156 — certainly a complete list of its rectors survives from 1479 to the present day.

Unfortunately no major burgh schools still occupy 17th-century buildings (George Heriot's School does in Edinburgh, but it was not the original burgh grammar school, which was the Royal High School). In most cases, modern burgh schools do not even occupy the original site of grammar schools. Haddington, for example, boasted a grammar school as early as the 14th century, but the main building in the Nungate was demolished in 1578 and rebuilt elsewhere. This, in turn, was demolished in 1755 when a new

Culross in the 1690s, by Slezer. Its prosperity depended on sea trade using the River Forth. The harbour has gone, but the houses still straggle uphill to the Abbey Kirk, preserving the town like a 17th-century time capsule.

building was opened in Church Street, which was itself replaced by the present Knox Academy, again on a totally new site. In the same way, the location of Stirling's original grammar school is now the Portcullis Hotel, close to Stirling Castle.

Some hints of the former existence of burgh schools still linger, but they are few and uncertain. Commerce Street in Elgin was once called School Wynd, and at Dunfermline near the East Port there is a Commerce School Lane — but it refers to a later Victorian school, for no 17th-century burgh ever had a 'commerce school'. School Wynd at Kirriemuir lies in the oldest part of the town and runs into Kirk Wynd, where one house still has a marriage lintel stone dated 1688 — which fits the early 17th-century gravestones in the kirkyard, and which may suggest a school long before the time of the famous Webster's Seminary.

Street names with 'college' in them tend to be misleading. They often refer to collegiate buildings associated with pre-Reformation cathedrals and abbeys, or to university colleges. Thus Sir Walter Scott's birthplace in College Wynd, Edinburgh was actually in a street which led to the university and has nothing to do with any school.

Apart from streets reflecting trades or crafts, such as Glover

Street at Elgin and Tanyard Lane at Cumnock, or those called after local proprietors, such as Gladstone's Land in Edinburgh or Thompson's Close at Lanark, quite a few other place names survive to tell something of the past. They can often fill in many more corners of a burgh way of life now totally gone, rather like pieces of a jigsaw together making the whole picture.

At St. Andrews a narrow lane called Butts Wynd leads from North Street towards the Scores, while at Crail a modern housing estate stands upon the Bow Butts. Those names recall the old archery practice areas in some burghs — an important feature of towns in the days when warfare still occurred and even ordinary citizens needed to be reasonably proficient at arms. Indeed James VI even had to pass a law compelling people to practise their archery instead of playing football because they were not skilled enough archers.

Bow and arrow practice was sometimes also held in kirkyards; gravestones were doubtless seen as ideal targets. At Crail and Tullibody (near Alloa) some stones still display the clear chipped marks of arrowheads, and sharp-eyed visitors elsewhere will surely find more. It should be noted, of course, that streets such as the West Bow in Edinburgh or Bow Street in Stirling have nothing to do with archery, but are so called because of their bow or curved shape.

Near some burgh kirks there are still some place names which refer to 'glebe', as at Crail and Falkirk, for example. The glebe was an area of open ground, usually about four acres, which was attached to every kirk manse as an additional 'perk' to the poor salary which the minister received. He could pasture a few animals there, or grow food, or sublet it to someone else for some additional income. Many glebes have recently come under the speculative eye of property developers — an attractive open space in the middle of a busy burgh has little chance of surviving undisturbed nowadays, especially when so many churches are struggling financially. The temptation to sell long-held glebes to meet repairs or running costs must be considerable, but every time it happens, another piece of history is lost.

Some burghs such as Falkirk, Jedburgh and Edinburgh have a street known as the Pleasance. Although some far-fetched explanations exist for this, the meaning is quite simple. As the name suggests, this was originally a pleasant area of ground, not crowded, built-up or used as a dump for the burgh's stinking refuse — in some ways the predecessor of public parks today. This was usually just outside the walls of a burgh, generally close to one of the gateways, so that a Pleasance today would be another clue to a burgh's limits in the 17th century. Later in the 18th century the expression 'comely park' meant much the same thing — an area of attractive land beyond the edge of the town. Since most communities had expanded by then into Georgian suburbs, the area of a comely park was further away from the centre of the town — like Comely Bank, Edinburgh — and should not be confused with a pleasance.

The word 'Row' is quite common in many burghs, and simply means a street or row of houses. By the 17th or 18th centuries some old rows were becoming fairly dilapidated, even ruinous, especially in the 'bottom' or poorer parts of towns. In some cases, such as Lauder or Glasgow, the name 'Rottenrow' therefore appeared, and has survived even when the street was rebuilt. In the same way 'New Row', as at Dunfermline, suggests the first tentative expansion of a town into a new street, usually just inside the burgh limits and often near a gateway. The very use of the word 'row' usually ties it to the 17th and 18th centuries rather than a later period, when avenues, drives and crescents began to sound better than rows and bows. On the other hand, New Row has become New Road at Coldstream and no doubt in many other burghs.

What else might survive? The word 'nether' is still quite common, as in the Netherbow Port at Edinburgh (now demolished) and the Nethergate at Crail or Dundee. This means 'lower' so that the Netherbow Port was a gateway lower down the slope of the Royal Mile. In the same way 'Townhead' indicates the opposite, upper, area of a burgh, as at Cumnock or Biggar. Loans or Loanings were country tracks, outside towns.

Most burghs also had street wells which provided inhabitants with their water. In some cases, such as Linlithgow and Edinburgh, these still survive, but elsewhere they have generally disappeared. Even where streams once provided water, these have been piped under modern high streets, as at Lanark or Kincardine-on-Forth for example. In Falkirk, East Bridge Street still exists but there is now no bridge, not even a stream, because the East Burn has been piped underground. In many towns, walls, burns and bridges still feature in street names, even where the original reasons have disappeared, but they are still valuable and interesting clues to the

John Knox's House and the Netherbow Port in Edinburgh, about 1760. Notice also the street well, which still stands today.

past. Fountains, or references to them, tend to be more recent and should generally be ignored.

Many burghs also had their own corn mills at one time, often owned by some local landowner but used by the townspeople.

Other towns sometimes owned their own mills: Tain possessed several, which were rented to various landowners and the income added to burgh revenues. Most burghers, tenants of these landowners, were bound by their leases to take their corn there, and nowhere else. Like street wells, the physical remains of mills are usually now lost but street and place names remain. These include references to Myln or Mylne (which used to be pronounced 'mill'). One word of caution, however: some 'mills' may refer to the cotton, flax or woollen mills of the later Industrial Revolution, but the difference will usually be fairly clear from the general type of burgh, or the style of the street and its houses.

Finally, there were dovecotes, or 'doocots' as they are better known. Their purpose was to provide a supply of food during the lean winter months, when grain and meat were scarce. Doocots were more often found on private land, but some did exist in burghs, usually owned by individual people rather than by the community as a whole. It is known, for example, that one stood on Glasgow Green in 1653 because there were complaints from the owner about boys 'chapping on the door' to frighten the birds. In the same way, Hawick's records for 1621 name three local men who 'have from January to November worn hagbuts and pistolets, have shot and slain great numbers of their neighbours' proper doves, and use the same for revenge upon all persons against whom they bear quarrel'. Punishments for killing pigeons or doves, or destroying doocots, were very severe; in 1567 they included forty days in prison for a first offence, the loss of the right hand for a second offence, and subsequent execution if anyone were daft enough to persist in this line of vandalism.

Remains of these interesting foodstores still survive at Portpatrick, Haddington, Crail, Prestonpans and elsewhere, but it must be admitted that the best dovecotes tend to be found in rural areas, especially on estate farms or in the grounds of hotels, country houses and castles. Dovecote Lane in Lanark recalls another example of a burgh doocot, but having survived into the 20th century this one was pulled down some years ago. Other examples, such as the fine dovecote dated 1647 at Westquarter, near Falkirk, may now be found in built-up areas, but may originally have been sited on private estates which have only since been swallowed up by urban development.

It should now be possible to explore old burghs with a better understanding. Having found the high street and burgh ports, and perhaps worked out the rough boundaries of the town, the next step is to locate the market area, the cross and the tolbooth. Other features should then fall into place — the kirk and perhaps its glebe, a reference to the school or a surviving well, and a scattering of other clues such as the tron, the butts, the pleasance, the mill, or whatever. It is surprising just how much of an old burgh can still exist!

Naturally, streets and buildings do not tell the whole story of a town's past. That needs to be filled in with people. Fortunately, burgh records are full of characters, real folk who lived and died and had their business in burghs. Their lives are explained in the next chapter.

CHAPTER 4

The Social Classes in a Burgh

From earliest times it is clear that there was a distinct 'pecking order' in burgh society. It is said of 18th-century Edinburgh that there was very little snobbery, that high and low lived easily together down the same closes or up the same spiral stairways, but that does not mean that people did not 'know their place'. The distinctions between property owner and tenant, merchant and craftsman, apprentice and servant, freeman and unfreeman, were sharply drawn and strictly enforced.

There was some limited scope for upward movement in society but this was rare — few people made it from rags to riches in a Scottish burgh. Most men were born, lived, and died in the same social rank as their fathers, and knew that their children would probably do likewise. Most women married into a social level much around their own.

Topmost rank in a royal burgh was the king himself, at least theoretically. In practice he was rarely, if ever, there, unless the burgh contained a particular attraction such as the palaces at Linlithgow and Falkland or the castle at Stirling (which were particularly enjoyed by James IV, V and VI). After 1603 and the Union of the Crowns, when James VI became king simultaneously of Scotland and England, most kings preferred the delights of London to the hardships of Scotland and stayed mainly in the south. Visits to royal burghs became rare events celebrated with great decoration and festivities (which, curiously, were actually called 'solemnities' in most burgh records).

By their charters, royal burghs were allowed to govern themselves — to regulate local affairs of law and trade — but that still left the king with authority over higher matters of state, especially land ownership and obligations to the crown. Since their own visits were so rare, kings usually appointed a representative in their place — some local lord to whom an honorary title such as 'keeper of the castle' could be given. In earlier centuries such an important dignitary might have been made provost, or sheriff, but by 1650 this practice was quickly fading. In effect the king's representative had a very limited influence on burgh affairs. Moreover, as the

The gateway to Linlithgow Palace, a favourite royal residence. It is early 16th century and resembles the West Port at St. Andrews (page 35). *Photo:* Craig Mair.

decades passed, kings made grants of land ownership to many burghs, and their control lessened.

Burghs of barony were quite different. They did not govern themselves except with permission from the superior landowner. The extent to which the feudal overlords showed an interest (some might say *interfered*) in burgh affairs varied from place to place and from generation to generation. It often depended upon their personal whim or inclination; some local lords were content to be consulted on a fairly honorary basis, while others took a personal, active, part in the workings, for example, of the barony court and the kirk, the appointment of ministers and schoolmasters, the granting of permission to build dykes or arm men, and so on.

Slightly lower down the social ladder came the heritors — men who actually owned property which could be passed as an inheritance to their children. They were the real men of importance in a burgh, the ones who formed the town council and had real day-to-day power.

Many heritors were local lairds who did not generally live in town, but who maintained a local 'town house' for occasional use, which gave them the technical right to be called citizens of the burgh. These men were often very powerful landowners of vast estates, sometimes highly titled, like the Duke of Hamilton or the Earl of Roxburghe. But there were others of more modest standing; by 1650 the Reformation had seen the Church lose most of its abbey, monastery and church lands, and in burghs a large part of this was acquired by merchants, craftsmen and less important lairds — heritors of lower rank. Indeed, whereas merchants had once rented land, by 1650 many now owned their own properties. The heritors in most burghs were therefore a mixture of a few very powerful and important landowners and a larger group of regular town-dwellers, mostly merchants and some of the more successful craftsmen.

As with the superiors of some burghs of barony, the more important landowner heritors did not always choose to interfere in burgh affairs; that again depended on personality or whim. Many were, in any case, preoccupied with higher matters of state politics or estate management. To some, burgh affairs were even rather petty and boring — an obligation in which they had to show an occasional interest. This seems to have suited most burghs, for they preferred in any case to be left alone to run their own affairs, and to keep 'landward' heritors at arm's length except at their invitation.

Since burgh councils preferred local lairds not to interfere and those lairds were often happy to let it be so, relations with many landward heritors were generally good. Examples of this crop up in many burgh records. At Elgin, for example, a meeting of local heritors was convened to discuss 'the building and repairing of the new church and providing a manse, and the Earl of Murray to be written to that effect' — in other words, he was being informed as a matter of courtesy, but with no expectation that he would attend unless he had some strong objection to the plan.

In some areas, where no single estate dominated the locality, there could be quite a few surrounding lairds. In the case of Peebles, the burgh records for the 1680s (to select just one decade) reveal regular dealings with Lord Yester, the Countess of Morton, Lord Douglas, Lady Blackbarony, the Earl of Traquair and various others. They also show that the council certainly did not stand in awe of such people; in 1689 they *allowed* the Countess of Morton to cut turfs on the town common, for the roofing of a building she was in process of having erected; to a letter from Lady Blackbarony they ordained 'the provost and baillie Plenderleith to answer the

The Argyll Lodging at Stirling, an outstanding example of a nobleman's town residence from around 1630. The courtyard and entrance porch are particularly impressive. *Photo*: Craig Mair.

Lady Blackbaronie's letter in her terms, that they wonder upon what account her ladyship quarrels our possession of our own property, and declaring we will use it at our pleasure'. In other words, they rejected her complaint, even with a touch of defiance.

Among those heritors who were burgh residents, there were clear subdivisions. Most obviously, merchants regarded themselves as superior to craftsmen, and in most royal burghs they still held sway over burgh affairs in the council. Even within the merchant class there were clear distinctions between a simple shopkeeper, such as a butcher or baker, and someone who traded overseas, who needed greater administrative skills, more capital, and was usually better off. There were also divisions among craftsmen; most notably, shoemakers and metalworkers or 'hammermen' regarded themselves as superior to the others.

Down to the level of craftsmen, most men were usually also burgesses — property owners and local taxpayers. To a greater or lesser extent they could be 'cessed' on their properties, and they were also liable to certain obligations, including a call to arms if required — indeed Stirling council decided in 1628 that 'no burgess be admitted hereafter until they first produce their armour sufficiently in presence of the council'.

The liability to taxation varied from a regular local tax, similar to the rates levied on householders in more recent times, to occasional exceptional demands; the Banff records for October 1683 show that when the town was 'stented' or taxed for a contribution of £500 to the college at St. Andrews, it raised half of this sum from local heritors and the rest from the town's own burgesses. At Forres, the usual regular 'rate' in 1659 for the burgh's 129 burgesses was between one shilling and ten shillings per month; the average was about three to four shillings, which provided the burgh with a total monthly income of £20:6:0d Scots. (Scottish currency is explained in Appendix 2.)

No man could be a trader or shopkeeper in any burgh if he was not also a burgess and a 'freeman' (or entitled to vote for the burgh council). The proof of being a burgess was possession of a burgess ticket, which, if the applicant was considered satisfactory, was generally presented at a short ceremony upon payment of a fee of entry. To lose the right to have a burgess ticket was therefore a terrible thing and deprived a man of his livelihood as a merchant. This did happen from time to time, generally for gross misbehaviour. When it occurred the feeling of devastation to the offender must have been terrible. In 1697 the Elgin burgh records minuted that William Paul was to lose his freedom as a burgess, 'his burgess bill to be publicly destroyed, and fined 500 merks. To be kept in the tolbooth until he pays this fine'. He must have been particularly hurt, because his only offence had been to mount a campaign against the re-election of the provost!

Lanark has a similar, but even worse, example lurking in its records. An unfortunate citizen called David Anderson was accused of insulting baillie Matthew Gemmell — a grave error, for Gemmell was also the judge in court and quickly found him guilty. The punishment which followed saw Anderson have his burgess ticket torn up at the cross in front of a crowd summoned by the town drummer, then fined £5 and jailed for twenty-four hours (longer if he did not pay up), then ordered to stand at the tron next market day from 10 o'clock to noon with a paper pinned to his chest describing his crime, and then to return to prison until he publicly apologised to baillie Gemmell and gave him satisfaction. It must have been some insult!

Provost Ross's House at Aberdeen. Solid, large and close to the harbour and its trade, this was the late 16th-century home of a wealthy merchant (Provost Ross himself was an 18th-century merchant). The dwelling is the oldest in Aberdeen and now houses the Maritime Museum. *Photo*: Craig Mair.

Usually included as burgesses somewhere among the merchants and craftsmen were the town's professional people. Although Edinburgh had numerous advocates and academics, and other university towns were also well served with teachers, most burghs had at least some sort of doctor and a grammar school teacher. In 1714 even a small burgh like Selkirk had two writers (or lawyers), one doctor and three teachers.

Occasionally women burgesses were allowed — many brewers and publicans were women, for example — but sometimes this was only permitted on a temporary basis, as illustrated by some examples from Edinburgh. In 1660 a supplication was received from Issobel Dickiesone, relict (or widow) of a burgess, who had forfeited the privileges and freedoms of a burgess's widow by subsequently becoming pregnant. She begged the council to reconsider its judgement ('humblie submitts herselfe to the discretioun of the Counsell'); it agreed to restore her rights on payment of a £40 fine. Then in 1673 liberty was granted to a relict of

Detail of a window in Sir George Bruce's 'Palace' at Culross. His initials are carved into the stonework. The half-shuttered windows are typical of most houses and reflect the expense of glass panes in the 16th—18th centuries.

Andrew Kinnear, late minister at Calder, to 'trade as a burgess during her lifetime'. Sometimes the daughters of deceased burgesses were allowed to trade until they got married, and if they were too old, still there was a chance. In 1708, for example, the council 'granted licence to Elizabeth Skeen, daughter to the deceast Mr Thomas Skeen, advocat, to trade in this city, liberties and privileges thereof, and that during her life, she being unmarried', and to 'Margaret Mowbray, daughter to the deceast Mr Patrick Mowbray, late clerk to the chyrurgeons (surgeons), for all the days of her life, she being unmarried'. A decent humanity runs through these extracts, much finer than the petty vindictiveness of Lanark's baillie Gemmell.

Quite often, honorary burgesses were created. These were usually people with whom the burgh wanted to ingratiate itself, or whom the burghers thought might be useful or friendly to them one day. Stirling, for example, created two burgesses in 1617, as the records show: 'James Reid, one of the grooms of his Majesty's slaughterhouse, is received and admitted to the liberty and freedom of a neighbour and burgess of this burgh, and that grattis. Resolved, Master Myllingtoun, one of the purveyors of his Majesty's wines in the wine cellar, to the liberty and freedom of a neighbour and burgess'. Was it mere coincidence that King James VI visited the burgh soon after? In the same way, Edinburgh seems to have fallen over itself to create a string of presbyterian generals burgesses whenever they came anywhere near the city: the covenanter General Alexander Leslie in 1640, Lieutenant General David Leslie 'and many other officers in the army' in 1647, and then the Cromwellian General Monck in 1654.

Most burghs made local aristocratic landowners and any other important figures honorary burgesses almost as a matter of course. They received no extra rights or privileges from this — just a ceremonial parchment tied with a ribbon — but the gesture was important. Thus at Lanark, for example, a string of law lords, sons of earls and others joined the regulars, Lord Douglas and the Duke of Hamilton, as honorary burgesses. It was a useful precaution, and so inexpensive for the burgh funds!

Beneath this top-dressing of burgesses and their invited friends swelled a larger mass of 'unfreemen'. These included apprentices to burgesses, the servants of burgesses, scholars, 'stallingers' or non-burgess tradesmen who paid rent to be allowed to erect a market stall, skilled labourers, manual workers and casual workers, generally in that order. A surviving tax list for Selkirk in 1694/5 lists that town's inhabitants by their occupation, and for some reason includes the burgh piper, the boatman, and surprisingly even the miller, among the 'cottars without trades' or unskilled men — a revealing insight into class attitudes. The chief criterion seems to have been first the possession of property, failing which the possession of a skill or craft, then 'the rest'. Widows of burgesses seem to have been slotted in somewhere between the craftsmen and their apprentices or servants.

Some burgh records show how burgesses guarded their privileged social position from intruders. In 1633 the Convention of Royal Burghs, meeting at St. Andrews, passed an act whereby merchants who were in partnership with unfree skippers of trading ships, especially if they also lived in unfree ports (non-royal burghs), were to disengage from any bargains or agreements, under pain of

John Cowane was a 17th-century Stirling merchant who made a fortune trading with Holland. This statue stands above the door of the Guildhall, built between 1634 and 1649 with money left in his will. See page 89. *Photo*: Craig Mair.

a £100 fine. In the same way, business partnerships between free and unfree men were frowned on, because this was seen as one way an unfree man could worm his way into the burgess class. Another way was for an unfreeman to have his son apprenticed to a burgess — he might never benefit, but the son would become a fully qualified craftsman one day and thus probably become a burgess. Regulations about this varied from time to time — when trades were dwindling, anyone might manage to fix up an apprenticeship, but when trades were strong, laws would suddenly appear to favour the sons of burgesses. At Stirling, for example, the council passed an act in 1671 by which the entry fee for an unfree apprentice to the

Hamilton House at Prestonpans, the 17th-century house of a wealthy merchant-laird. See also page 177. *Photo*: Craig Mair.

rank of burgess was set at 500 merks — prohibitively high — whereas that for the son of a burgess was only ten merks.

One sign of the rivalry between merchants and tradesmen was the appearance of guilds (sometimes spelled 'gilds'). As early as the 13th century the merchants of Perth, Aberdeen, Stirling, Elgin and elsewhere formed themselves into associations, elected officials, and were eventually even granted royal charters acknowledging their rights. Berwick seems to have provided the early model, and in Dundee's charter of 1327, for example, the guild was to exist 'as freely as ever our burgesses of Berwick have and enjoy theirs'.

The most important right was that of being entitled to vote for the town council, and to be a member of it. In fact, many merchant guilds *were* the town council. In 1372, for example, reciprocal trading arrangements were made between the merchant guilds of Dundee and Montrose — the sort of administrative decisions normally made by a burgh council. By 1403 Edinburgh's election of guildry officebearers was, in practice, the election of the town's council. This seems to have been so in several burghs.

On the other hand, there were some burghs where exports and trade were not of great importance, and where merchant guilds

The tools of a blacksmith hammerman on a gravestone in Larbert kirkyard, Stirlingshire. Many craftsmen were wealthy enough to afford a decent headstone when they died. *Photo*: Craig Mair.

therefore did not appear. For example, apart from the annual export of a few bales of wool, Lanark was never a trading burgh — its strength lay in its craftsmen, where shoemakers (or cordiners) were especially numerous. In Forfar the cordiners were also very important, as were Selkirk's 'soutars'. Elsewhere weavers, hammermen or some other group of craftsmen may have been more important; the bonnetmakers of Kilmarnock were already famous in the 1650s, for example. In such towns, where crafts were more important than trade, merchant guilds sometimes did not exist. Instead, there were trade guilds, or 'incorporated trades'. They served a similar purpose, by regulating the town's affairs, choosing the town council, supervising burgh tolls and markets, and looking after the welfare of guild brethren and their families, such as 'decayed' widows or orphans.

Any group of craftsmen could form a guild if there were enough of them in the burgh to make one worthwhile. There were seven incorporated trades at Linlithgow, for example, namely the bakers (who also made ale), smiths, cordiners or shoemakers, weavers, wrights, fleshers or butchers, and tailors. In 1620 the shoemakers lost the right to make their own leather, and thereafter tanning became a separate industry. Coopers existed (they made wooden plates as well as barrels), but they were not incorporated. At Lanark, the first guilds included cordiners, weavers, hammermen, tailors, dyers, skinners, waulkers, butchers, glovers, wrights and masons. There were not enough maltmen or coopers to form guilds, and within fifty years those of the butchers and glovers also became extinct. Similarly at Linlithgow the waulkers died out as a guild in 1639. These crafts and trades still existed, of course, but there were too few members to make guilds viable. Each guild then elected a representative, known as a Deacon, and from these deacons one was elected (even in merchant-dominated burghs) as the Dean of Guild to serve on the council. His function is explained in Chapter 5.

In due course many trade guilds were also acknowledged by the Crown and given official charters. In 1660 the Lanark tailors had their seals renewed, and the preamble to this document is typical: 'Formerly the Deacons and freemen of the said Craft had a seal of Cause granted to them by the baillies and council of the said burgh for the time, acknowledging them of old to be a trade and a member of their incorporation'. Numerous clauses then went on to detail working conditions, duties, rights, infringements, and allowed them to 'elect and admit yearly a Deacon with boxmasters (treasurers) and officers, who shall be defended by the provost, bailies and council in all their lawful acts and statutes'. Details of crafts and trades are in Chapter 8.

As times changed, so did circumstances in many burghs. Trade might dwindle or improve, and so the importance of merchants and craftsmen could see-saw. In practice, most burghs moved to a position in which there were both merchant and craft guilds, generally rivals, but sharing the right to elect the town council and to be members of that council. Merchants always believed that they were superior to mere craftsmen, but in reality they often depended on the output of those same craftsmen for their exports, and a grudging kind of mutual co-existence seems to have settled over most burghs. It is noticeable, however, that merchants usually occupied the most important positions on town councils.

In theory, guilds may have been about political power, but in day-to-day practice one of their most useful functions was in caring for the widows and children of members who died. At a time when there were no old-age or widows' pensions guildry funds were a lifesaving source of charity for many people left destitute by a sudden or premature death. The Stirling guildry records mention how in 1661 several widows, 'relics of brethren who are in great necessity', were given monies, 'as much as seen fit', and again, in a slightly different vein, they refer in 1653 to a 'distressed chapman' or pedlar who was given £10 because he had lost all his goods at Dundee and had a wife and children sick with ague.

Finally, it is worth mentioning that some towns had no guildry at all, and that about half of all guildries were not established until after the Reformation. Such burghs still functioned, of course, but since neither merchants nor craftsmen were organised into guilds, perhaps because there were not enough to make guilds feasible, local burgess-lairds tended to hold power and dominate town councils. Stranraer, for example, was a burgh with only 279 adult inhabitants in 1684, and consequently was easily dominated by the local Kennedy lairds, whose tower-castle still stands in the centre of the town.

CHAPTER 5

Town Councils

What exactly were the town councils which ran Scotland's royal burghs? By their charters, royal burghs were allowed to elect their own governing bodies; in other words, there was no question of feudal control such as existed over burghs of barony or in the countryside. Burgh councils were completely independent and were entitled to resist the demands of local lairds or gentry if they wished. Laws made by various monarchs repeatedly declared the independence of burghs and prohibited interference from outside landowners, as was noted by Banff's burgh council in 1670: 'The magistrates and council, finding and considering that in times bygone barons and gentlemen have screwed themselves in the office of the magistracy and government of this burgh, contrary to the acts of Parliament, and by the admitting of them to the said offices the common good of the said burgh is dissipated, the liberties thereof much infringed, and the place reduced to great poverty; for preventing such prejudices in after times therefore statute and ordain that the election of the magistrates of the burgh be made conforming to the eighth Act of Parliament of King James the Sixth, that no person be elected provost or bailies but such as be burgesses, actual residents and constant traffickers and such persons who will lose and win in all the affairs of the burgh'.

Most town councils consisted of about twenty members, from whom a number were elected by the rest to official positions, rather similar to the arrangement of District Councils today. The highest office was that of Provost, but in many respects this was an honorary post which varied from place to place. Originally the provost was the king's representative, often the sheriff, in a royal burgh. By 1650, however, the king's direct influence had greatly waned and the position of provost had changed. In some burghs he was still the chief magistrate, but in others the provost was no more than a local dignitary or burgess-laird, given the title as a courtesy.

In some burghs the office (with a grander-sounding title of Lord Provost) was held, like a hereditary title, by the most important local family; Peebles' first Lord Provost appears in the records for 1555 and was John, Lord Hay of Yester, the first of a succession of

This little statue of a burgh provost sits like a Toby jug in a niche at Ceres in Fife. He is said to have been the last church-appointed provost of this burgh of barony — which would date him to around 1578, though the figure was carved by John Howie, an 18th-century local stonemason. *Photo*: Craig Mair.

Yesters. At Lanark the candidates for provost in 1582 included Lord Somervell, the various lairds of Dalzell, Carmichael, Hamilton, Leviston, Cunningham, Bannatyne, and James Lockhart of Lee who was actually elected. By the 1590s, however, John, Lord Hamilton had become almost a permanent fixture as provost and the first of many more Hamiltons to follow on later. In the same way the Menzies and Gordons monopolised Aberdeen, as did the Scotts of Buccleuch at Selkirk, the Learmonths of Dairsie at St. Andrews, and so on. Some local noblemen had no serious interest in burgh affairs and chose a burgess to act for them; at Edinburgh when local dignitaries were invited to become provost, a local burgess was also appointed 'president' and would actually perform the day-to-day functions of the provostship.

By the 17th century the burgesses in many towns were electing someone from their own number to the provost's post. It was still essentially an honorary position and was usually given to someone who would make a fitting public figure or representative for the burgh. The post usually circulated round a select group of cronies who chose each other year by year. On the other hand Burntisland varied between a burgess provost and a lord provost. Some burghs had no provost at all; Linlithgow and Lanark did without until 1540, and at least nine burghs still had no provost even in 1708, which only shows how unimportant and purely ceremonial the office generally was.

Below the provost in rank came the bailies, or burgh magistrates. Unlike the provost, whose function could be different from place to place, bailies had a specific and identical role in every burgh — indeed, when a burgess took his oath, it was to the king, the *bailies* and the community, and did not include any mention of the provost. Their earliest function was to collect the king's taxes (except customs on trade, which were collected by the customer), but by the 17th century they had evolved into law officers. Sometimes this meant work as a Depute Sheriff in court, but in day-to-day terms it often involved little more than settling petty disputes. Most bailies were ordinary merchants (hardly ever craftsmen), so many squabbles were settled simply by asking a bailie to adjudicate between townsfolk at his shop door. In Lanark, however, there were so many interruptions to business that two actually complained of this and said they did not want the job. One, called James Gray, was eventually imprisoned in the tolbooth in 1605 for his lack of public spirit!

On the other hand, bailies had considerable authority and most enjoyed the status. In particular, as Depute Sheriffs, bailies had the power of life and death in the courts — woe betide anyone who even just insulted a bailie, or any little boy who threw a clod of earth at one, for punishments could be severe. The case of Bailie Gemmell at Lanark was not an isolated example. It followed, of course, that bailies themselves had to be men of high character and complete honesty, and if a bailie was discovered to have been secretly breaking the law himself, the scandal was all the greater.

Below the bailies there ranked a number of other officials. Among them was the burgh treasurer (or 'thesaurer' as he was often spelled), whose job was to supervise and guard the town's money, in the days before banks. The surviving account books of many burghs go back to well before 1600 and reveal a wide variety of sources of income. Explained simply, royal burghs paid a cess or lease to the Crown in return for their privileges, raised mainly by the burgh heritors and from trade tolls and customs. However, burghs could also add to their income in other ways, and this money was known as the Common Good, to be used for repairs or projects which would benefit the entire town. Ayr's accounts for 1616, for example, show the Common Good being used to pay Andrew Morris for rebuilding part of the tolbooth stair (£9: 2s), George Fultoun for slating the kirk and pointing the council-house (£22), John Smyth for going to Irvine about the casting of the town bell and for its delivery (£4: 10s), Laurence Porter for cleaning the streets (£6), and so on.

Common Good income came from such things as the lease of mills, from ferry dues, from the hire of a mortcloth or bellringer at funerals or from the subletting of common grazing lands or fishings. Some privileges were even auctioned to burgesses by public roup; the right to collect customs dues, or to run the town mill (which everyone was obliged to use) were examples. Usually any burgess winning, say, the right to the local salmon fishing also had to offer some property (other than his own house) as security, but thereafter he would have the monopoly of all local salmon fishing and selling for a year and would expect to make a profit from the business. The burgh, meanwhile, obtained an annual income from the auction of its various concessions.

On the whole this system worked well but it was open to abuse on occasion. Town councillors could benefit themselves by not increasing the rent on the burgh's mills or other properties; Inverkeithing was once fined by the Convention of Scottish Burghs for not raising its rents for nineteen years! By law, customs could not be let for more than one year at a time, and fishings for a maximum of only three years, so that the rents could be increased from time to time. In the same way, it was found in 1590 that Aberdeen had not sublet its concessions for thirty years — the magistrates and their friends had simply pocketed the various sources of income, to the detriment of the Common Good fund. As the Convention investigators wrote, the burgh had been 'thirled to serve one race of people, as if it were a burgh of barony'.

Another important official was the Dean of Guild. He represented the guild members and was responsible for ensuring that trading regulations and standards were properly enforced. The Dean of Guild Court could punish offenders, such as those who traded outwith the correct hour' or whose workmanship was shoddy. For example, Robert Strachan, a merchant at Keith, was fined £10 by the Dean of Guild's court at Banff in 1663 for having faulty weights: 'his quarter weight was found one ounce light, and his pound weight was found twelve drops light'. In later years this court came increasingly to handle building and planning controls as well.

Lesser officials included the Master of Works, responsible for building work and repairs such as to bridges. The Master of Works was not always a burgess or even a council member, for this was a job which ideally should be given to someone with building experience such as a stonemason. At Lanark, however, the local wigmaker was appointed on one occasion! Part of the Master of Works' remit included care of the burgh's tools, and the supervision of workmen employed on council business. It was not a popular post — not only was it frequently unpaid, but the master was often out of pocket since he had to pay any workmen himself first, and then claim the expense back from the council.

Then there was the Burgh Clerk, who kept the records (and thanks to whom so much is known about burghs today). The clerk was very important because, although the councillors were burgesses, many could not write. In 1681, for example, when Elgin's councillors had to sign the Test document (an oath of loyalty to the Protestant faith), only a few could actually write their own names, and the local Notary had to sign for twenty-seven more 'because they cannot write, except Alexander Winchester, who subscribeth A.W.' The surviving records of so many burghs bear witness to the careful and laborious work which generations of clerks undertook over the centuries.

Another important official was the Fiscal, who was responsible for legal prosecutions and was usually elected annually. Some burghs created several at one time — in October 1601 Paisley burgh council appointed four, for example. The fiscal was usually helped by 'officers', who were the nearest thing then to policemen or jailors. These officers were supposed to guard the tolbooth, and to ensure that there was peace and quiet on the streets, or at night.

Most burghs needed only four officers, each delegated to a particular area of the town, but in emergencies they could co-opt more men from among the townsfolk, and in that event the 'officers' became more like military captains. In the 1690s, for example, during the 'seven ill years' when Scotland suffered from terrible famine, burghs found themselves swollen with people from the surrounding areas looking for food. During this period Banff organised night watches of its streets and adjacent fields, undertaken by officers each with ten men, with orders to apprehend all vagrants and thieves.

In addition, there were Inspectors of various sorts. In the 14th and 15th centuries most burghs had ale-tasters and 'flesh-prisers', appointed during the summer months when meat and drink would appear for sale in the town. By the 17th century these had developed further, and covered a wider range of market commodities. There were ale- and wine-tasters whose job was to inspect the quality of alcoholic drink offered for sale within the burgh, and to ensure that it was sold within the correct hours. The work of the 'Visitor to the fleshmarket' or 'Appreciator of flesh' similarly involved the control of quality and trading times, but also included a check on the way meat was cut up by the burgh's butchers. In the same way there were often fish-prisers or 'visitors and judgers of fish', timber-prisers, and so on.

There were also Lyners, or 'Lynsters', whose function was to check all boundaries within the burgh. They led the ceremony of riding the marches, but also adjudicated between burgesses when disputes arose over property demarcation. At Selkirk, for example, only one property in 1714 was divided from its neighbour by a dyke, 'the ancient walls known as Cowans Walls'; all others were marked by stones placed there by the council, or by trees and other natural features. Encroachment by one man on his neighbour's land would have been quite feasible. At Lanark the Moss Divider had the task of supervising peat-cutting on the burgh commons; this was permitted only during the month of May, when the year's entire fuel supply had to be cut, and was another occasion when arguments could arise over bounds and encroachments.

Some burghs included a Poinder among their officials. In 1604, for example, Paisley appointed a man 'for poinding and apprehending of all horse, ky [cattle], and other bestial eating any other man's corn or grass [other than] their owners'. His job, in other words, was to seize all animals grazing illegally on someone else's land. In 1653, for example, Peebles burgh council ordered 'all the goods (except the town's) to be houded and poynded off Venlaw and Homildon' which were part of the burgh's common grazing lands.

Many burghs had officials to supervise various aspects of the Common Good. Some towns had a hospital or charity almshouse, for example, so there was a hospital-master. Stirling's hospital originally stood on the site of the later High School, and then moved to the building now called the Guildhall, but once known as Cowane's Hospital after John Cowane, a wealthy local burgess who endowed the building. In the same way, there were variously bridge-masters, pier-masters, kirk-masters and others, depending on the kind of burgh. Some ports such as Ayr, Glasgow, Irvine and Aberdeen also had water-bailies, whose job was to regulate all goods landed in the harbour, to ensure that all duties were paid, to prevent smuggling, and even to supervise the dumping of ballast stones so that these did not silt up the navigation channel.

Finally, other men employed in the service of the burgh included the clock-keeper and the bellman or town-crier. These duties were sometimes undertaken by the same person, as at Elgin in 1703 when the council appointed James Russell bellman with the proviso that 'he shall keep the town's clock so right in her going as that she shall not go half an hour wrong backward or forward in twenty four hours time. . . .' In addition, Russell was to ring the bell at 8 p.m. and 4 a.m. daily as a sort of public alarm-clock service.

Larger burghs sometimes also had an executioner. At Lanark he was known as the 'Executioner of the Laws' in the 17th century, but by 1737 was recorded simply as 'the common hangman'. For centuries there never was a hanging in Lanark and his main job was actually to administer public whippings. This persuaded the burgh in 1730 to economise by doing without an executioner; when the need for one then arose in 1733 the town had to borrow him from Hamilton, which cost them £6: 16s — hardly an economy, since the Lanark hangman's annual salary in 1729 had been just 25 merks plus £5 for a house. Like Stirling and several other burghs, Lanark also employed a minstrel, and every burgh also had either a piper or a drummer.

The drummer's job was similar to that of the bellman. In many burghs, council regulations were advertised round the town 'by

Cowane's Hospital in Stirling, built with money left by John Cowane, a wealthy 17th-century merchant. The building was originally an almshouse for elderly guild brethren, but later became the Guildhall. See also page 77. *Photo*: Craig Mair.

tuck of drum'. The annual reappointment of a drummer crops up regularly in most burgh records, as at Stirling in November 1642 when Duncan Ewing was appointed burgh drummer, conditional on his good behaviour, at £60 Scots yearly plus a livery of clothes every one or two years. Ewing had to promise to tuck his drum nightly at 7 p.m. and each morning at 4 a.m., beginning at the Lady Vennel and through the whole town. His wages were to be paid by raising £20 from the guild brethren, £20 from the craftsmen, £10 from the maltmen and £10 from a mixture of the burgh wrights, masons, coopers, slaters, and others. Even the drum itself was a considerable item of expenditure for any burgh council anxious to watch every penny; Elgin's records for 1641 mention that 'Robert Hardie when he goes to Edinburgh, provide a drum for the town of Elgin'. In other words, at a time of difficult communications and high transport costs, it was too expensive to send away for one. Some burgh drums still survive in local museums, such as at Irvine and Aberdeen.

Burgh pipers were the characters in any town; their music

D

Linlithgow's town drummer, a figure on the burgh's mercat cross.
Considering how many drummers there must once have been, surprisingly
little sign of their existence survives in Scotland except for an occasional
drum in a museum.

brightened up fairs and markets, and their colourful personalities
would make a book in itself. Habbie Simpson, the 16th-century
piper of Kilbarchan, is perhaps remembered best of all, thanks to
Robert Sempill's poem of his exploits, as in this brief extract:

> And at horse races many a day,
> Before the black, the brown, the gray,
> He gart his pipe, when he did play,
> Baith skirl and skreed:
> Now all such pastime's quite away
> Sen Habbie's dead.

Habbie Simpson, the much-loved piper of Kilbarchan, gazes down from a niche in the town's kirk steeple. This 19th-century statue replaced an earlier wooden one. *Photo*: Craig Mair.

Another well-known piper was Rob the Ranter, who played at fairs in Fife. A poem of the time describes how he met Maggie Lauder at Anstruther Fair, for example.

Most pipers were dreadful rogues, particularly fond of a drink or the company of lassies, and as often as not to be found sobering up in a tolbooth cell. Burgh councils could not be seen to condone such behaviour, and pipers were regularly sacked, at least until they went through the motions of showing abject repentance for their excesses. Then they were quickly reappointed in time for the next wedding or fair, for like all politicians, town councillors well knew how to be popular with ordinary folk.

Last of all there were the town herds — Paisley had two, for

example — whose duties were to keep an eye on the burgh's cattle
and sheep during the grazing season on the commons, to stop them
from wandering on to the unfenced agricultural rigs or strip fields
where they might trample the crops. These herds were often
appointed on a seasonal basis, usually from Beltane (Whitsunday)
to Lammas (August 1st). At Lanark the end of the grazing season
was signalled by blowing a horn, after which animals were supposed
to be kept in byres or allowed only to forage in the corn stubble on
the rigs.

And so burgh councils up and down Scotland were elected and
ran their town's affairs. In 1673 the Elgin burgh council consisted of
seventeen burgesses, comprising the Provost, four bailies, the Dean
of Guild, the Treasurer, the Clerk, two Fiscals, two Visitors to the
Fleshmarket, a Master of the Hospital, and four officers. The
Peebles council of 1684 consisted of seventeen burgesses plus two
local lords as extraordinary members, and included a Provost, two
bailies, Dean of Guild, Treasurer, a clerk, several officers and a
Keeper of the Keys (or jailer). By a local Act, Stirling's council in
1620 came to consist of twenty persons, of whom the Provost, four
bailies, Dean of Guild and Treasurer were all to be merchants and
guild brethren, plus an additional seven merchants and seven
deacons of crafts. The gradual involvement of craft deacons in local
government can also be seen at Lanark, where the council for 1712
consisted of six merchants and eleven craftsmen.

In general, only about one third of a burgh's council stood for
election each year. Those standing down that year could not be
immediately re-elected but had to wait until the following year's
election to stand again. Nevertheless, in most burgh records the
same names reappear regularly, and it is clear that most towns were
dominated by a small group of the most powerful burgesses, voting
for each other. Sometimes there was serious rivalry between families
both seeking local burgh influence and prestige. At Forres, for
example, the Dunbars and Tullochs jostled for power for well over
a century, and when Sheriff Dunbar of Moray was shot dead in 1611
there were many who suspected the Tullochs were behind it.

Burgh council meetings were originally known as Head Courts
and were supposed to be held three times a year, at Michaelmas
(October), Christmas and Pasch (Easter). Elections were generally
held in October, when new burgesses were admitted, stallingers
had their licence to erect market stalls reviewed, town lands were

Dysart tolbooth, an excellent example from Fife. Town councils all over Scotland normally convened in the burgh tolbooth. *Photo*: Craig Mair.

feued or rouped, market regulations were updated and the most important local laws or Acts were passed. On these Head Court occasions burgesses were obliged to attend, wearing their armour, on pain of a fine if they were absent.

That was the theory, but in practice most burgh councils met weekly, often on a Monday, and usually ceremonially summoned by the burgh piper or drummer or the ringing of a bell. At Forres the council arranged in 1658 to have the town bell rung at 7 a.m., when meetings were supposed to begin. In Peebles a council statute warned that 'if any member of the council be not present at the meeting after the prayer be said and calling of the roll, without a lawful excuse or licence had of before from one of the magistrates, [he] shall pay for the public use [i.e. the common good] two shillings

Scots; and ordaines a box to be made for keeping such fines to the use of the public'. Meetings were usually held in the tolbooth, but this was not universal. The Elgin burgh records, for example, hardly ever indicate where the council convened, but one rare reference mentions 'At Elgin and within the South Aisle of St. Giles Church, thereof the forsaid twenty third day of July, 1683 years, a meeting about James Cumming's yard etc.'

CHAPTER 6

Burgh Courts and Punishments

Burgh courts clearly had great powers. Most day-to-day affairs of life were controlled in some way by local regulations. In essence, burgh councils were there to enforce parliamentary laws first, and then to supplement them with a host of local laws or Acts designed to deal with the lesser matters of burgh commerce, buildings, dress, behaviour and so on. On top of this, the Kirk had great sway over people's moral behaviour (even if it did not actually break any law), but this is dealt with separately in Chapter 10.

A sample dip into the burgh court books of some Scottish towns gives a good flavour of the wide range of municipal affairs regulated by the council. Many, such as building controls, street cleaning or education still come under District or Regional authority even today, forming unbroken links which, in some cases, go back for many centuries.

Building regulations were very common. The Banff records for 1655 mention that 'the magistrates and council give power and warrant to James Smith to edify and build a stair and passage to the front street for accommodation of his new house, the said stair not exceeding thirty-six inches to the door'. Similarly, the Stirling records for 1599 state that 'it is statute and ordained by the bailies and council that no person or persons presume to take on hand to build, edify or big, any house or work with this burgh or territory thereof in any time coming, without [having first received] the advice and consent of the council of the said burgh . . . under the pain of twenty pounds money to be paid by any person or persons contravening the same . . . to the common good of the said burgh'.

Instances of burgesses being made to pull down unauthorised extensions and outside stairs crop up regularly in burgh records, just as they still do in local newspapers today. One example was Alexander Cunningham, a Stirling merchant, who was discovered in 1629 to have encroached on the street near the cross by erecting a wooden extension, and who was given just forty-eight hours to take it all down again under pain of a £40 Scots fine.

Other aspects of what might be called the general appearance of burghs were also strictly controlled. In 1696 Aberdeen burgh council

A halberd or axe, once used by the burgh officer and found a few years ago in a disused room in the Inverkeithing tolbooth. It is now on display with a more ceremonial example in the local museum.

passed an act against the keeping of pigs, 'being an unseemly kind of beast', and ordered that none should be allowed within a quarter mile of the town. Elgin's council likewise acted against the proliferation of dogs in the burgh by ordaining that 'no bitches be kept within the burgh under the pain of six pounds money'.

Middens or dungheaps were a common cause of complaint in burghs; people generally threw their slops and waste out into the street — 'ane midding stead fornenst the door' as the Tain records put it. As these grew bigger they eventually obstructed traffic, and councils were then forced to take action. A typical instance was at Peebles in 1671, when the council warned inhabitants: 'keep any midden or muck upon the king's causeway, at any time hereafter, under this certification that it shall be lawful for any neighbour within the same to intromet [interfere] and lead away such muck found upon the said street, lying above eight days time, for his own use'. (Middens made good manure and were highly prized and valued by townsfolk, who spread them on their lands.)

Eventually road sweeping was introduced, as at Aberdeen where the council finally got round to 'appoynting ane scaffinger for keeping the streits clene' in 1675. Similarly, Elgin's records for March 1681 show the burgh treasurer paying John Findlay £20 Scots monthly for keeping the streets clean, while at Ayr the streets were swept by David Huntar who, in 1623, was paid £6 out of the Common Good for his services.

Water supply was another problem. In 1706, following a very dry summer, Selkirk's burgh council agreed a cost of £95 Scots with a plumber called Campbell for piping water to the Cross. This included the cost of 'casting the ditch for the pypes, building a little lodge round the font and a big trough at the Cross for gathering water'. Similarly, Linlithgow's Cross Well was repaired by the council in 1659 following damage by Cromwellian troops.

The variety of other interests regulated by burgh councils is considerable. In 1652 members of the Forres council interviewed Thomas Tulloch for 'tilling land in the north side of the Cloven Hills, which was the town's Commonte, and putting up a fence for bestial etc.', which was followed a few months later by a new law stating that 'any inhabitant found pasturing his bestial in his neighbour's corn or grass under cloud of night, the same shall pay for every beast 20 shillings of a fine'. By contrast, in 1589 Glasgow's council 'statut and ordained that all creamers [i.e. stall-keepers] of woollen cloth stand above the cross, or pay a fine of 16 shillings, unless they are freemen. The butchers below the cross have to stand beside their own merchandise before their own doors'. Yet again, Lanark's council passed a law designed to prevent house fires by insisting that malt kilns and tallow melting (for making candles) were to be outside the burgh ports. Similarly, in 1653 Stirling's council ordered the treasurer to provide the town with buckets for fire-fighting, and in another case ordered ladders to be hung along the walls of closes, to facilitate rescues and firefighting when required.

Punishments for those who offended local or national laws were handed down by the burgh courts. Broadly speaking, these were matched to the person concerned and the crime committed, so they varied widely in different circumstances. Another factor was the town's ability to pay for certain punishments; prison sentences, for example, were generally quite short since the burgh had to provide a jailor, food and perhaps even fuel for any prisoner locked in the tolbooth.

Executions (other than for witches, explained in Chapter 10) were also surprisingly rare — in most burghs except Edinburgh there might be only one or two in a person's entire lifetime. When they did occur, executions were usually by public hanging; since the dropping trapdoor was not invented yet, death was therefore an agonisingly slow strangulation by knotted noose, with the executioner sometimes hanging on to the victim's feet to speed up the process. Beheading was perhaps a quicker death, assuming that the axeman was both sober and accurate. However, the axe on show at St. Andrews Museum has such a short handle that the blows cannot have been very powerful; success presumably depended on the weight and sharpness of the blade. At the Royal Museum of Scotland in Queen Street, Edinburgh there is also a guillotine, incongruously known as the Maiden. Though first used in the late 16th century, it still looks a gruesomely effective instrument even today. The blade of another Maiden can also be seen at Provost Skene's House in Aberdeen. In many places females were sometimes executed by drowning, especially in burghs of barony where the feudal superior perhaps had the right of 'pit and gallows'.

Punishments must be kept in perspective, however, for comparatively few people were executed. Most people were likely to suffer a spell in the jougs or stocks, where they learned their lesson through public ridicule. At Hawick in 1676, for example, Adam Brown, found guilty of 'the most insolent degree of all

Stirling's original beheading axe, now in the local museum. The 'beheading stone' survives on a nearby hillock, although executions were more commonly performed near the tolbooth. *Photo*: The Collections of the Smith Art Gallery and Museum, Stirling.

degrees of insolence and contempt done against the bailies', was fined £20 Scots and made 'to lie in stocks during the bailies' will and pleasure'.

Another typical, and attractively cheap, punishment was banishment from the town. In 1658 at Elgin, Jannet Coutes was 'ordained to be jouged and banished with a paper on her head to show her fault, which is swearing, lying and slandering'. Similarly in 1654 Isabel Taylour, found guilty of theft at Forres, was 'banished off the burgh liberties thereof, and if she is found within the liberties thereof in any time thereafter, she is to suffer death without doom'. In 1675 at Fortrose a thief was ordered to be publicly scourged or whipped by the executioner and then immediately banished from the shire.

Fines were also common, since they could be set according to the offender's means and usefully added to the burgh's revenues. Record books are full of examples, such as the weavers who were each fined £20 Scots at Hawick in 1683 for making cloth too narrow, or the three Peebles youths who, in 1665, were each fined 40 shillings Scots for assaulting James Caitcheon, plus another thirty shillings for the repair of his torn cloak. Then there was councillor Thomas Young who was fined £40 Scots at Lanark for persistent failure to attend council meetings, or James Keith and Mary Smith who were fined at Banff for having premarital sex.

Some punishments could be horrifyingly brutal. At Fortrose a woman was convicted of reset and ordered in 1698 to be scourged through the burgh, receiving twelve lashes in each of the town's

The Stirling stocks. Not many wooden ones survive, although there once
were many all over Scotland. Those at Hamilton were burned for firewood
during the Second World War. The principle was the same as for those at
Crieff (page 56). *Photo*: The Collections of the Smith Art Gallery and
Museum, Stirling.

four streets. At Banff in 1658 John Henderson was taken to an
upper room in the tolbooth and there whipped by two officers for
insulting a magistrate. Worse still, in 1604 at Edinburgh, for
murdering a farmer Robert Weir was tied and spreadeagled on a
cartwheel and had his back broken by the burgh hangman.

At Stirling in 1546 John Fischair (Fisher) was found guilty of
stealing clothes and was sentenced to be nailed by an ear to the
wooden post of the tron, to have the other ear cut off, to be branded
on the cheek, to be whipped through the streets, and then to be
banished from the shire under threat of death if he ever returned.
He may, of course, have been a persistent criminal who had been
punished before, but it does seem a very vindictive punishment.
Sometimes an offender was allowed to pull himself free by ripping
his ear, as at Castle Grant on Speyside in 1692, where one man was
sentenced 'to be nailed by the lug with an iron nail to a post, and to
stand there for the space of one hour without motion, and to be
allowed to break the griss (gristle?) nailed without drawing of the
nail'. This form of punishment was sometimes opposed by burgesses,
not because of its cruelty, but because so many people came to
watch the victim pluck up courage to tear himself free that it
disrupted burgh life — 'children played truant from school, the

This extraordinary example of a branks was worn like a helmet, with the long point representing the tongue. Women who spread malicious gossip were often punished by being made to wear a branks. This example, and the one on page 149, are at Montrose. *Photo*: Angus District Libraries and Museums Service.

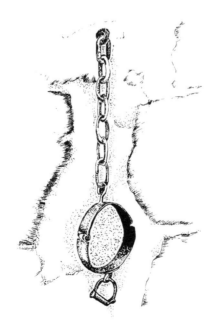

The jougs at Ceres hang outside the tolbooth and are exactly typical of most others all over Scotland (see page 147). They were locked round the neck of an offender, thus inflicting public ridicule and disgrace.

weavers left their looms, the women threw their spindles down', as one writer described it.

Elsewhere, some people had their noses broken, a process performed with an iron frame fitted with clips which held the cartilege of the nose, apparently between the nostrils. At Carluke, for example, a persistent local thief was 'pilloried, his lug nailed and his nose pinched'. And of course there were any number of other punishments — human cruelty and ingenuity seem to know no bounds — so people were publicly stripped and flayed, had their hair shorn (a favourite for adultresses), had a hole burned through their tongue, and so on.

One last matter which greatly exercised the burgh courts was the question of wandering beggars. There were beggars in every town, some genuinely in need because of being crippled or blind or whatever, but others fit and of working age who were not considered to be *bona fide* destitutes. Times and fortunes could, of course, change and work or food might be in short supply so that even the 'able-bodied' poor may well have been sometimes in desperate straits.

Many burghs allowed a number of citizens to become licensed beggars or 'gaberlunzies', shown by wearing a lead badge or token with the town's stamp on it, and sometimes also by wearing a blue gown. This arrangement usually applied only to cripples or the elderly, and occasionally to little children, and it was invariably emphasised that this was a privilege which could be withdrawn at any time for unsatisfactory conduct. Nevertheless it also helped to identify outsiders or vagrants as unlicensed and therefore offenders.

Sometimes the wandering poor were tolerated, but every so often the burgh authorities would clamp down, either by organising a sudden mass round-up of strangers or by making an example of one or two. Thus in 1697 the four bailies of Banff were ordered to search the town for beggars and 'to banish all loose vagabonds who cannot give an account of their manner of living, summarily without process'. At Lanark the problem of 'vagrants, thiggers, randy beggars and Egyptian [gypsy] sorners' seems also to have cropped up regularly, as in 1654 when Margaret Gordoun was banished from the town for being drunk and 'speaking vainly and idly in asking kisses from noblemen, gentlemen and others in a scorning way'.

This beggar's token is marked 'M. Gordon, Keith' and is typical of those worn by 'official' beggars in most burghs. *Photo*: The Collections of the Smith Art Gallery and Museum, Stirling.

Nevertheless, in spite of the risks, the streets of every town were full of sad, pathetic folk who sat on the forestairs or by the closes with outstretched hands, or who solicited or got drunk or said they were shipwrecked sailors or did odd jobs when they could. Typical of most towns, Dundee's records stated clearly that any beggar not actually born in the burgh would be burned on the cheek and banished from the town. For many people the threat of being branded, usually with the tolbooth key, was a risk they ran every day. For them, life was always a fine balance between people's instinctive charity and their suspicion of strangers or idle wasters.

CHAPTER 7

Merchants, Shops and Markets

The greatest benefit to any royal burgh in 17th-century Scotland was that it had certain privileges which other towns did not enjoy. For burgess citizens, the most important of these was the right to trade and to collect tolls or customs from outsiders coming into a burgh to sell their goods.

By this time, many burghs of barony had been founded and were steadily eating into these trading privileges. Many allowed craftsmen to work there, and had the right to hold markets or annual fairs, but royal burghs still held on to the greatest advantage of all — the right to import from abroad and to send goods overseas. That was the *real* moneyspinner; exclusive access to foreign spices and fabrics, wines, brandies, furs and ivories, for sale to Scotland's gentry, made far greater fortunes than the humdrum sale of home-produced candles or shoes or rough cloth to ordinary folk ever did. And so there appeared, within the merchant class in any burgh, subdivisions between those merchants who traded abroad and perhaps even owned some ships themselves, those who went with horse and pack round more distant parts of Scotland, and the more modest vendors of local products who stayed mostly at home.

Some powerful merchants were very rich men, fit even to marry royalty, such as one who married James III's niece during the 15th century. Many were based in Edinburgh, through which most overseas Scottish trade passed, but they could also be found living in ones and twos in any of the more important burghs. Sir George Bruce made a fortune trading coal out of Culross, for example, and built for himself a house known today as the Palace, close to the mines which were the source of his wealth. John Cowane of Stirling became rich from the trade through Holland, benefiting from the royal preference for Stirling Castle and the constant demand for wines, spices, textiles and other commodities which this generated. Likewise, Sir John Wood of Largo made his fortune in London and left £70,000 on his death in 1659.

Scotland's greatest merchants, however, lived in Edinburgh. During the 16th century bailie John MacMorran was probably the

Sailor's Walk in Kirkcaldy, a reminder of the town's wealthy sea captains and the North Sea trade with Europe. *Photo*: Craig Mair.

richest of all, with shares in nine trading ships and huge debts owed to him at Dieppe, Bordeaux and elsewhere when he died in 1595 (shot by a schoolboy in an affray at the Royal High School). A generation later Patrick Wood died with an estate worth over £100,000, including debtors in Poland, Spain, France, and the Canary Islands, plus shares in four ships, saltpans in seven towns, a ropeworks, butter, herring, wool and potash ventures. Sir William Dick of Braid, Provost of Edinburgh in 1638—9, was even wealthier, 'in Scots money a millionaire twice over' as one historian has put it, and mostly won from continental business ventures.

Cargoes for such men came into sea and river ports mostly on the east coast, benefiting burghs such as Perth, Dundee, Aberdeen, Leith, Montrose, Arbroath, Culross, Crail and Stirling. During the 17th century Scottish trading ships were still pathetically small; in 1656 a report for Oliver Cromwell by the English civil servant Thomas Tucker listed only four east-coast harbours where there were owners of vessels weighing more than ten tons burden. Fewer than one third of all east-coast ships noted by Tucker weighed

Three dignified and prosperous-looking 17th-century Glasgow merchants, every inch the picture of solid confidence. *Photo*: Craig Mair, courtesy of the Glasgow Merchants' House.

more than one hundred tons and the largest was an exception at two hundred tons.

Harbours were just as simple, being at best a couple of wooden jetties but more often simply a natural river bank or coastal bay. (The remains of stone quaysides have been excavated at Aberdeen but the dig was too small to reveal much.) Whatever the kind of harbour, vessels simply moored alongside and then rode with the tide, for there were no dock gates or harbour basins. At the time of Tucker's report, Leith was the most important Scottish trading port, largely due to the import of huge quantities of wine — in 1692 over one third of Edinburgh's income came from duties paid on claret and port landed at Leith. Even the northern English counties traded wine through Leith. The port's extensive wine vaults, rediscovered in 1981, date back to the 15th century at least, but the actual harbour facilities were very elementary, 'a convenient dry harbour into which the Firth ebbs and flows every tide, and a

Part of Lamb's House in Leith, rescued in the 1950s from neglect and dilapidation. There are very few signs now of Leith's great merchants or its old trading days. *Photo*: Craig Mair.

convenient key (*sic*) on one side thereof, of a good length, for landing goods'.

Edinburgh's wine importers were, of course, extremely wealthy men and for centuries had a good run for their money, until the 19th century when high taxes and cheap whisky killed the trade. The current revival of wine drinking, and even the appearance of a new, very enjoyable, Leith Claret in 1985, have therefore helped to rekindle links with Scotland's trading past.

The top rank of merchants also had a social position to uphold. They had to dress well and live well — any prospective merchant had by law to have very substantial means before he could engage in foreign trade, for to be seen walking about in the streets of Bruges or Bordeaux wearing anything less than the finest clothes would have brought ridicule on Scotland itself. In 1551 Edinburgh's council complained of the 'lichtleing' or belittling of Scotland's reputation in France and Flanders because of merchants there 'clad in vyle array'. Moreover, there were even some merchants who descended to petty trade in 'parcels and remnants of cloth' which the English refused to do because it would dishonour their country.

Even at home, merchant burgesses could be fined for not keeping up appearances. It was often an offence, for example, to wear a blue bonnet, for this was usually worn by ordinary folk. The Peebles records of 1664 ordered that 'members of the council shall buy and wear hats at all occasions when they are called to wait upon the magistrates, and when they come to the council' on pain of a heavy fine if they did not.

By the 1650s the first small 'factories' had begun to appear, often the result of joint-stock ventures founded by merchants seeking a use for the monies raised by trade. A small woollen factory was opened at Glasgow in 1635. In 1650 another mill was opened in the same street; during the next few years its water lade was enlarged and shiploads of the best Spanish wool were even imported to supply its needs. By 1700 at least three woollen or linen companies operated from Glasgow, one of them employing 1400 people. By the 1680s there were also four candleworks at Glasgow, plus a silk weaving and dyeing workhouse and at least one 'soaperie', using the product of four Glasgow merchant-owned whaling ships as the raw material for soap-boiling.

17th-century industries existed elsewhere too. There were rag-paper mills at Dalry, near Edinburgh, cloth mills at Dean on the Water of Leith, waulking mills and stocking mills at Aberdeen and weaving sheds in the border burghs. Lace was woven at Hamilton under the guidance of French artisans brought in by the Duchess of Hamilton, and at Stirling a special kind of lining cloth called shalloon was manufactured (so called from the town of Chalons in France). Although salt panning declined after the 1660s in the face of cheaper and purer foreign alternatives, coal mining still thrived along the shores of the Forth. By the 1660s there was a developing glass works at Leith and in due course potteries, ropeworks, sugar mills, breweries, distilleries and other enterprises added to a growing list of industries in Scotland.

This development of early industry might convey an impression of bustling progress in Scottish burghs, but the picture was variable. In many places there were terrible difficulties, which saw the

Culross 'Palace' — the fine residence of Sir George Bruce, who made a fortune from the coal trade to Holland. This wing dates from the 1590s, but a newer extension was added in the 1610s. King James VI stayed there in 1617. The building's original painted wooden panelling survives in most rooms. *Photo*: Craig Mair.

decline of all but the strongest trading burghs. For example, during the period from the union of crowns in 1603 to the union of parliaments in 1707, Scotland increasingly felt the effect of English foreign policies. Queen Elizabeth's wars against Spain and Portugal were inherited and continued by James VI and this disturbed long-established Scottish links with Portugal. As King of England, Charles I went to war with France, interrupting Scotland's long French association through the Auld Alliance. During the Cromwellian period, when Scotland was briefly united with England, there was war with the Netherlands which hindered Scotland's trade through the staple port at Veere. Charles II continued this war, and Scotland's trade continued to decline. Then when William of Orange arrived from Holland, relationships with the Netherlands were restored, but war began again with

France. In other words, Scottish trade suffered greatly from wars waged by England after both countries shared the same king.

In addition, the Covenanting and Cromwellian periods saw widespread destruction of Scottish east-coast towns, either by the royalist troops of the Duke of Montrose, or by Cromwell's army commander in Scotland, General Monck. In 1644 Montrose's army sacked Aberdeen for four days. Dundee was similarly destroyed by Monck's soldiers in 1651. Fifty years later, Dundee had still not recovered from this terrible period — in 1612 the city paid eleven per cent of the king's cess on royal burghs but by 1705 this was down to just four per cent.

Even smaller ports were ruined by the covenanting wars. Kirkcaldy, for example, was destroyed by Monck, while the ships in Stonehaven harbour were burnt by Montrose. In 1656 Dysart's council reported that the town, once a flourishing burgh royal, 'came to decay by the intestine and unnatural war against Montrose where the most part of the skippers and traffickers [merchants] were killed and destroyed'. This refers to the battle of Kilsyth in August 1645 when Montrose won a decisive victory, and many raw levies from Fife, including a number of sailors 'who never fought on land before that time', were slaughtered in the rout which followed. Such events had a terrible effect on trade, and on the prosperity of merchants and traders. St. Andrews especially dwindled to a trading obscurity from which it never recovered, so that in 1705 its cess was only one tenth what it had been in 1649.

By the 1690s Scotland's trade was still languishing and many ports were in decay and despair. In the 1670s Anstruther was so poor that no-one could be found to hold the position of bailie, since this carried with it responsibility for the burgh's finances and debts. Consequently, the sea walls became so neglected that they were washed away in a great storm about 1670 and the harbour was destroyed. In 1695 the harbour at Irvine was also so decayed and filled with rubbish that the burgh had to ask parliament to pass an Act giving it power to impose an additional duty on all malt ground at the town mill for the next ten years, the money to be used to improve the harbour.

To find out just how serious the wider picture was, in 1691 the Convention of Royal Burghs organised an enquiry into the state of every royal burgh's trade. Town after town reported a sustained slump in all trade, both inland and overseas. Haddington, Renfrew,

A view of Edinburgh from the village of Dean, as illustrated by Slezer in the 1690s. It shows how small the burgh was, and how much the inhabitants still farmed agricultural strips around the town.

Lauder, Peebles, Selkirk, and Annan all agreed that their inland trade was not enough even to be worth listing. Dumbarton's accounts books showed only the petty import of small purchases from Glasgow. Rutherglen and Dingwall reported no trade at all. Leith's list of vessels was down to just twenty-nine ships. Anstruther reported that it now had no fairs, no markets, no ships or merchants, no trade, and only one fishing boat. Glasgow's list of ships stood at eight tied up in port and seven at sea, but uncertain ever to return. Perth's burgesses tried to revive trade with a new vessel, but it was wrecked in the Tay estuary on its first commercial run, with the total loss of a cargo worth £20,000 Scots. Undaunted, the Perth merchants built a new ship at Leith, but after two or three voyages its skipper sailed off with a cargo worth £10,000 Scots and was never seen again.

Little did Perth's merchants realise that with the coming of the 1690s an even worse period of history was about to unfold. During this decade Scotland endured both nationwide famine and economic ruin, in what has often been called the King William's Seven Ill Years — a Jacobite analogy with the biblical famine of ancient Egypt, as if this Scottish disaster was a curse from God for the exile of James VII in 1688.

As with other mainly agricultural, north European countries, periods of dearth were not uncommon. In 1623 the crops failed for two seasons and caused famine all over Scotland. Then in 1634—36 they failed again in northern Scotland; one report stated that 'multitudes die in the open fields and there is none to bury them. . . . Some devour the sea ware [weed]; some eat dogs . . . and some have desperately run in the sea and drowned themselves'. From 1695—1699 this dreadful scene returned to the whole of Scotland in yet another catastrophe, heaped on top of years of trading decay and military destruction. In country areas as much as one third of the population died and thousands became wandering homeless beggars forced to eat grass or the flesh of disease-ridden animals. Fletcher of Saltoun, writing at the time, estimated that as many as 200,000 people were now vagrants, out of an estimated population of about one million.

Even in coastal trading burghs, where overseas connections and the organisational skills of merchants ensured a slightly better picture, people nevertheless died of starvation, even in the streets. They died in small burghs all along the Fife shores, in the prosperous port of Aberdeen, even at Leith, in a disaster which was to become as firmly etched on the Scottish memory as the famine of the 1840s came to be for the Irish.

In the midst of this terrible period, what was seen at the time as a great hope then emerged — the Company of Scotland Trading to Africa and the Indies, as it was grandly titled. A group of Scottish and London merchants aimed to rival England's famous East India Company by establishing Scottish colonies and thus developing trade. It was hoped not only to obtain precious cargoes of gold and ivory but to stimulate Scotland's own woollen and manufacturing enterprises by selling overseas.

At a critical moment the English government bowed to pressure from the East India Company and prohibited the London directors from investing in the venture; it fell to the people of Scotland to make the scheme work. £400,000 Sterling had to be found, and in a 'heroic and fatal decision' as one historian has called it, the people rallied round. Stimulated by everything from national fervour and the hope of economic recovery at a time of despair, to simple anti-English bloodymindedness, folk of every rank gave what they could — one rough and ready calculation has estimated as much as half of all the capital in Scotland went into this one venture. Some among the Scottish upper crust made very substantial payments into the fund — the Duchess of Hamilton, for example, subscribed £3000, Sir Robert Chiesly paid £2000 and the Countess of Rothes gave £1000, but there were many more eager to have at least a minimal stake of £100 in the venture; one director wrote that 'they came from all corners of the kingdom, rich, poor, blind and lame, to lodge their subscriptions in the Company's house'.

Burghs also contributed; the Incorporated Cordiners of Edinburgh and the Coopers of Glasgow were just two of the burgh guilds which added their funds to the rest. The burgh councils of Edinburgh and Glasgow, Inverness and Aberdeen, St. Andrews, Paisley, Selkirk and several other towns all promised money. Lanark's council raised £100 by a combination of £50 from the burgh's funds, £25 from the Guildry and £25 from the Incorporated Trades. Burgh councils, like the hundreds of individual investors who also contributed money, saw in 'the Africa Company' the chance of making a profit and stimulating trade — burghs more than others hoped that their languishing fortunes would rise in a desperately needed general revival of Scottish trade.

The rest of the story is quickly told. The attempt to found a new colony at Darien, in modern Panama, failed in the face of tropical disease, poor leadership, ships lost at sea, Spanish attacks on foreigners they regarded as intruders, and deliberate indifference to the plight of a dwindling band of desperate survivors by the English in Jamaica. The scheme collapsed and the money was lost. Lanark's £100, Aberdeen's £300 and the rest sank with the hopes of all Scotland.

After the Union of the Parliaments in 1707 the money was repaid from England's great wealth to those who had suffered. Lanark's council received £115: 17s 4d 'on account of the money put in by the Royal Burghs to the African Company', but it was scant compensation for the psychological blow which rocked every Scottish investor and ruined the livelihoods of merchants and burgesses up and down the land. At a time of declining trade, partly due to English policies, the Darien fiasco came as a disaster.

Foreign trade may have been patchy and sometimes very slack, but day-to-day business did continue, and people went on making a living. Below the exclusive class of burgesses with access to foreign goods came merchants who would regularly load a packhorse or waggon and set off to peddle their goods round the country. Some seem to have reached into England and Wales, and even to Ireland. Their business was clearly on a smaller scale than that of merchants who traded overseas. In fact some were so financially modest that a few packmen could not even afford a horse, and so carried their loads on their backs. In 1581 a Glasgow packman (but also a burgess) was attacked on the Island of Mull by some local MacLeans, severely wounded and robbed of his pack of merchandise worth three thousand merks.

More likely to survive unscathed, but less likely to make a fortune, were the merchant shopkeepers. In Scotland those who bought and sold things, including people like butchers, bakers or even publicans, were merchants. Craftsmen who made things and then sold them were only tradesmen, because they practised only a skill or trade. They were regarded as lower in status because they did not take the same financial risks or require to have the same administrative expertise as merchants. In England the meaning was different; a retailer or shopkeeper such as a butcher or baker was a tradesman because he traded goods for money, whereas a person who made something was a craftsman.

Evidence of merchant shopkeepers survives all over Sotland, especially in graveyards where many tombstones still display the merchant symbol of a figure 4, sometimes reversed or standing on top of a letter M. Many stones also show the working tools of a butcher or baker, or a pair of weighing scales, or even a portrait of the shopkeeper at his counter. Excellent examples of merchants' stones survive in many burghs including Perth, Dundee, Culross, Alloa, Stirling, Bo'ness, Edinburgh, Peebles and elsewhere.

Strict regulations governed almost every aspect of shopkeeping. Foremost was the need to prohibit all but proper merchants from having a shop at all — tradesmen were eventually allowed to sell their wares, but only from temporary market stalls, and they had to sell the goods personally, rather than through an employee. Examples of non-burgesses being caught and punished for selling staple goods crop up in many burgh records, as at Stirling where, in 1670, a sergeant at the castle was fined for selling tobacco to the townspeople instead of only to the garrison troops — he claimed ignorance of local regulations, so the fine was withdrawn and he was let off with a severe warning. Elgin's records for 1654 refer to a complaint from members of the Guildry 'against Andrew Adame merchant burgess of Aberdeen, for selling staple goods to

The piazza-style arches of Andrew Ogilvie's house at Elgin, built in 1694. Ogilvie was a typical wealthy merchant. *Photo*: Craig Mair.

unfreemen within their liberties. He is fined one hundred pounds Scots and is ordained to remain in ward until payment'. Similarly, Charles Cruickshank was fined £12 Scots at Banff in 1736 'for selling merchant goods within this burgh, he not being a burgess thereof'.

In 1688 Edinburgh's town council passed an Act against 'unfree persons who vend their goods all the days of the week in this city, both in public and private, without having any regard to the market day, the market times or place . . .' and who were, of course, affecting the livelihoods of proper merchants. This Act went on to complain that these people 'did daily and hourly vend and sell sundry sorts of merchandise, such as webs of linen and woollen cloth, plaids and suchlike, which ought to be sold by freemen burgesses only . . . they, their wives, bairns, and servants, going up and down all the streets and vennels of this burgh to the private houses, selling webs and plaids and suchlike merchandise, to the great hurt and damage of the freemen of this burgh'. It was then advertised 'by tuck of drum through this burgh, pier and shore of Leith' that the penalty for this would be the confiscation of all goods, and an additional punishment to be decided by the magistrates (who were, of course, merchants).

Stirling's town council viewed the problem so seriously that they took it to the Court of Session at Edinburgh in 1696. Alex Cudbert, a glover by trade, was encroaching on the Guildry's privileges by keeping an open shop where he sold brandy, wine, hock, sugar, raisins and other foreign staple commodities, and when brought before the Provost and Bailies he refused to stop and 'answered in hectoring expressions'. Thereafter, the Dean of Guild and an ex-Provost appealed at the courts in Edinburgh, where the Lords of Session, having referred to a copy of King David's charter to Stirling, agreed that a craftsman could not also be a merchant without first renouncing his craft, and that anyone doing so in Stirling could be arrested and imprisoned.

The protection of this exclusive right of burgesses to be shopkeepers and traders went on in Scottish burghs until the Burgh Trading Act of 1846, which finally made it 'lawful for any person to carry on or deal in merchandise, and to carry on or exercise any trade or handicraft, in any burgh or elsewhere in Scotland, without being a burgess of such burgh, or a guild brother, or a member of any guild, craft, or incorporation'. Until then, town councils, through their merchant or craft guilds, controlled all trade.

Licensing hours, for example, were specified, as often was the price of drink. In 1693 Lanark's town council passed one of many laws on drinking when it stated that those found drunk or haunting taverns after 10 o'clock at night could be fined three pounds Scots or put in the jougs for six hours, with a rising scale of punishments thereafter for persistent offenders. Banff's council passed an Act in 1657 against any brewer or alehouse-keeper selling drink to the servants of burgesses after 7 o'clock, on pain of a fine of £5 Scots. A law at Forres prohibited brewers from raising the price of drink beyond the ability of common people to pay, and this was set at one shilling and eight pence for a pint of ale and two shillings for a pint of beer.

There were also strict regulations against sharp practice by shopkeepers. The Stirling bakers were warned in 1638 for making baps and loaves which were too small, for example, and for future reference a sliding scale of prices and loaf weights was added to the council minutes. In 1667 five Peebles bakers were each fined ten merks 'for baking and selling of wheat bread lighter than the table'.

Similarly, Stirling's town council passed an Act in 1618 against the 'blowing of flesh' by butchers, 'either by their mouth or by their oxters' under the pain of confiscation of all such flesh, to be given to the poor. It seems that butchers all over Scotland were in the habit of inflating their meat with a sort of bagpipe, to make it look bigger than it was — perhaps it was just as well for the poor that germs were still unknown!

The actual shops of these butchers and bakers were usually found towards the centre of town. At Linlithgow there were one or two in niches under the mercat cross, and at Lanark under the tolbooth, but most were located down nearby side lanes or along the High Street. In some cases, however, the ovens for baking bread were situated near, or even outside, a burgh port, well away from housing as a fire precaution. It is well known that a baker's oven started the great fire of London in 1666, but the risk was just as great in Scotland. Consequently, John Turnbull, a baker in Peebles, was ordered in 1658 to 'be watchful and careful of his oven, that no danger come to the town thereby'. Butchers' slaughterhouses were also sometimes required to be discreetly hidden from common gaze or smell. The fleshmarket at Lanark was right beside the Tolbooth, next to the 'ass-midden'; the resulting blood or discarded offal and putrid smell were so offensive that the council eventually had a wall built around the site. In some towns the butchers' working area was known as the Shambles — the well-known street at York is justly famous, but there was also a Shambles Wynd at Forres until it was renamed Caroline Street, and more examples exist elsewhere for sharp-eyed visitors to discover.

As well as having shops, every burgh had the right to hold regular markets and fairs. The exact number of these varied from place to place and was specified by the terms of each burgh's own particular royal charter. Selkirk had a weekly market and five annual fairs. Linlithgow had six annual fairs and a weekly market on Saturdays (changed in 1645 to Fridays because of frequent drunkenness which was thought unsuitable for a day just before the Sabbath). Ayr's weekly market was also on a Saturday, with a fifteen-day fair at the feast of the Nativity of John the Baptist, to which was added in 1458 a second fair for four days at the feast of St. Michael. In fact, fairs could vary from one day to well over two weeks, depending on the town concerned.

Many fairs had colourful names which happily were not swept

away by the Reformation. At Banff, for example, the Hallows Fair continued to be held on Hallowe'en, while at Peebles the Beltane Fair was still held every May, the Trinity Fair every June, and so on. The Muckle Mermass Fair at Thurso thrived for many years and attracted merchants from all over Scotland. At Fortrose the St. Boniface Fair is still held every August and there are still Lammas Fairs in various Border towns. Many fairs still retain interesting local features; at South Queensferry the Burry Man Fair features a man dressed in a costume completely covered with prickly burrs, who strolls through the streets — an ancient local custom.

Fairs were originally held on days of religious significance, which could vary from year to year, just as Easter still does. Most burghs eventually began to standardise their fair days, however, and Lanark's records for 1696 show how Whitsunday Fair was thereafter fixed on the last Wednesday of May, the St. James Fair on the last Wednesday of July, and so on. Many burgh records contain similar minutes of council decisions. At Peebles, for example, the burgh fairs were also standardised in 1696 so that the Trinity Fair became the first Tuesday of June, with all the other days being arranged likewise.

Most fair days occurred during the farming season, when there was likely to be a surplus of produce to sell and when people from surrounding areas might think it worth travelling in to town — Elgin's fairs were sometimes publicised at Nairn and even Inverness, for example. Some fairs were held during winter months, however, including one in early January at Aberdeen, the St. Leonard's Fair on the last Wednesday of November at Lanark, or the St. Andrews Fair on the last Tuesday of November at Peebles.

On fair days the whole town centre, sometimes the entire burgh itself, was filled with jostling crowds, herds of animals, market stalls, entertainers and musicians, peddlars shouting their wares and alehouses overflowing with customers. It was a holiday as much as a market. In many burghs horse races or archery competitions were held on the common lands outside the town, and these are described in Chapter 14. Many burghs also designated separate areas of town for the sale of different kinds of livestock, often close to the burgh gates to avoid the indiscriminate mingling of cattle, sheep, horses, pigs and so on. At Largs the St. Colm's Fair, held on the first Tuesday after June 12th (the supposed birthday of St. Columba), began to attract such large numbers of Highland folk,

The St. Boniface Fair at Fortrose, complete with bellringer and public proclamation. This event has been revived in recent years and is held around the ruined cathedral. *Photo*: John McLellan, Culbokie.

who came by ship to sell their cattle and buy essential goods, that the fair was held on the Common.

The weekly market days held by most royal burghs were more functional. This was when everyday essentials were offered for sale at stalls by craftsmen and merchants who did not have a shop. These were the 'stallingers' who had to apply annually to the council for permission to erect a market stall or trestle table from which to sell their goods. Banff's records for 1682 minute how a flesher, or butcher, had to pay twenty shillings Scots each year for a stand, while 'every man not an ordinary flesher' had to pay thirty shillings Scots. In 1664 a local Act at Edinburgh specifically prohibited packmen from setting up stands, until they became burgesses (which was unlikely because of the cost of enrolment). This was followed in 1665 by another regulation which insisted that those coming to sell goods and claiming that they were free burgesses from other towns had to produce not only their burgess tickets but also a testimony of proof from their local Dean of Guild or bailies. Moreover, those claiming to be servants or apprentices, sent by some burgess master, had to produce a certificate signed by their master and confirming that the goods were being bought for personal use only.

Outside vendors could also bring their goods into town for sale, but they usually had to pay a custom stent or toll on their merchandise before they could enter the town. Burgh records frequently include lists or tables of the charges payable on a whole range of goods. A long list would be repetitive, but in 1612, for example, the tolls charged on Stirling Bridge included twelve pence for each puncheon of wine, eight pence per barrel of beer, two pence per load of flour, and so on. By 1660 the tolls on goods coming into the port of Banff covered everything from three shillings and fourpence per load of cloth or two shillings and sixpence per load of timber, down to one shilling per horse, eight pence per carcass of beef, fourpence per mutton carcass, four pence for each pair of wheels, and twopence for each pair of shoes.

Market regulations were controlled by the burgh council. Hours of business were strictly specified and in some burghs a bell sounded the start of selling — 'No man to buy or sell before the ringing of the bell at 9 o'clock in the morning' as Banff's records mentioned in 1682. Elgin's records for 1653 similarly state, 'It is ordained that the Friday market shall not begin until eight hours in the morning and that no commodities to be sold before then'. Stirling's market began at ten o'clock but in many burghs it was as likely to begin as early as seven, since people rose and went to bed earlier than today.

Many local regulations dealt with forestalling — attempting to buy provisions before they reached market and therefore before tolls were paid on them. Lanark's records specifically included among the goods which it was illegal to forestall such things as fish or flesh, butter, eggs, cheese, hens, skins, hides and all other merchant goods. Often associated with this was the second serious offence of regrating, or bulk buying to hoard supplies and thus force up market prices. Such activities harmed the common good in burghs and were severely punished — the confiscation of goods and a fine at the very least.

Another vital aspect of trade control was the question of weights and measures. This needs some preliminary explanation, however. During the 12th century the first burghs were Berwick, Roxburgh, Stirling and Edinburgh; these were then formed into an association

The Stirling Pint Jug, or Stoup. It actually held about three English pints. Stirling was guardian of Scotland's liquid measures until 1707 when Imperial measures were introduced following the Treaty of Union with England. *Photo*: The Collections of the Smith Art Gallery and Museum, Stirling.

or court, which regulated many aspects of burgh life thereafter. In due course Berwick became English and Roxburgh fell into decay, so they were replaced by Lanark and Linlithgow in 1369. One of the most important functions of these four towns was the guardianship of Scotland's weights and measures.

Since local weights and measures could vary, national standards from which copies could be made were needed. Edinburgh therefore kept the standard ell, which was 37.2 inches long and by which the length of everything from cloth to land was measured. One example of an ell, dated 1500, can be seen at Inverkeithing Museum. Linlithgow, on the other hand, looked after the standard firlot, by which grain was measured, and which looked like the lower part of a sawn-off barrel. There was actually a graded series of measures, which ranked through chalders, bolls, firlots (sometimes called

E

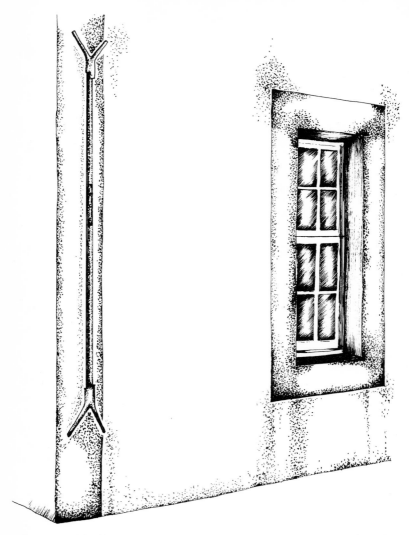

The Dunkeld Ell dates from about 1700. It is fastened to a wall in the market square and was used by traders to measure lengths of cloth. Edinburgh was the guardian of length measures until 1707.

bushels, and which equalled eight gallons), and pecks. Stirling had charge of liquid measures, and the Stirling Jug or Pint Stoup (which actually held nearer three modern pints) became the national standard. Finally, Lanark guarded the set of national weights, originally made of stone but after 1567 of brass or lead.

Every burgh was supposed to have a set of weights and measures, exact copies of the originals and obtainable only from the guardian burgh concerned. These were usually kept by the Dean of Guild, who used them to check the weights used by merchants in the town. From time to time these became worn or were lost and were therefore replaced, again by sending off for new copies. Burgh records are full of references to weights and measures, such as at Elgin in 1656, where the Dean of Guild was ordained 'to visit the firlots for all grains, the stone weight and other weights of that sort, the ell wand [stick] and the stoups and to report'. In 1697 Stirling's Dean of Guild was ordered to get a 'stand of Lanrick weights, from an ounce and downwards, for the use of the guildry'.

The exclusive right to make Scotland's weights and measures was a privilege jealously guarded by the four burghs. It provided work for the craftsmen and an income for the town; Lanark, for example, used to stamp its weights with the town crest of a double-headed eagle as a sort of trademark of authenticity. The town still has one or two early examples which, at the time of writing, were stored in a strongroom at the public library.

All this disappeared with the Union of the Parliaments in 1707, however, when Scotland adopted English imperial weights and measures. For a time the same four burghs continued to make the new standards, so that Banff's accounts for 1709 include the purchase of a complete set of all the new measures, including brass weights from Lanark and 'Item four jugs from Stirling of fine metal from an English gallon to a pint. Item one bushel from Linlithgow, English measure of metal, one peck of oak wood, hooped with iron etc'. The Queen Anne bushel is still on display in Banff's local museum. Indeed early imperial measures can be seen in many museums, but they do not convey the same feeling of Scottish history which the older, but rarer, measures do. By 1750, however, the exclusive manufacture of weights and measures by the four burghs began to disappear. In 1758, for example, Glasgow made its own weights from a load of scrap metal, and by 1764 Lanark's neighbour Hamilton began to manufacture them as well. The monopoly was lost and a part of history faded away.

Armed with a correct set of weights and measures, burgh officials

These stone weights are kept in the museum at Forfar and were once used at markets, perhaps on a tron weighbeam. Lanark held Scotland's original weights. *Photo*: Angus District Libraries and Museums Service.

used to check those used by market traders. If nothing else, it was a good excuse to prosecute rival stallholders in those non-burghs where markets were nevertheless held. It is easy to imagine the feeling of satisfaction at Banff, for example, when in 1663 the local magistrates fined Robert Strachan, a merchant at Keith, £10 for having 'weights that were too light and not sufficient'. To avoid argument, an ell was sometimes fastened to a public wall near the market place. Some still survive today, including one on the town-house wall at Dumfries and another on the shaft of the Kincardine mercat cross, now standing in the square at Fettercairn. The remains of another can also be seen in the grounds of Dornoch cathedral. Bulky weights were checked by using the burgh tron, already explained in Chapter 3. Nowadays Regional Councils still have an inspector of weights and measures, usually attached to the Trading Standards Department, and still performing much the same duties as those once carried out by the Dean of Guild's officials.

With a little imagination, it is not difficult to visualise 17th-century traders measuring things out in a bustling Scottish marketplace. In some markets today cloth is still dispensed from

The Little Cross at Elgin, dated 1733 but with a shaft which may be much older. The first cross was erected in 1402. The arched building behind is 17th century, and was a banking house from 1703—22. *Photo*: Craig Mair.

the bale by holding one end in the middle of the chest and then stretching out an arm sideways to its full length — the vendor will probably call it a yard or a meter, but it was also the traditional way of measuring an ell. Electricians often measure cable flex in the same way — so the 17th century is still alive today, under our very noses! In Holland, where this market practice also survives, cloth is actually still measured by the ell; even the word is still used.

CHAPTER 8

Crafts and Trades

During the 17th century, burghs were almost entirely self-sufficient except for the foreign luxuries sometimes bought by richer people. In the case of towns like Selkirk or Lanark with no foreign trade, almost everything needed by the people derived from local produce — wool, hides, horn, fat, timber, bark, straw, heather, stone, slate and so on. The only other materials likely to be needed were salt, possibly some glass, gunpowder and iron bars for making into products such as cooking pots, nails, barrel hoops or tools and weapons.

As a result, there was a variety of crafts and trades in any burgh. In a small place like Selkirk, these included weavers, tailors, fleshers, cordiners, maltmen, and hammermen — in 1694 the Selkirk hammermen included wrights, coopers, blacksmiths, stonemasons and a coppersmith. In larger burghs the variety of crafts was even greater; in 1658 Elgin had, in addition to those at Selkirk, lorimers (who made spurs and horse bridles), pewterers, skinners, tanners, glasswrights, glovers, and even a golfclub maker. By the 1690s they had also been joined by a gunsmith, while in 1702 James Bradie, pirivick maker (wigmaker) was admitted a burgess and freeman of the burgh. Gentlemen who wore wigs also had to have their heads regularly shaved (or 'barberised' as it was called, since this was done by a barber). In most larger towns there was also likely to be a saddler, a candlemaker, a slater, a cutler, and possibly a silversmith or jeweller. Other occupations which were not crafts or trades included the town musician, the ferryman, the miller, the schoolmaster, lawyers, constables, possibly an apothecary, and the gravedigger (who at Elgin in 1695 was paid 14 shillings Scots for each adult grave, 7 shillings Scots per child, and was required to dig the graves of the poor for nothing).

Lanark is a good example of a typical small burgh. According to a surviving list of the number of craftsmen who took the Oath of Allegiance in 1693, the town contained thirteen smiths, fourteen wrights and masons, fourteen tailors, seventeen shoemakers, nine glovers, twelve weavers, four waulkers (cloth finishers) and a glazier. In addition there were certainly some bakers, a slater, a gunsmith

Two brewers carrying a barrel. A detail from a headstone in Dalmeny kirkyard. *Photo*: Craig Mair.

and, it seems, even an artist. The Lanark smiths included blacksmiths (because of the growing number of horses), makers and menders of ploughs, and the town clock keeper. Butchers were in decline, perhaps because of the famine years of the 1690s. Selkirk in 1694 had a similar situation — twenty-two hammermen, forty-seven shoemakers (for which the town was famous), twenty-two weavers and seven tailors, but only six butchers.

As with merchants, burgh councils exercised strong controls over trades and crafts. Burgh records are full of regulations on such things as where tanning was permitted, quality controls on bleaching, inspection visits to the fishmarket, the price of spun wool, and so on. John Lead, for example, was fined £3 Scots at Banff for selling bad mutton, while Alexander Tarres was fined thirty shillings Scots at Elgin in 1639 for selling overpriced shoes.

One of the worst offences was forestalling — attempting to buy goods before they reached market, usually before dues had been paid on them and the price was therefore cheaper. Food was especially liable to this, and Lanark's records for 1658 specifically prohibited the forestalling of fish, meat, butter, cheese, eggs, hens,

A plaque to Robert Spittal, tailor to the King, on a 17th-century house wall in Spittal Street, Stirling. The scissors were a mark of his trade and can also be seen on gravestones. The wording is easy to follow when a V is read as a U. *Photo*: Craig Mair.

skins and hides. If convicted, an offender could expect confiscation of his goods and a fine. At Elgin in 1636, for example, William Coban was 'fynit in tuentie four pundis' for forestalling.

Along with this went the even more serious offence of regrating — bulk buying to create shortages and thus push up market prices. This was regarded as a self-centred act against the town's common good, as at Peebles in 1663 where a grain merchant refused to offer his stock for sale because he believed the going rate was too low — this was followed by a severe fine, but in some burghs persistent (three times) offenders could be banished from the town.

Another activity which exercised the merchant burgesses of many towns was smuggling, 'a practice scandalous in itself and highly prejudicial to the nation in general and to the fair trader in particular' as the Stirling council said, 'and which if continued in must tend to the ruin of this part of the kingdom . . .' In other words, smuggling affected the pockets of burgesses. Unlike regrating, ordinary people did not regard it as much of a crime and all sorts of folk from schoolmasters and lawyers to craftsmen and even kirk ministers had a finger in the smuggling pie — 'the national vice' as one historian has called it. All over Scotland toll collectors turned a blind eye to much of this business, encouraged no doubt by the occasional token of gratitude from those who ran the risks. The most lucrative contraband goods tended to come from abroad, often from France or Holland, so that rocky and lonely coastlines such as those of Fife, Angus, Ross-shire and along the Solway perhaps saw more clandestine business than elsewhere.

The penalties were severe and people were hanged — merchants and burgh barons saw to that — but even after the union with England in 1707, when the new British government decided to clamp down and drafted hardened English tax collectors into Scotland, smuggling went on well into the nineteenth century. In due course whisky-running especially became such big business that two or three Inverness coppersmiths actually hung the sign of a whisky still outside their doors as an indication of the craft which they followed!

Another aspect of crafts and trades which came under the control of burgh councils was the question of apprentices. Regulations depended on the general level of trade and availability of work; in general, when times were hard, local laws were passed to restrict masters from taking on too many boys, and when possible to favour the sons of existing craftsmen. Restrictions also ensured that there were never too many apprentices for the amount of business available to give them a living. At Selkirk, for example, the poll tax roll for 1694/5 shows only four apprentice hammermen, thirteen apprentice cordiners and five apprentice weavers and so on.

Local craft guilds set the standards for apprentices in each burgh. These included such things as supervision of the quality of instruction, or ensuring that apprentices were properly fed and clothed. The length of apprenticeship could be up to seven years, but more typically it was five, as at Stirling. At Lanark it was three years, followed by a spell of two years as a journeyman (from the French *la journée* because such workers were paid per day, unlike apprentices who were not paid at all).

If all went well this would be followed by an 'essay test' in which the intending craftsman would be asked to show proof of his skills by making a 'masterpiece' before being admitted a full member of his craft guild — 'that each craft apprentice, before being admitted to the Guild, must make an example of his work, the same to be passed as satisfactory by three expert craftsmen of the Guild' as the Dunfermline hammermen insisted in their 'Rules and Regulations' of 1570. For the cordiners of Aberdeen in the 1690s this consisted of one pair of boots, two pairs of shoes and a pair of slippers. One Dundee baker was asked to make a selection of biscuits, rolls, loaves, mince pies, puff pastry apple tarts, prune tarts and a veal pie. In 1735 John Baillie, a prospective silversmith at Inverness, was required to make a silver sword hilt, a silver teapot of china fashion, and a raised decanter in silver — extremely difficult work.

Even if he passed the essay test, an apprentice might not always receive automatic admission into a craft guild. Regulations at Stirling in 1660, for example, laid down that any prospective entrant had to pay an admission fee of one hundred merks, and have a stock worth at least £1000 Scots 'wherewith he may be able to trade'. In 1671 the entrance fee was increased to three hundred merks for 'strangers', who also had to have £2000 worth of stock to set up in business.

Crafts existed in every burgh but there were some places where specific centres of excellence sprang up. Pistolmakers worked in the Canongate and at Dundee; two pistols dated 1611 and made by James Low of Dundee were owned by Louis XIII of France and are now displayed at the Royal Museum of Scotland in Queen Street, Edinburgh, while another pair by the same maker can be seen at the Hermitage in Leningrad. Around 1650 Doune began as another centre of pistolmaking and a fine collection of Doune weapons can be seen at Inverness Museum. Edinburgh developed as a town of goldsmiths, jewellers and clockmakers — George Heriot or 'Jinglin Geordie' was a goldsmith who made such a fortune that he tore up a debt of £2000 owed by King James VI and still founded the hospital school which continues to bear his name. In the 1670s a French clockmaker called Paul Roumieu established such a reputation that his fourth-floor house and workshop in the West Bow was known for a long time as Clockmaker's Land. Edinburgh and Aberdeen also became centres of printing because of the university colleges there, while Wemyss in Fife made glass, and silversmiths were especially skilled at Inverness and Tain.

On the other hand, there were some skills which Scotland simply could not produce. Tapestries and embroideries, for example, still came from France and Flanders, often from Arras which virtually gave its name to the art. Fine glass came from Venice, as it still does, while many tolbooth and kirk bells were cast in Sweden or Holland. The Inverkeithing town bell, dated 1667 and on display at the museum there, was just one of a great many bells made by Johannes Burgerhuys of Zeeland, for example.

17th-century towns were alive with the sounds and smells of work. The ringing of the blacksmith's hammer contrasting with the finer tapping of a slater, the smell of cattle and ox hides soaking in bark at the tannery, the tang of roasting malt drifting over from the kilns by the burgh gates — it must have been quite an experience. Nowadays, apart from the occasional smithy, as at Kippen, or specially restored weaving shop, as at Kilbarchan, little atmosphere of craftsmanship remains. There was a time when skills were all around, and were a part of normal life. The nearest equivalent today might be a craft colony or an eastern bazaar, where craftsmen still sit hunched up in tiny shops practising many ancient crafts and skills, and the surrounding streets and alleys are filled with the sights and sounds and smells of work and everyday life intermixed.

Signs of various trades and crafts can be found in many old graveyards, especially those where the stones are durable and have not worn. Fife, Angus, Perthshire, Stirlingshire and the Lothians are particularly fruitful areas. The graveyards at Dundee, Perth and Stirling, St. Andrews, Culross and Alloa all contain particularly good examples of craftsmen's headstones, but the best example in a small burgh is probably the Tulliallan kirkyard at Kincardine-on-Forth, where the stone is hard but workable and a wonderful cross-section of 17th-century craft and merchant stones survives.

During the 17th and early 18th centuries many stones were inscribed with only the year date, the initials of the husband and wife (her maiden initials), and the symbols or tools of his or her occupation. Sometimes symbols of mortality were also added, including skulls, crossed bones (nothing to do with pirates!), hourglasses, angels' wings, Adam and Eve figures, or even the monstrous face of a 'green man', but for the purposes of this book it is the symbols of work which are important. These can sometimes look rather strange because so many occupations are no longer seen every day, but they are actually quite easy to interpret when the jobs themselves are understood.

Many baxter or baker stones feature a sheaf of corn or a row of buns, and sometimes the crossed paddles which were used to slide loaves into a hot oven. The tailor's hot pressing iron, scissors and

sewing needle have hardly changed at all over the centuries and
are easily recognised, as are the butcher's carving knife and cleaver,
or the shuttle used by weavers. The gauntlet made by a glover
might also be easily spotted, but some glovers' stones show rows of
buttons or buckles, which these craftsmen also made. Maltmen or

A selection of gravestones from the Forth valley, where the stone has worn well.

brewers often chose a long-handled shovel and sweeping broom as their symbols — tools used for turning the roasting malt barley and stirring the brewing ale. In many burghs women were traditionally

This is the stone of a shipwright from Kincardine-on-Forth. He appears to be using a caulking hammer and chisel — a common job in any 17th or 18th-century shipyard. *Photo*: Craig Mair.

alehouse keepers, and often maltsters, but sometimes the baker or miller would double as maltman since he already dealt in grain. This might result in a stone with, say, the crossed paddles of a baker side by side with a maltman's broom. The tools used by stonemasons, carpenters, slaters and coopers have not changed at all since the 17th century and would be quickly recognised by people in those occupations today — a whole assortment of mallets, chisels, saws, pliers, compasses and set-squares can be found on gravestones all over Scotland.

Finally, there are stones with crowns on them. Only two crafts were entitled to use the crown as an emblem — the cordiners or shoemakers, and the hammermen (which included a wide variety of sub-species from goldsmiths and armourers to bucklers and blacksmiths, even saddlers and glaziers). This reflects the antiquity and importance of these two craft guilds, which in many towns were regarded as the most senior of the Incorporated Trades. Most cordiners' headstones show a semi-circular leather-cutting knife placed below the crown, with perhaps an awl or a shoe last elsewhere else on the stone. Most hammermen stones similarly have a hammer

The symbol of the Elgin hammermen, once in the old kirk of St. Giles but now in the local museum. *Photo:* Craig Mair, courtesy of Elgin Museum.

below the crown, but the size and type of hammer then tells more exactly which metalworking occupation the person followed. A griddlemaker's hammer at Culross, for example, would be quite different from that of a gunsmith or a cutler. Blacksmiths, incidentally, often doubled as clock-repairers, dentists, and even bonesetters!

CHAPTER 9

Burghs and the Reformation

The religious issues apart, the effect of the Reformation on church buildings was disastrous — Archbishop Laud, on seeing later the remains of Dunblane Cathedral, is said to have called it the 'Deformation'. Violence and destruction flared up so often during the one hundred and thirty years from 1560 to 1690 that buildings, especially church properties, in almost every burgh suffered at one time or another. By the end, virtually every friary and monastery was empty and in ruins, cathedrals were pillaged and often roofless, and a priceless heritage of exquisite medieval architecture was lost.

One of the first casualties was the beautiful cathedral at St. Andrews, in its day one of the finest medieval monuments in Scotland, but destroyed from June 11th-13th 1559 by a calvinist mob including John Knox himself. In an orgy of vandalism the cathedral's fine vestments were ripped to pieces, all statues and other signs of idolatry were smashed, and the lead was stripped off the roof so that the building soon decayed and crumbled to a ruin. Today only fragments of its walls survive to indicate what splendour there once was.

The last victim of this period was probably Dunkeld Cathedral, ruined in a battle on August 21st 1689. Twelve hundred lowland protestant troops resisted a siege by five thousand highlanders fresh from victory twenty-five days earlier at Killiecrankie, but only by stripping lead from the cathedral roof to turn into ammunition. The Jacobite highlanders in occupation of the town were finally driven off by setting fire to the houses, leaving all but two buildings in Dunkeld burnt to the ground and the cathedral in ruins. Today, the choir has a roof once more and is the local parish church but the nave still stands an empty shell, a relic from the closing days of the Reformation.

Cromwell's troops were the cause of some damage — much of Linlithgow was razed to the ground, for example, and the tower of Stirling's Holy Rude church is still peppered with bullet marks from General Monck's siege of the castle in 1651 — but the worst perpetrators of vandalism were the Covenanters. Many saw it as a mission to erase all sign of 'popery', so they went about smashing

Dunblane Cathedral, beautifully restored today but vandalised and much neglected during and after the Reformation, to the extent that Archbishop Laud called it the 'Deformation'. Cathedrals at Elgin, St. Andrews, Dunkeld and elsewhere suffered similar destruction.

stained-glass windows and statues, even defacing effigies of past bishops on their tombs. To some, beauty and splendour were distractions from proper worship rather than an offering to the glory of God. To others, churches had to be 'cleansed' from the detestable worship of idols. And undoubtedly there were also those who enjoyed destruction for its own sake.

In 1560 St. Machar's Cathedral in Aberdeen was looted by a crowd of reformers, who wrecked everything which was easily accessible, even the library. In 1568 the regent Earl of Moray removed the bells and stripped off the lead roof — the ship carrying this booty was too heavy and sank half a mile out of port, in an ironic twist of fate. Then in 1640 the Covenanters again turned on St. Machar's, and with still greater zeal removed even the high ceiling of the nave which was painted with a magnificent procession of church dignitaries led by the pope. But at least the building still stood in a usable, if dilapidated, state. Other churches were not so lucky. Arbroath Abbey was destroyed and made roofless. Stonehaven's church was destroyed. Cambuskenneth Abbey at Stirling was

Stirling's 15th—16th-century Kirk of the Holy Rude, where both Mary Queen of Scots and James VI were crowned. During the Reformation its many chapels and altars were wrecked and today only one survives. *Photo*: Craig Mair.

dissolved in 1559 and was pulled down to become a local source of building stone. Kelso Abbey, St. Mary's Church at Dundee, the Franciscan friary at Dumfries, the Cross Kirk at Peebles, St. Giles at Elgin, St. Nicholas at Aberdeen — the list of buildings ruined during the Reformation could go on and on, like a lament.

In other cases, churches were re-used for presbyterian worship. However, the needs of a Church of Scotland congregation were rather different from before. All that was required was a gathering place, no matter how plain, where everyone could clearly see the minister as he preached. Vast choirs and naves were unnecessary. Transepts and elaborately carved rood screens blocked the view.

Stained glass, hangings, paintings or candles were generally removed. But at least some churches survived. Paisley Abbey stood for years with only half of the church roofed and the rest falling into ruin. Dunfermline Abbey, Dunblane Cathedral, St. Machar's at Aberdeen, Dunkeld Cathedral and others limped along in a state of semi-dereliction until more recent times.

On the other hand, some survived only to suffer a lingering death after all. Part of Jedburgh's Abbey nave and transept was converted into a parish church in 1671, but then the main arch collapsed in 1743 and the building was finally abandoned in 1875. Holyrood Abbey in Edinburgh became a parish church during the Reformation, but then in 1688 James VII unwisely had it converted into a Roman Catholic Chapel Royal, which more or less ensured its destruction a year later when the king was deposed and exiled. Even then it did not yet die; in 1758 a new roof of flagstones was fitted, but this collapsed in 1768 to leave the building in ruins at last. Elgin Cathedral's story was particularly sad. In 1567 the lead was plundered from the roof but the church struggled on. Then in 1640 its rood screen was demolished by Gilbert Ross, the 'detestable bigot' minister of Elgin. But it was not until Easter Sunday 1711 when the central tower collapsed and left the place little more than a ruin that the church, described by many as the most beautiful medieval cathedral in Scotland, was finally abandoned to the plunderers of dressed stone.

The Reformation also saw the end of many of the educational and charity buildings once associated with the Catholic Church. Grammar schools, song schools, alms houses, hospitals for the aged and infirm, leper colonies, hospices for travellers in lonely places — almost all were swept away, to disappear for ever. Most burghs with a monastery, abbey, friary or convent also had a hospital for the needy. They existed at Dunfermline, Peebles, Glasgow, Dunbar, Elgin, Dundee, Annan, Cambuslang, Arbroath and so on, in a vast network of houses which must surely have played an essential part in the social services of any burgh. Some larger burghs such as Stirling or Aberdeen had several hospitals. By the time of the Reformation there were at least four in Aberdeen, including St. Anne's for poor ladies, and six or seven in Edinburgh. A similarly long list of burghs once had alms houses. Linlithgow's were burned by Cromwellian troops but, one way or another, by 1690 the alms houses at Peebles, Aberdeen, Brechin, and elsewhere had all gone.

It is not always realised that in medieval times leprosy was a disease common across Scotland. It may have killed Robert the Bruce in 1329, and did not greatly diminish until around 1600. This required the provision of isolation colonies, usually run by friars and invariably located outside any burgh. Such places existed at Dundee, Stirling, Elgin, Haddington, Aberdeen and elsewhere. Edinburgh's leper hospital stood at Greenside beside the Calton Hill near the top of Leith Walk. All of these disappeared during the Reformation when the friars, who supervised them with a sense of charity stronger than that of self-preservation, were dispossessed and thrown out.

A few churches survived almost unscathed. Glasgow Cathedral, resting place of the bones of St. Kentigern (or Mungo), was reprieved 'until ane new kirk be biggit'; happily, as one writer has said, 'it remained unbiggit long enough to allow hot heads to cool' and thus it still stands today. The priory at Whithorn survived because the monks there judiciously adopted episcopalian worship when necessary, so the building remained intact and became a parish church in 1690. At Edinburgh the Cathedral of St. Giles, scene of much of Knox's rhetoric and high drama during the Reformation, was renamed the High Kirk of Edinburgh and converted into four separate churches inside, but at least the external appearance remained unspoiled.

What happened when a previously Catholic church was commandeered as a parish church? All 'popish' trappings were, of course, removed or obliterated. In 1649, for example, the Synod of Dunblane ordered the demolition of a cross in the grounds of Dunblane Cathedral. Religious out-buildings such as chapter-houses or sacristies were sometimes demolished, and inside many private chapels or altars were wrecked — the Town Kirk in Perth had thirty-seven such altars, St. Michael's at Linlithgow had twenty-six, St. Machar's at Aberdeen had thirty-eight and St. Giles in Edinburgh had forty-four, so a lot of dismantling must have gone on.

Many then had extra 'lofts' or balconies added by local carpenters to create additional seating space for the congregation. At Dunblane Cathedral a gallery or loft was added in 1653, and another (with an outside stair) in 1664. Similar lofts were added to churches all over Scotland. At St. Machar's a surviving wooden screen which had once stood behind an altar to St. Katherine was dismantled in 1646 and reused to build a loft across the west end of the nave. At the Holy Rude Kirk in Stirling a number of lofts and galleries were built during the 17th century, for the use of the Guildry, the Trades, the burgh magistrates, the grammar school, various local lairds and gentry. How far this work destroyed the original interiors of churches depended on the fanaticism of the congregation, the sensitivities of the workmen, and the amount of money available for the conversion. Some lofts were so simply made that they have been dismantled since with hardly any sign of their former existence.

In some places such as Prestonpans, Lauder or Burntisland, purpose-built new parish churches were erected. These were usually plain, oblong buildings, unadorned with any decoration — sometimes even without plaster on the rubble walls. Unlike most medieval churches, there was no need for them to face east, or to have a high altar. Communions were rare events, generally held only once every two or three years, so there was no need for a permanent communion altar — a table could be set up when required. There was generally no organ and the singing of psalms was done unaccompanied, often led by a precentor who sang each line for the congregation to copy. There were also very few permanent seats in 17th-century churches. Most people brought a stool or kept a chair for their own use during services.

The most important requirement was to place the minister's pulpit and baptismal font in clear view of everyone. As burgh populations grew, cross-aisles were eventually added, but since the pulpit was usually placed centrally, and above the height of the congregation, this cruciform arrangement did not obstruct anyone's view. In many kirks lofts were added, usually for specific groups of people who could pay for their construction. In Tulliallan Kirk, built in 1675 at Kincardine-on-Forth, there were eventually three lofts, used by the local colliers, seamen and laird's family. Many lofts had their own outside stairs and these can still be seen in many places. The little kirk at Gargunnock near Stirling has three outside stairs and is an excellent example.

Kirkyards from this period can be very interesting. In pre-Reformation times they were almost like social gathering places. Sheep often grazed among the headstones, people practised archery, and even fairs were held there. Kirriemuir still has a number of houses with windows facing into the kirkyard, from where refreshments were served during fairs. The St. Boniface Fair at Rosemarkie and Fortrose was held in the grounds of the cathedral and was happily revived again in recent years. Dunblane also seems to have held its fairs in the cathedral grounds, for in 1659 the local council had to pass a law ordering that fairs, even those held on Whitsunday, Lawrence and Hallowday, should no longer be held there. At Dundee the local incorporated trades began to hold meetings in the Grey Friars churchyard, which became known thereafter as the Howff or meeting place — a name retained today.

For all their austerity of church decoration, post-Reformation folk certainly wanted elaborate and often showy gravestones. While many merchants or craftsmen were content to have the emblems of their work on their stones, those who could afford it often went for ornately-masoned headstones with a wide variety of figures, mortality symbols, decorative foliage and so on. The Howff stones at Dundee convey a distinctly ostentatious impression of merchant power and wealth. Those at St. Andrews (especially the stones now kept under cover) and at the Greyfriars burial ground at Perth have a similar feel. Unfortunately, gravestones in the West of Scotland were often cut from less durable sandstone and many have not lasted so well.

Nowadays kirkyards generally look very trim and tidy, with the stones standing in neat rows and the grass cut and well cared for. In the 17th century things were quite different — stones stood around anywhere, sloping, leaning, fallen over, and certainly not in regimented rows. Only grazing animals kept the vegetation short. Many graveyards were also much more hilly and uneven than they are today. The headstones around St. Andrews Cathedral, for example, have been landscaped, re-erected in straight lines, and the whole burial site levelled from its earlier hummocky state.

There is no doubt that in most districts the Reformation was accepted, but it is also true that under Calvinism everyday life became plainer and more serious. The fun and games of fairs and markets was suppressed. Singing and dancing and wearing bright clothes was often frowned on. Traditional religious festivals and processions died out and left Scotland the poorer for it, as is obvious when compared with the colourful events much photographed by tourists in Roman Catholic countries today.

One popular occasion was the procession of Corpus Christi, on the Thursday after Whitsunday. At Lanark this always included a number of pageants or tableaux, rather like the floats in a modern

Gala Day parade. First came the Nativity, and then a scene of Christ's Passion, both simple visual, almost instructional, reminders of Bible events for an uneducated population. Next came the Three Wise Men, mutated by tradition and folklore into the Kings of Cologne, followed by St. Martin's Chapel (included because St. Ninian was taught by Martin of Tours before coming to light the first spark of Christianity in Scotland). Finally there was a scene which seems to have varied between St. George and the Dragon and Robin Hood and his Merry Men — an opportunity for the burgh craftsmen to have a part, dressed up in green and carrying bows and arrows. At Lanark the town preferred Robin Hood to St. George, mainly because the dragon needed so many annual repairs that it became unpopular.

Regular processions of this kind were useful religious reminders to people. Medieval folk did not all go to church regularly so parish priests kept religious teaching alive by organising street pageants, plays and processions. These were performed in the open air simply because there were no public halls in which they could be staged. They were rather like the Miracle Plays, Moralities and Mummer Plays performed by Trade Guilds in many English cities, most notably at York, Newcastle, Norwich, Coventry, Chester and Wakefield (where they were known as the Towneley Plays). There were equivalents in Scotland, such as the pageant of 'Halyblude' held in Aberdeen at Candlemas, where members of various crafts and guilds had long-established parts to play — the smiths and hammermen playing the Three Wise Men, for example. Sadly, Reformation burgh life was never quite so colourful or lively.

CHAPTER 10

The Kirk's Role in Burgh Life

The Reformation became rooted in different places at different times, but once the presbyterian church *was* established, Scottish burgh life was never the same again. A more serious attitude was introduced, and an obvious sign of this was that everyone was now required to attend the kirk regularly and to do no work on the Sabbath. Similarly, clothing became more subdued, and personal behaviour was expected to become more restrained. Even Christmas was not celebrated, for this was considered too Episcopalian.

Many of these changes were enforced by the new kirk sessions, which perhaps need a word of explanation. The Church of Scotland retained the parish system used by the Catholic church but instead of having a priest sent to them by the local bishop, the congregation chose their own minister. The minister and his flock then decided upon a number of worthy people to act as kirk elders. These elders and the minister formed the kirk session, a sort of management committee on behalf of the congregation, which enforced church attendance and dealt with a wide variety of social matters ranging from care of the poor and the provision of education in the parish to the punishment of sinners and petty criminals. The minutes or records of session meetings now form, along with burgh court and council records, an invaluable source for the study of burgh history. Some kirk minutes go back to the 1560s, making it a fascinating experience to open the handwritten pages of such old records, there to discover the day-to-day life of a burgh, set out just like a diary.

From the very start of the Reformation, pressure was put on people to respect the Sabbath as a day of rest. Dundee's burgh records for 1559 illustrate this: 'The town council command that Sunday be kept as God's day and that no merchants, craftsmen nor street-sellers open their booths and sell anything. Also that no inn-keepers, brewers or bakers open their booths and sell bread, wine nor ale during the preaching on Sunday'. The Dunfermline kirk session records for 1570 instruct 'no blacksmith to work on the Sabbath, unless it is to shoe a stranger's horse'. At Aberdeen, those who winnowed corn on a Sunday could be fined twenty shillings

Kincardine church, a typical post-Reformation parish kirk built in 1675 and used until the 1830s. The collection of 17th and 18th-century gravestones is one of the best in Scotland. *Photo*: courtesy of Kincardine Local History Group.

and were expected to make an act of public repentance. At the peak of Puritan observance during Cromwell's occupation, almost everything was banned on Sundays, including dancing, listening to 'profane music', baking bread, brewing ale, washing, or travelling anywhere.

In many places kirk elders went round the burgh just as the Sunday service began, to apprehend those who were not in church. In 1621 at Stirling, John Smyth was accused of breaking the Sabbath by 'wandering through the fields unnecessarlie in time of sermon'. At Kincardine-on-Forth the elders were instructed by the session to go 'after the ringing of the third bell through the town of Kingcardine and see there were no persons profaning the Sabbath'. This particularly meant combing the town's taverns for drinkers, and the banks of the River Forth for fishermen at the salmon cruives or basket nets. The excuses offered by those who were caught were sometimes quite ingenious; one group of Kincardine men claimed in 1700 that they had only gone out to their nets to check that they had not been washed away 'after the extraordinary storm that day'. Sunday fishing must have been a problem all along the river, for at Alloa a number of men and women were fined one shilling each for the same offence in 1666.

The enforcement of Sunday observance led on to the regulation of many other aspects of behaviour. Adultery, fornication, drunkenness, Sabbath-breaking and other moral offences were upgraded by Scotland's parliament into civil offences by a series of Acts passed between 1560 and 1620, and the Kirk was given authority to apprehend and punish offenders. Although they included fines, Kirk punishments were often designed to humiliate or embarrass the offender, and to produce a public scene of repentance. The most important feature was the stool of repentance which was located in front of the minister's pulpit in every church, so that everyone could see the offender and hear the preacher's words. Then there were the jougs, often fastened to the kirkyard gate or by the door of the church itself; examples survive here and there, such as at Stobo Kirk near Peebles, or on the ancient kirk tower at Abernethy. Whippings were sometimes administered, rough sackcloth was sometimes worn, and in extreme cases there was the last resort of excommunication, which at St. Andrews in 1573 included an order against anyone else speaking, eating or drinking with the offender, inviting him into their house, or even selling him anything, on pain of a similar excommunication.

Those who refused to accept the will of the Kirk faced sterner punishment in the civil courts; for example, adultery was punishable by the offender being made to stand bareheaded and barefoot at the kirk door, and then on the stool of repentance, every Sunday for up to six months or more, and to this might also be added a public flogging and perhaps a fine. On the other hand, anyone who refused this could be executed by the civil courts.

Some moral offences such as greed, pride, gluttony or hypocrisy were not easy to detect and do not occur often in kirk records. Other crimes were much easier to discover and crop up regularly. Far and away the greatest number of punishments were to do with fornication and adultery — from 1560 to 1600 the kirk session at St. Andrews dealt with someone on a sexual charge roughly every fortnight, while in 1566 two-thirds of all the crimes brought before the Canongate kirk session in Edinburgh were for sexual offences.

Anything thought to encourage licentious behaviour was also suppressed, so that even funeral wakes and wedding feasts (where 'promiscuous dancing' was likely to occur) were restricted. In 1683

These jougs hang outside the Kirkcudbright tolbooth and are typical of many in Scotland. Many offenders were sentenced by the kirk session rather than the burgh court. Jougs were often placed at the doorway of a kirk — the church at Kincardine was once an example. See also page 101. *Photo*: Craig Mair.

Elgin burgh council ordained that none except friends and relations of 'the defunct' were allowed to attend lykewakes, on pain of a £5 fine, presumably because when such events were open to all and sundry, they became little more than 'fruitful seminaries of all lasciviousness and debaushtrie'. 'Penny weddings' were also widely condemned. On such occasions, anyone who contributed a penny or so towards the expense of entertainment and food became a 'guest' (there could be as many as two hundred people), so the possibility of excessive drunkenness and immorality was very high. The Kirk had no wish to stop 'legitimate jollification' but it regarded penny bridals as little better than orgies and clamped down firmly; at Kincardine-on-Forth the session resolved in 1705 that parishioners would not even have their banns proclaimed until they had first paid a bond of £40 Scots against any promiscuous behaviour, including dancing, at the wedding party. In 1623 at Aberdeen, James Proctor was actually obliged to accept a legal undertaking that there would be no 'pyping, fiddling, dansing, truble, bancatting nor no uther kynd of ryot' at James Leslie's wedding.

In larger burghs both elders and bailies regularly invaded the brothels which thrived in many closes and side streets. 'Harlotrie' was a serious problem in 17th-century towns. If caught, the least a man could expect was a stint on the stool of repentance, although he might also have been whipped, shaved bareheaded or made to wear sackcloth. Women were treated more harshly; in Edinburgh, where the problem seems to have been greatest, prostitutes were first ducked 'in the deepest and foulest pool of the town' and then banished from the burgh. Any return from banishment could result in death by drowning. If a girl became pregnant, she was usually made to reveal the name of the father, who was then strongly pressured to marry her, but in addition she was likely to have her hair cut off, and both would usually have to make a full declaration of repentance, often in sackcloth, in the kirk.

Another very common misdemeanour was street-fighting or even just insulting or arguing loudly in public. Drunken brawls, even gang fights with swords or dirks, did occur; Robert Birrell, an Edinburgh burgess and diarist, recorded in 1568 how 'at two o'clock in the afternoon, the Laird of Airth and the Laird of Wemyss met upon the High Street of Edinburgh; and they and their followers fought a very bloody skirmish, where there was many hurt on both sides'. Common street insults were, however, more likely. One man from Kilmarnock who had insulted his wife in public was obliged to kneel in front of his congregation, hold his tongue between his teeth, and cry out 'False tongue, thou lied!' — in fact a common punishment in most burghs. In 1610 Catherine Lyne was charged at Aberdeen with abusing Bailie Forbes by calling him 'suetie hatt, clipit brecis and blottit hippis' (in other words, 'sweaty hat, short trousers and bloated hips'), for which she was actually banished from the town.

It should be emphasised that kirk sessions did not only pick on ordinary folk. Magistrates, bailies, elders and even ministers were just as likely to be summoned to the stool of repentance for drunkenness, profanity, lewdness or any other offence for which they were caught. At Kincardine, for example, the kirk treasurer was found drunk coming home from Culross Fair, for which he was suspended from his duties as elder and treasurer and given a public rebuke on the stool of repentance by the minister; four months

A branks from Montrose. Women were often punished by the kirk for spreading gossip, scolding or slandering, and had to wear this mask on Sundays. Some branks had a metal tongue which prevented the offender from speaking. *Photo*: Angus District Libraries and Museums Service.

later, having led a satisfactory life thus far, he was called again to the session where he again professed his full repentance and was voted back into his previous posts.

The humiliation and public exposure which was part of Kirk punishment was, of course, unpleasant and much has been made of this ever since, but the motive was not one of tyranny or small-minded vindictiveness. The Kirk's aim was to save a soul from eternal damnation, to see a sinner repent and resume a proper place in Christian society. In many cases punishment also included pastoral help from the minister, including scriptural guidance, and perhaps also a continuing watch on the conduct of some offenders — not to take some perverse delight in catching them transgressing again, but to help keep them on the straight and narrow. No doubt there *were* vindictive elders who were glad to see some persistent nuisance get his just deserts in the jougs or the stool of repentance, but that was not the aim of the Kirk in general.

Apart from its concern for public moral welfare, which affected everyone in burgh life, another important aspect of the Kirk's work was in caring for the poor. A body of 'poor', including orphans, the blind, the aged or infirm and such like, always existed in every burgh, but during times of economic hardship or famine this number always grew with the influx of beggars or destitute people from elsewhere.

This human problem was handed on to the Kirk, especially since the alms houses and hospitals of pre-Reformation days were now mostly swept away. However, since church lands were now also lost, the Kirk did not have the same flow of revenues which the Catholic Church had once enjoyed, and it fell upon members of the congregation to support the poor in their particular parishes by offering regular Sunday donations in church. High and low born were supposed to give what they could according to their means, but if local gentry or heritors 'forgot' to contribute, there was little the minister could do about it. He might condemn the rich from his pulpit, but in some cases it was the taxes paid by these same people which ultimately paid his salary and many thought it more prudent to say nothing. 'It's the poor who maintain the poor' became a fairly accurate saying in some parts of Scotland.

It was up to the kirk session to disburse as sensibly as possible what funds there were in the Poor Box. People were usually interviewed by the elders, and if found to be genuinely needy, would then receive a small cash sum, or whatever else was deemed appropriate, such as shoes, coal, or even the cost of a funeral. For example, Kilmarnock's kirk session minutes for 1692 recorded a donation 'to Bessie Miller, to buy blankets to her, £1 Scots'. Sadly, a later entry that year added, 'To Robt. Barr, for making Bessie Miller's grave, two shilling, and fourtein shilling of charity, £2.13s.4d Scots'. Every parish kirk record book contains hundreds of similar entries, for the poor were everywhere and so was the spirit of charity. At Aberdeen the congregation of St. Machar's supported eleven regular paupers in 1621, but when an enquiry in 1636 discovered another thirty-five who were 'not provided with kail and fuel and other necessaries of good neighbourhood' they were unstintingly added to the list. In 1692 there were eleven needy people in Kincardine receiving aid, including a baby left by its mother and one old man with an epileptic son. In May 1699 the kirk session of Stirling's Holy Rood kirk minuted a long list of starving people who received temporary help during the famine of

Most wealthy citizens saw it as their Christian duty to help the poor and needy, often by endowing the local guildry hospital for 'decayed brethren'. The Glasgow Merchants' House still recalls many of its members who gave charity in the past. *Photo*: Craig Mair, courtesy of Glasgow Merchants' House.

that time, ending with 'John Miller, likewise taken into the roll of weekly pensioners and allowed 6d a week'. In other words, these famine victims were over and above the regular list of poor who were given charity.

Famine put great pressure on burgh kirk resources, and it might be supposed that there would be little sympathy for those additional poor who drifted into town from elsewhere looking for alms. In fact, many records show that even when Poor Box funds were under severe strain, these 'stranger poor' were still somehow cared for or, if necessary, given a decent burial. In 1711 the Kilmarnock kirk session noted, 'Given to a stranger at the Kirk door, 8s Scots', and again in 1712, 'Given to a paralitick man, a stranger, 15s Scots'. Similarly, in 1660 at Peebles four shillings was given to 'Ane poor man, with ane young child in his arms, called Dankin Magill'. On the other hand, there was always the suspicion that some beggars were no more than idle wasters or vagabonds. Unless times were unusually hard, or they were manifestly disabled or sick, those aged between around 13 and 70 were liable to be chased out of town and punished if they returned, as described in Chapter 4.

Another matter in which the Kirk played an active part was education. In a sense this was related to the problem of poverty, since money from the Poor Box was sometimes used to help pupils pay their school fees.

During the Reformation many of the old Catholic-run schools were closed. However a great number also survived, especially in burghs, to reappear as Grammar Schools run by the burgh councils. Examples, with their earliest recorded dates, include Dumfries (1481), Perth (c1150), Kirkwall (1486), Brechin (1485), Leith (1521), Peebles (1464), Dundee (1434), Kirkcudbright (1455), Montrose (1459), and Kirkcaldy (1569) — but the list is really much longer. At Forres, for example, the first reference to a school in the burgh records was in 1582, when John Forrester was appointed the master. During the 1590s the local minister was then given charge, but in 1608 the two posts were separated again and thereafter most of the teachers were graduates employed by the burgh council; of the thirteen schoolmasters who served the school during the 17th century, five came from Aberdeen University.

Most small burgh schools had only one teacher but sometimes there were more. In 1612 the Stirling burgh council appointed 'Johnne Thomesoun, son to Robert Thomesoun the bellman, to be a doctor (ie teacher) in the grammar school, under master William Wallace, principal master, for teaching the bairns in reading of the English tongue, and grants him in fee the sum of ten merks yearly'. The term 'doctor' had, of course, nothing to do with medicine and generally did not even imply that the teacher had gained a university doctorate — it meant simply 'teacher'. John Knox's vision of a proper school in every parish may not have been achieved in his lifetime, but by about 1650 there was at least a school in most burghs.

Inevitably the Reformation did cause an acute shortage of

teachers for a time. A weeding-out process went on all over Scotland, identifying those priests and academics who would not unreservedly embrace the new Protestant way; this inevitably resulted in the loss of many good teachers. For a time, low-calibre people were sometimes all that could be found to tide things over. Until the situation improved, the curriculum in many schools often consisted of whatever the teacher happened to know — hopefully, but not always, some Latin, English, Arithmetic and perhaps Music. From the Kirk's point of view reading was the most important subject, for family Bible study was an important part of Presbyterian life, especially now that the Latin Bible had been translated by command of James VI. One big step forward in schools came in the 1590s with *Dunbar's Rudiments*, a Latin grammar written by Alexander Simpson, the minister and schoolmaster at Dunbar. This was followed in 1612 by another Latin grammar, this time written by Alexander Home of Dunbar, which was so highly thought of that it was ordered to be used in all schools. With books like these and a slowly improving supply of university graduates, education recovered. In a few places even the old song schools, once attached to abbeys and cathedrals, reappeared as music schools — Elgin's records for 1692 mention 'John Taylor, master of the musick school', while in 1636 a census made by Aberdeen's burgh council included a master of the song school.

During the 17th century education came steadily to be regarded as an important part of burgh life, but although they were graduates and were helping to establish the Scots as amongst the most literate people in Europe, school teachers were not well paid. To make ends meet, many had to find other part-time work. Thomas Mure, the school 'doctor' at Kilmarnock in 1647, was appointed the kirk precentor, for which he would have received a small annual consideration. At Stirling in 1620 William Row, who was a teacher at the grammar school, was paid an additional 6s 8d per quarter for teaching music to the town's children. Elsewhere schoolmasters acted as clerks to kirk sessions, gave private lessons (sometimes including even sword fencing) to the children of wealthier burgesses, did a little farming or ale brewing, and sometimes even dug graves. On the other hand, unsatisfactory teachers were liable to be quickly dismissed by burgh councils seeking high standards and good value for the salaries they paid. At Stirling, Andrew Matsone was dismissed as English teacher at the grammar school for negligence

F

and laziness, while in 1672 the entire staff was sacked, following 'manifold complaints against the master and doctours of the grammar schoole'.

Although burgh councils actually controlled schools in towns, the Kirk always had an important influence in educational affairs. Many town councillors were also kirk elders and, with the minister, they ensured that the curriculum reflected the correct biblical teachings, beginning with the Catechism but including a suitable selection of approved literature. In addition, it was the minister (a university graduate himself) who often interviewed prospective teachers for their academic and spiritual suitability. Even the school buildings were sometimes provided by the kirk; at Kincardine-on-Forth in 1694 the kirk session erected the burgh's first proper school building in the grounds of the kirk itself, shouldering the cost because the chief local heritor was in financial straits and a school was needed meanwhile. In 1708 the kirk session also built a dwelling house for the school master.

The Kirk could also put strong pressure on parents to send their children to school. Alloa's session records for 1671 minute that 'it was ordained that intimation should be made the next Sabbath from the pulpit to parents to be more careful educating their children at school', while at Kilmarnock in 1677 the session appointed the elders to 'bring a list of the boyes fit for the school, that their parents may put them to school'. At the same time unofficial dame schools and other private establishments were usually suppressed, unless to educate girls in simple reading and arithmetic, with perhaps some sewing and, of course, religious instruction. Parents could also be brought before the session if their children were persistent truants.

Perhaps more importantly, kirk sessions regularly paid the school fees for poorer pupils in burghs all over Scotland. Selkirk's records mention 'two poor boys sent to school at Newark'. At Kilmarnock the session recorded that it would meet 'the quarter payments of the poor whom they list to be put to school'. In 1694 Dumbarton's kirk session minuted that it would 'give 20 merks for the maintenance of John Anderson at the Colledge' — presumably Glasgow University. At Kincardine the session decided in 1692 that the parents of children who were 'capable of learning and are not able to pay their quarter's wadges are to put them to school and the Session will pay for them'.

The Kirk's work in aiding the poor and encouraging education was very much to its credit, but one matter for which it must surely stand indicted and ashamed was its merciless persecution of witches. This is not the place to describe the relentless searching out, mostly of women, which happened in Scotland, but it must never be forgotten that about four thousand people died in terrible agony in the market places of Scotland's burghs, tortured until they confessed to being witches, then murdered that their souls might be saved.

Persecution swept the country in four phases, in the 1590s (when King James VI himself led the campaign), in the 1620s, the 1640s and during the early 1660s. Though some areas, particularly the Highlands and Perthshire, escaped the attentions of witch-hunters, burghs in every part of Scotland were the scenes of many deaths. At Aberdeen, twenty-four women and two men were burned in 1596—97 alone. In 1659 at Dumfries nine women were strangled at the stake and then burned to ashes — their executioners were then given free ale as a reward. The diarist John Nicholl records that in Edinburgh during 1658 at least one man and eleven women, including 'a maiden', were burned on the Castlehill. They died on Paisley Green, on the shore at Pittenweem, the gallows knowe at Selkirk, the Witch Hill at St. Andrews, at Bo'ness, Dundee, North Berwick, Forfar, Perth and most other burghs. The last to die was a woman strangled and burned in a barrel of pitch in the streets of Dingwall in 1727. Thereafter, the frenzy died away, but not until a terrible stain had marked Scotland's burgh history for ever.

There is, however, an exception to this shameful catalogue of cruelty. It is said that in 1649, eleven women, accused by another at Peebles of witchcraft, were brought by the Marquis of Douglas to Lanark and incarcerated there in the tolbooth. This required the town not only to feed and guard them, but to pay one George Cathie to torture them to get them to confess, which greatly angered the bailies because of the cost involved. It was said that a similar case at Aberdeen had cost the town £65, plus another £11.10s for burning the victims afterwards, which was an alarming precedent. Eventually, the eleven at Lanark were all acquitted — it would be nice to think that, for once, the cost of a burning worried the bailies more than the saving of some souls.

CHAPTER 11

Military Matters

From the days of Robert the Bruce, when it was commanded that every man who owned goods worth more than one cow should possess a spear or bow, ordinary people were expected to take up arms if required. Scotland was a rough and dangerous land, so it was up to every burgh to look after itself. In 1424 James I ordered every man to learn archery, and each town to establish a practice area or 'butts', so that the king could call upon a force of civilian, but trained, bowmen for his army if necessary. Slowly, ordinary people became at least vaguely skilled at arms and accepted that at some time during their lives, though they were perhaps butchers or bakers in normal circumstances, they might be called upon to fight.

Over the years wars, civil wars and invasions occurred so often that most burghs organised a force of local civilian defenders to repel danger when it threatened. Burgesses were usually required to possess armour and weapons, and were expected to man the town's defences when any crisis occurred. At Stirling in 1628 no man could even become a burgess until he had produced his armour before the council. In 1679 Peebles burgh council ordained that every burgess in the town was to provide himself with a 'stand of sufficient armes, to wit, one pike and one sword, or one musket and firelock . . . upon pain of twenty merks Scots money for each person that fails'. In other words, in a land racked for centuries by wars, but without much hope of being protected by a regular army, it was up to the burghs to see to their own defences.

To ensure that their ramparts and militia were kept in good order, burghs were supposed to hold a 'waupenschaw' or weapon-show four times each year. In practice these troop reviews were often neglected, and tend only to occur in burgh records when there was some risk of the town being attacked. Most seem to have been pretty ramshackle affairs. At Lanark, for example, each burgess was supposed to turn up with a steel helmet, a 'jak' or steel breastplate, a sword, pike or Lochaber axe, and ideally a musket, so that he could be classified as 'furnished' or fully equipped. However, there never was a waupenschaw at Lanark where every man was properly 'furnished'. At the muster of 1581, for example, which is fully described in the burgh records, of the 155 men who paraded, fifty-two were furnished (though some had no jak), seventy-two had spears, twenty-nine had axes, one man had a musket, and very few had steel helmets.

Stirling's attitude was more practical. In 1666 when a Covenanter rising in the south-west led to an armed march on Edinburgh, the council decided to have the burgh 'put in a posture of defence'. Four bailies were therefore sent through the town to 'require every fencible neighbour to have arms, and upon Tuesday next to muster them, that it may be known who wants and who has'. Fortunately for Stirling's townsfolk, the Covenanters were defeated at Rullion Green and their precautions were not tested.

This sort of thing happened everywhere — from the time of Mary Queen of Scots to that of King William, most burghs were thrown into panic at some time or another and found themselves cleaning up rusty old pikes or woodwormed muskets. When James VII was exiled in 1688 Banff examined its arsenal, stored in an upper room of the tolbooth; it consisted of fifteen muskets, one hundred pounds of rough lead, twenty-eight pounds of musket balls, four militia coats and one and a half bandoliers. Not surprisingly, the burgh council hurriedly ordained the Treasurer to 'dress the guns that they be kept from rusting'.

Even if there had been enough guns in a burgh, its defences would have been unlikely to hinder a determined enemy. Walls and gates could force ordinary travellers to enter the town at the gates, and some may even have been enough to deter marauders or armed mobs, provided the burghers looked well-armed and determined, but few towns were strong enough to stop an army from entering if it wished. As mentioned in Chapter 2, many burghs did not even have a proper stone wall, but depended instead on an earth rampart, a ditch, or a perimeter of garden walls. In places such as Edinburgh or Stirling where there was a strong castle, this may well have held out against an enemy but the town itself was usually captured. This then obliged the castle defenders to fire at an enemy hidden among the houses of the burgh, which the townsfolk must have watched with great dismay. The impression is that most burghers preferred to offer little or no resistance if hostile forces appeared, for fear that the town would be damaged and the town's finances would then be ruined. After all, most armies came and then moved on, but townsfolk would have to

Part of the walls of Stirling burgh. The bastion has been converted into a dovecot at some time since the 18th century. See also page 33. *Photo*: Craig Mair.

clear up the mess and pay for repairs afterwards if there was any fighting. The advice of the minister at East Anstruther was probably not uncommon when he counselled his flock that 'it was aye best to jouk and let the jaw gang ower' (which means that it was always best to duck and let the water dash over).

Some towns did choose to resist, and even found that it paid off. When part of the highland Jacobite army of 1715 threatened the burgh of Dumfries the local population, swelled by volunteers from the whole south-west area of Scotland, armed itself with everything from muskets or pikes to pitchforks and scythes, and placed a guard on the town gates. Two rows of trenches were dug around the town and a local stream was dammed so that it could be diverted to flood these ditches if required. Then with bells and drums kept ready to sound an alarm when the warning came and horsemen keeping lookout around the town, all but two of the burgh gates were bricked up. Local ministers and doctors went on standby to help should any fighting occur. With the nearest Jacobite troops only three miles away, the alarm went during the night of October 31st, and in pouring rain the defenders waited to face the

Highlanders. Candles lit up most house windows to prevent any clansmen from somehow sneaking in under cover of darkness. Two hundred reserve militia waited in the High Street, ready to assist wherever the attack was strongest. Then, nothing happened. No enemy appeared — when told of the strength and determination of the burgh defenders, the Jacobites had turned away and destruction was averted.

In a few cases damage was caused by local feuding families, which was difficult to foresee or avoid. In 1593, for example, a party of Maxwells took refuge from their ancient enemies the Johnstones by gathering in the Old Kirk at Lochmaben — so the Johnstones burned the place down and in one moment of bloody rivalry the royal burgh lost its kirk. By the 17th century, however, such clan-like warfare was declining.

That is not to say that people in burghs did not get involved in the passions of the Covenanting period. Many townsfolk took sides and went off to fight, sometimes with disastrous results. In 1645, for example, the men of Anstruther decided to join the Covenanters. Sixty-three marched off from the tolbooth 'accoutred with steel caps and pikes' to fight in the Battle of Kilsyth against Montrose, where with three inexperienced regiments of townsfolk and sailors from Fife they were almost all slaughtered or captured. The effect of this disaster was so strong that for the next twenty years only one man from Anstruther enlisted in the army.

Similarly, for all their desire to avoid destruction, some towns were dragged into various campaigns. In 1644 Aberdeen was looted by Irish troops from Montrose's army; burgh records indicate that about 160 people were butchered including bailies and merchants but also innocent women and children. Dundee was also pillaged, first by Montrose's men in 1645 when, for a day, they ransacked the shops and warehouses of many merchants, and then by Monck in 1651 when the covenanter General Lumsden made a last stand in the steeple, the rest of the town having been destroyed in a siege. About 800 men and 200 women were then coldbloodedly executed by the Roundheads — an event as dreadful as any ordered by Cromwell in Ireland, yet strangely forgotten today.

In 1746 one arch was knocked out of Stirling Bridge by General Blakeney in an attempt to hinder the Highland retreat to the north — Stirling folk had no sympathy for Prince Charles, but to lose the use of the bridge was a heavy blow. All but two houses in Dunkeld

Dundee in the 1690s, by Captain J. Slezer. The town was totally destroyed by General Monck in 1651, when one thousand inhabitants were executed.

were burned to the ground in 1689, while in 1645 most of Stonehaven was burned down by Montrose. And these are just a few examples.

At Falkirk the local Livingstone family supported the King against Cromwell, so when Monck's men came to Falkirk in 1650 there followed a short siege of the Livingstone home at Callendar House. When the defending garrison refused to surrender, artillery was brought up and, in the words of an English officer's letter, 'we made a breach upon Kallendar House even in the face of the enemy we stormed it and lost a captain of foot, our gunner Robert Hargreave of your troop and 2 or 3 private soldiers. More were slain in the storm. We slew the enemy about 50 persons, and such as had quarter given them were most of them wounded'. A local street close to Callendar House is still called Monck's Road and marks where the English army camped.

On the other hand, campaigns sometimes moved so swiftly that troops often did little more than pass through some burghs, though even one day's looting and debauching could be devastating. At Aberdeen, for example, where some citizens signed the Covenant and others did not, the result was that every time an army marched in, the troops plundered the houses of those 'on the other side'. The bishop's palace was ransacked twice in as many weeks by Covenanter troops as occupation of the town see-sawed between rival armies.

On other occasions, however, the enemy came to stay, and then a

Callendar House, Falkirk, scene of an attack by General Monck's troops in 1651. This view dates from around 1820, by which time the house and grounds had been greatly altered. *Photo*: Falkirk Museums.

burgh would find itself occupied. The entry of the 9000-strong Covenanter army into Aberdeen in March 1639 was colourfully described by John Spalding, a contemporary local historian: 'They came in order of battell, weill-armed both on horse and foot, ilk horseman having five shot at least with ane carabine in hand, two pistols by his side, and other two at his saddle toir; the pikemen in their ranks with pike and sword; the musketiers in their ranks with musket staffs, bandolier, sword, powder, ball and match; ilk company had their captins, lieutenants, ensignes, sargeants, and other officers and commanders, all, for the most part, in buff coats and in goodly order. They had five colours of ensigns, they had trumpeters to ilk company of horsemen, and drummers to ilk company of footmen; they had their meat, drink, and other provision, bag and baggage caryed with them'. The picture is one of a strong and determined force which no ordinary town could have resisted.

Similarly, in 1745 Jacobite troops entered Stirling (whose gates were reluctantly opened since the walls were not defensible) and from among the houses set about bombarding the castle, which was

161

held by royalists. During this siege the gates were locked by the Highlanders to prevent all movement of the local inhabitants. People were also warned by proclamation not to go near the castle area, or to help the families of soldiers, on pain of execution by shooting. In due course a royal army approached the town so the Jacobites retired, but not before they blew up the church at St Ninians, which had been used as a powder magazine.

Occupation raised all sorts of questions as to how far locals should co-operate with troops billeted in the town. Some answers may never be fully known, for in some cases the records of suspended burgh councils are missing. Peebles' records are blank from early November 1650 to 29th May 1651, the period when Cromwellian troops took over the burgh just after the Battle of Dunbar. Lanark's records from 1615 to 1652 contain only a few entries, as if written during odd months of calm in an age of general upheaval. However, the kirk records, referring to the same period after the Battle of Dunbar, noted on November 28th 1650 that 'the enemies came to the town of Lanark, being about the number of four thousand horse, and so [we] were forced to go away in haste out of the town'. Lanark's council records did not resume properly until March 1652. Stirling's records were also interrupted in the same year, while at Forres it was again the kirk records which noted how 'on 10th December 1651, a garrison of the English Army had but lately entered the town and was not yet thoroughly settled and accommodated therein'. Other periods of upheaval can also be followed by reference to missing burgh records.

A fair picture can nevertheless be drawn of life in an occupied burgh. First was the reality that the town was, indeed, *occupied*, and that the population would have to get used to living under military law. Depending on the political or religious attitude of the town, the burgh council was sometimes suspended and orders often came from an imposed army command, as in 1654 when 'an order under the hands of Robert Overtoune and Lieut. Colonel Blunt . . . was published at the mercat cross of Elgin', or at Stirling in 1655 when there was 'produced to the magistrates and council of this burgh an order given forth by General Monck . . . authorising and requiring Colonel Read, governor, to cause and give notice . . . etc.'.

In many cases the first thing an imposed military command did was to order billets for the troops. Of the 9000 Covenanter troops who marched into Aberdeen in 1639, for example, about 1800 were left there under the command of the Earl of Kinghorn. It is unclear how the burgh, which did not have a large population, was expected to find accommodation for so many soldiers, but a payment of 6s 8d per man per day was promised by Montrose. This money does not ever seem to have been paid, but on the other hand, when Montrose demanded a tax of 100,000 merks from the town, this does not seem to have been paid either; the burghers complained of poverty and poor trade, and seem to have spun this excuse out until the Covenanters retreated two months later.

A note jotted on the flyleaf of the Peebles burgh records indicates an occupation by Cromwellian troops. '*8 September 1657*: That pairt of Captane Blissetts troope come to Peebles; removed 17 October 1657. *22 October 1657*: That pairt of Captane Turnours troop, in Lilburnes regiment, come to this burgh; removed Weddensday, 19 May, 1658. *24 September 1658*: The forsaid pairtie entered to their winter quarter; removed 8 May, 1659.' In other words, the burgh was under almost continuous occupation by English cavalry troops for two years.

Stirling's commanding strategic position meant that in times of trouble it was among the first burghs to be occupied by troops. As elsewhere, many soldiers ran up bills only to disappear leaving them unpaid. Stirling's records show the town clerk James Norie being sent off to Paisley in 1667 'with the accounts of quarterings due by the lord Carnegie's troop to this burgh and to get payment thereof before they be disbanded'.

At Lanark, a royalist force under the Earl of Strathmore came to town for twenty-one days in 1679, part of an army sent to deal with the Covenanter rising of that year in south-west Scotland. Strathmore's troops were mostly Gaelic-speaking Highlanders who wore native dress and carried their traditional weapons — the culture shock to the folk of Lanark can only be imagined. Although several Lanark men joined the Covenanters' rising and fought at the battles of Bothwell Brig and Drumclog (for which at least two were eventually hanged), the occupying Highlanders behaved well and caused no trouble. By contrast, the Angus Regiment which was stationed in the surrounding area seems to have been an ill-disciplined crowd of thieves which eventually marched off loaded down with shoes, pots, pans and such like plundered from its unfortunate hosts, leaving an unpaid quartering bill of £3544.

One of the last lowland towns to see a Highland army was

Dumfries, when four thousand Jacobites under Bonnie Prince Charlie marched in on December 21st 1745 during the retreat from England. Like every other army in every other time, the officers found comfortable lodgings while those ordinary soldiers who could find no-one to threaten for accommodation, made a field camp roughly where the Shakespeare Street car park now lies. The burgh council, meanwhile, received a demand for £2000, 1000 pairs of shoes, 200 horses and 100 carts, to be handed over within twenty-four hours or the troops would be allowed to ransack the town. Despite frantic efforts by local cordiners to made enough shoes, and pleas to local gentry for loans of money, neither were produced on time so the Jacobites took matters into their own hands and, as one local historian has described, 'gentlemen were upended in the street and the shoes wrenched from their feet'. At that point, news came that pursuing Hanoverian troops under the Duke of Cumberland were close at hand so there was a hasty packing of gear and on December 23rd the Highlanders moved out, taking Provost Crosbie and Walter Riddell with them as hostages for the money. When this was eventually paid, the two men were released at Glasgow and the town could breathe easy again. Indeed, thanks to the intervention of the local Duke of Queensberry, the burgh even received government compensation of £2848 for the demands made by the Jacobites.

Occupation also brought other changes. Cromwellian forts were built at Inverness, Perth, Ayr, Leith and Inverlochy in the star-shaped form of citadel ramparts used at that time — rather like the slightly earlier walls of Berwick-on-Tweed which still stand today. The intention was to enforce English rule in Scotland, and these forts were therefore used as bases for occupation garrisons. At Ayr this included commandeering the parish kirk of St. John the Baptist for use as a storehouse inside the fort; although 1000 merks was paid in compensation, the burgh nevertheless had to build a new church elsewhere.

Then there was the helpless feeling of watching occupation troops of whatever army behave as they wished, knowing that they were beyond the complaint of ordinary townsfolk. During the Cromwellian period, for example, the people of Linlithgow had to pay £30 ransom for their burgh records. At Anstruther 200 citizens were taken hostage against the good behaviour and cooperation of the townspeople; even so, the burgh was totally plundered and 'nothing imaginable that was transportable or moveable [was] left by them' — they even took the minister's hourglass and threw the kirk bible into the sea. In many places beds were requisitioned and some records refer to beds actually being carried out of people's homes for use by soldiers elsewhere. Soldiers also got drunk, which led to arguments and street brawls with locals. With soldiers in town, prostitution became a serious issue for kirk and council alike, as did the problem of young mothers abandoned by soldiers who moved on and never returned.

Officers had a particular habit of consuming large quantities of wine without ever paying for the pleasure. In some cases officers' wives and children were also billeted in towns, which was a particularly irksome drain on burgh resources since they could not be said to be soldiers on active duty. Horses were often demanded and sometimes a disproportionate amount of food was taken from some burghs, which caused hunger for townsfolk and ruin for some merchants. In 1690 Stirling's burgh council decided that since the burden of having horses commandeered often fell upon only a few burgesses, others would be required to share the demand by contributing horses to those who had lost the most. Selkirk's records reveal great hardships for the burgh during Cromwell's time, and at Linlithgow many merchants actually fled to Culross, presumably with their goods, for fear of looting. Little wonder that every burgh preferred to see the soldiers of *any* army go somewhere else!

Some towns found themselves housing prisoners of war. In 1645, for example, Montrose's brilliant campaigns were halted at Philiphaugh, just outside Selkirk; several hundred royalist survivors, including their camp-followers and families, were butchered by the Covenanters on the field of battle. A handful, mostly Irish women and children, were brought to the Selkirk tolbooth and locked up. Three months later, when passions had surely died down, they were nevertheless brought out into the market place and shot, watched by an indifferent population which remembered only that the local laird's son had died in battle against Montrose. Except for the execution of Dundee's population in 1651, the callousness of the slaughter at Selkirk was the worst episode in the whole story of the Covenanting wars. On the other hand, the Covenanters faced the same treatment themselves. At Dumfries, two Covenanters were executed in 1667 and their heads and right arms were then dangled from the old bridge as a warning to others. This clearly did not

The 15th-century bridge at Dumfries, beside which witches were burned on the Whitesands and from whose arches the severed heads and arms of Covenanters were dangled in 1667. *Photo*: Craig Mair.

work, for in 1685 another Covenanter, called James Kirko, was executed by shooting on the Whitesands — an event marked by a plaque today. Similarly, in 1679 about 1200 Covenanters were brought to Hamilton after their defeat at the Battle of Bothwell Brig. Some were subsequently executed at Edinburgh and elsewhere. It is an account of cruelty and counter-cruelty sadly repeated in far too many Scottish towns, for the Covenanting period opened deep and bloody wounds which have barely healed even today.

For most burghs of this period, the last experience of prisoners of war came during the Jacobite rebellion of 1745. At Stirling, for example, the records show that thirty-four Jacobite prisoners were deposited in the tolbooth by the Duke of Argyll in February 1746. Although the folk of Stirling were staunchly anti-Jacobite, they were clearly dismayed at having to look after these unwelcome Highlanders, for they sent a daily fee of £3.8s to Argyll to cover running costs. It is not clear if this was ever paid, but the records do mention that three weeks later the council appointed the town treasurer to pay Archibald Moir, 'jaylor of the burgh, thirtie shillings starling for his extraordinary pains . . . in attending the prisoners that were incarcerated in the tolbooth by the government since beginning of September last, cleaning the prisoners, serving the prisoners, and furnishing ane servant to his assistance for the better doing thereof . . .'

From time to time burgh men were also levied into various armies. Although there were always some with a liking for the military life, or were unemployed and could find no other livelihood, a fair bit of arm-twisting nevertheless went on. At Forres, for example, the records mention that eight men were 'nominated' for service in 1650 — more likely they were virtually press-ganged for action against Monck's Cromwellian army.

Wars in the Low Countries and against Spain were also costly and burghs were regularly ordered to supply both money and replacement troops. Peebles, for example, was ordered by Act of Parliament in 1657 to contribute £12 9s 9d Sterling to a national levy of £15,000 for war against Spain, while in 1694 the town was ordered to raise a contingent of men for King William's war against France. These demands were a serious drain on burgh resources, for trade was often slack, hunger haunted Scotland during the 1690s, and useful men were often taken off just when burghs could least do without their skills. But there was no avoiding the obligation — indeed any town which prevaricated could face a heavy fine which would have strained the coffers even more.

Fines did not deter cowards, however. In 1690 when Lanark was ordered to provide just one recruit, a lottery of suitably aged unmarried men in non-vital occupations resulted in Alex Wilson being picked. At first the fellow accepted his lot but then he must have had second thoughts for he ran away. To avoid the town being fined the magistrates paid James Buick four dollars to go instead. When Wilson later returned to the burgh he was promptly fined the same four dollars and jailed in the tolbooth until he paid up.

It was actually quite common to employ a substitute to do military service. Burgesses especially did so when they wanted to avoid duty in the local militia. At least one of the men levied from Peebles for service against France was also a hired substitute; the records mention that a Cumberland man was paid £3 Sterling by bailie Robert Forrester to take the place of Thomas Peacock, the payment being ten shillings immediately and the rest a year later 'provided the said soldier should not be found to be a deserter or taken away for some other misdemeanours'. The council also ordered the burgh treasurer to pay bailie Forrester the same again whenever he asked, 'for getting up his band on the terms above mentioned'.

At Lanark they eventually decided upon a better system for meeting the demand for levies. The most important thing was to avoid recruitment of the burgh's most necessary citizens, for these were not easily replaced. Accordingly, a list was made of all useful men who could possibly be levied — this came to fifty-three people in 1696 — and each man then paid fourteen shillings into a common fund. If any were subsequently called up, even into the local militia (known at Lanark as the Fencible Men after 1689), the fund would be used to hire a substitute. After all, army recruits were easily obtained, but a town's future could be ruined by the loss of its best craftsmen or merchants. In the same sense, therefore, when a company of Lanark men was drafted into the King's army to deal with the 1715 Jacobite rebellion, there was general relief when they all returned having 'unfortunately' missed the vital Battle of Sheriffmuir, and having consequently seen no action at all.

The men of Falkirk seem to have shared this sensible view. Seventy-three followed the local Earl of Callendar against Cromwell and were in the army which, ineptly led by the Duke of Hamilton, was routed at Preston in 1648. Although this Scottish army was badly mauled and suffered terrible losses, the Falkirk men fought their way through the English ranks and eventually found their way home. Tame surrender would not have been very helpful for their town or families.

Warfare seems to have been such a recurring nightmare during the 17th century that it might seem surprising that burghs could lead any sort of normal life at all. And yet burgh council and kirk minutes are overwhelmingly the record of day-to-day events, a concern for trading regulations and petty punishments. References to warfare appear only occasionally. Although many burghs were by-passed by conflict, even in places such as Aberdeen where fighting flared up repeatedly the impression is still one of a town doggedly pursuing its crafts and businesses, collecting its tolls, regulating its markets and punishing its wrongdoers. Armies came and went, and sometimes killed and looted. Trenches sliced through grazing land and artillery fired down the streets. Infant industries struggled through recession and plundering. And yet by 1700 the burgh was still there and its ships still traded. Everyday life carried on.

CHAPTER 12

Housing in Burghs

Apart from kirks and castles, houses are the most obvious and visible signs of history in towns today. However, most surviving old houses are quite different from the way they would have looked in the 17th century. For example, old houses did not have pretty gardens, rone pipes, door locks and knockers, sash windows, or often even harling. Most were not painted white, as 'quaint' houses tend to be today. Many windows had no glass, only wooden shutters.

Many roofs were either turfed or were thatched with straw, reeds or heather — pantiles may look more colourful and authentic nowadays, but a stroll through any picturesque Fife fishing port would show that many tiled roofs were originally thatched. (For many years Auchtermuchty remained a forgotten corner of thatched houses, but even these last survivors are now rapidly disappearing and will be gone within a generation.) On the other hand, the houses of most wealthier people were slated by the 17th century — many burghs included a 'sclaiter' among their craftsmen, as at Ayr where the burgh accounts show that George Fultoun was paid £22 Scots for slating the kirk in 1616, or at Lanark where the local slater was made a burgess in 1687. And yet, how many restored buildings have had the slates removed and replaced with pantiles because they look more 'historic'? In fact, wealthy householders looked on tiles as the corrugated iron of their day and would never have used them if they could have afforded better!

Above all, no house today can convey the filth and smell of a 17th-century street. Not only did folk throw their household waste and effluent out of the windows to be raked up with the street's animal droppings into a dungheap by the door, but there was an unwashed smell even to the people themselves. Hardly any town houses had lavatories. Clothes were rarely washed, and faces were hardly ever wetted — even Queen Elizabeth of England wore thick white make-up to cover spots and blackheads, and a wig to cover a balding head which must once have been verminous with lice. Many Scots still wore hats at meals, to prevent nits from falling into the food. The houses, streets and alleys of any Scottish burgh must truly have smelled disgusting.

As still happens in many towns today, 17th-century burghs tended to divide into areas of greater or lesser desirability. The most select part of a burgh was usually the top end, closest to the castle, palace, university, abbey or kirk, and if possible on rising ground above the other houses (which avoided the sight and smell of tanning pits or slaughter houses). Thus in 17th-century Edinburgh, the upper classes lived if they could at an address in the Castlegate or Lawnmarket, at the top end of the Royal Mile. At Stirling they lived close to the castle at the top end of Broad Street. At Aberdeen the finest houses congregated round the university in the Auld Toun. At Falkland they lived across the street from the palace. Dunfermline's top people lived near the abbey — if there wasn't one, as at Inverkeithing or Haddington, they gathered into an area around the kirk.

In most cases these were only town houses, sometimes occupied when a nobleman came into the burgh on business, but often rented out to someone else. Some were retained simply to qualify the owner as a heritor (which offered a certain influence and status in local affairs). Others were used seasonally, as at Maybole where there were 'many pretty buildings belonging to the severall gentry of the countrey, who were wont to resort thither in winter, and divert themselves in converse together at their owne houses'.

Good examples of surviving town houses still exist all over Scotland. Kellie Lodge, built around 1590 at Pittenweem, was once a burgh residence for the Earls of Kellie. Glencairn's 'Greit House' at Dumbarton, built in 1623, was a town house for the Duke of Argyll. Huntly House in the Canongate, Lady Stair's House at Edinburgh, Rosebery House at Inverkeithing, Abertarff House at Inverness, Plewland's House at South Queensferry, Lanark's Hyndford House, Kinneil House at Bo'ness, Queen Mary's House at Jedburgh, Sir George Bruce's 'Palace' (corrupted from 'place') at Culross, Haddington House at Haddington, Preston Lodge at Cupar and Old Gala House at Galashiels are further good examples of town houses from the same 16th or 17th-century period. The finest example in any burgh is probably the Argyll Lodging at Stirling.

These houses may only have been used occasionally by their proper owners but they were nevertheless supposed to convey an outward impression of wealth and importance. Most were three or four storeys high, which alone made them very conspicuous above

Mar's Wark, an impressive 16th-century nobleman's house at Stirling. It stands near the castle and Argyll's Lodgings (page 72) facing down the burgh's main street to the tolbooth and mercat cross. *Photo*: Craig Mair.

the much smaller homes of other folk. They were built of fine dressed stone, unlike the rubble which most other people used. They had lots of windows and chimneys, which indicated many rooms inside — another status symbol. Many also had balconies (again very select) and then, to emphasise the point, the family coat of arms, often accompanied by the initials of the owner, were carved on the outer walls or above the windows.

This desire for grandeur can be illustrated by the house which Sir Philip Anstruther built at Anstruther. In 1641 during the Civil War King Charles II is said to have travelled along the Fife coast and 'lodged att the Laird of Ensters house' (which was then Dreel Castle). Here, perhaps being more accustomed to fine living in England, he apparently called the laird's residence a 'craw's nest', which irked Sir Philip so much that when peaceful times came he decided in 1663 to erect a better house. This building was clearly intended to outshine all other surrounding mansions, for the instructions stated quite explicitly that the windows were to be 'as large and compleit as those in the hall of Kellie', while the fancy entrance was to 'conform to the principal gate of Balcarres', and

Kellie Lodging at Pittenweem, dated around 1590 — a good example of a town house but now all that's left of the burgh's original High Street houses. The 16th-century church and tower still face down the street, however. *Photo*: Craig Mair.

even the dovecote was to be 'of the quality of Sir James Lumsdaine of Innergelly his doocote'. In addition, the outbuildings included a stable, a brewhouse and bakehouse. Unfortunately the house was demolished in 1811, but the 17th-century doocot at Innergellie, though dilapidated, still stands and is worth a visit.

The 17th century was, as Sir Philip Anstruther's new house well illustrates, a period of transition for many nobles and landed gentry from living in a castle or manor hall to a more sophisticated family residence. Many 17th-century town mansions, such as Maclellan's House (or Castle) at Kirkcudbright, were still built with some hint of a great hall, perhaps with a fireplace, but most were little used. More popular now were the drawing room and the dining room, though it is clear from surviving furniture inventories that the function of these rooms was still uncertain; many drawing rooms were sparsely furnished with little more than chairs, and not even curtains, nor an occasional table, a cabinet, bookcase, hanging pictures or clock. On the other hand, there was often a chamber pot in the drawing room! Bedrooms now opened from an upper landing

The painted ceiling at Old Gala House, Galashiels — an excellent example of a 17th-century laird's taste. Although such ceilings survive in a few tolbooths and castles, hardly any now remain in private houses. *Photo*: Robert Sutherland, Ettrick and Lauderdale District Museum Service.

or corridor, and thus were moving away from the older habit of having interconnecting doors through which people came and went to their own rooms. Bedrooms often contained, as well as a bed, a table and chair and a chest (in which clothes were stored, because wardrobes were still unknown). Since the swivelled dressing-table mirror was not yet invented, the only mirror was probably hand-held. In most cases there was no bathroom, nor even a jug or basin of water in the bedroom; the only regular washing seems to have been of the hands from a basin in the dining room before a meal. Having a bath was an extremely rare event, and was done in a large tub.

As with the buildings, 17th-century furniture in such houses was also in transition from the heavy, carved oak of Jacobean times to the more delicate Dutch and Flemish fashions which began to appear during Covenanter times, following stronger contacts with the protestant Low Countries. The great long tables of medieval banquets were slowly supplanted by smaller, often circular or oval,

The Gyles at Pittenweem, once the home of a sea-captain trader but later the tenement home of several families. Now restored by the National Trust for Scotland. *Photo*: Craig Mair.

dining tables with drop-leaves and spiralled gate legs. Similarly, although Arras tapestries still hung on many walls they were gradually seen off by a growing fashion for portrait paintings. In the better houses, wood panelling was a feature which softened the lines of walls with carvings or even rounded, barrel-shaped ceilings. Some beams or panels were painted — the colours look attractively soft and faded today, but when fresh they were bright and vibrant and must have made a striking impression. The Palace at Culross is almost entirely panelled, and gives a fine idea of the original painted decoration which adorned many such houses. The painted chapel at Provost Skene's House in Aberdeen is another fine example.

Burgess houses were usually much simpler than those of the nobility, but by standing several storeys high and including frequent architectural embellishments, they still contrasted with the houses of poorer folk. Burgess wealth varied considerably from the sizeable incomes earned by merchants engaged in foreign trade to the more modest means of burgh shopkeepers. Houses therefore also varied, from some which were not much smaller than those of local lords,

Pan Ha' at Dysart, another sea-trader's house restored by the National Trust for Scotland. The date above the door is 1582. *Photo*: Craig Mair.

with perhaps even a courtyard and entrance gateway, to others which were little more than a couple of rooms above the shop.

In coastal towns quite a few merchant houses were built beside, or overlooking, the shore so that anxious shipowners could watch for the safe arrival of expensive cargoes. The 'castle' at Elie, Sailor's Walk at Kirkcaldy, Thompson's House at Inverkeithing and the Gyles at Pittenweem are all examples of this along the Fife coast. At Culross, the Study was a similar house, but situated beside the mercat cross away from the harbour; an 'Outlook Tower' was therefore built to provide a view over the rooftops of ships sailing up the Firth of Forth. The old kirkyards at Kincardine and Bo'ness are full of headstones carved with the sailing ships once owned by

Thompson's House, Inverkeithing, dated 1617 and built by John Thompson, a local merchant burgess. Later occupants included the Earl of Rosebery. *Photo*: Craig Mair.

17th-century merchants, and convey a clear picture of the importance these men must once have enjoyed, not to mention the high opinion they must once have had of themselves.

Trade was not confined to the shores of Fife. Loudon Hall at Ayr was erected by a local 16th-century burgess to overlook the harbour. Aberdeen's Provost Ross was a wealthy burgess and shipowner, and his harbour-side house is now the city's maritime museum. Lamb's House in Leith is situated near the harbour and once included warehousing space, perhaps with an eye to saving storage costs at the port or simply because the owner felt that foreign cargoes would be more secure under his own roof.

On the other hand, some wealthy merchants preferred to live

Detail of the windows at Hamilton House, Prestonpans (see also page 78). The date above the centre window is 1628. *Photo*: Craig Mair.

inland, perhaps to be nearer their customers rather than the seaports where their goods first arrived from overseas. Cross House at Linlithgow was erected around 1700 by Andrew Craufurd of Lochcote, whose family were prominent local burgesses. Hamilton House at Prestonpans is another equally fine burgess house, built in 1628 and well worth a look. Similarly, the fine three-storeyed building at 1 High Shore in Banff is a burgess house built in 1675, solid, reliable-looking, yet with an attractive corbelled turret at one corner and a sundial at the angle — enough to show that its owner was a person of substance.

Several lovely examples of 17th-century merchant houses also survive at Elgin, where they have been well restored. No 42-46 High Street has a series of five arches of the Italian piazza style, a feature repeated elsewhere so that there is an impression of great wealth in the town. Just for good measure, Andrew Ogilvie and his wife Janet Hay had their initials sculpted on the stonework of No 50-52 High Street — another arched house. Norrie's House at Stirling, built in 1671 by James Norrie, the town clerk, includes some fine stonework on the street front, indicating the original owner's desire for something rather better than the simple tenement buildings more

Another fine 17th-century merchant's house, at Elgin. See also page 115. It bears the date 1694. *Photo*: Craig Mair.

typical elsewhere in the burgh. Nevertheless, since rates were assessed by the length of street frontage, Norrie built his house narrow and upwards — four storeys and an attic high, but only three windows wide. This tall, narrow look is also a feature of Edinburgh's old town streets, around the Lawnmarket, West Bow and Grassmarket. John Knox's House and Moubray House are two well-known Edinburgh buildings once owned by local burgesses — Knox's House, which dates from around 1490, is now the last partly-timbered dwelling house in the city — but the best example of a merchant's house is Gladstone's Land, in the Lawnmarket. In 1617 Thomas Gledstanes, an Edinburgh merchant burgess (and ancestor of the famous Prime Minister), bought and reconstructed the property into a ground-floor shop with flats above; he and his

Provost Skene's House, Aberdeen. This is the Cromwellian Room and recreates the furnishings in a wealthy burgess's house from 1649—1660. Despite their high social rank, even burgess merchants lived simply and unostentatiously — the dishes on the table are of pewter, for example. *Photo*: Aberdeen Art Gallery and Museums.

wife occupied two floors and rented the remaining four flats to a minister, a merchant, a knight and a guild officer. The house is now a museum furnished for the period, and gives a clear idea of the lifestyle of a 17th-century merchant burgess.

A fine example of a burgess house is Provost Skene's House at Aberdeen. Sir George Skene (1619—1707) was a wealthy merchant who was elected provost of the city from 1676 to 1685. Perhaps in keeping with his elevated status, he converted an older fortified tower into a much more comfortable family house, with cosily proportioned wood-panelled rooms inside and a small courtyard outside. The main entrance door is surrounded by fine sculpted stonework, some of it in a thistle and rose motif which Skene added to mark the restoration of Charles II to the throne in 1660. It is a house which would not have disgraced any nobleman or absentee heritor, and yet to stroll around today the feeling is still one of a pleasant and manageable family home.

The rooms in Provost Skene's house have been arranged to show different periods of furniture, beginning with the Cromwellian period, then the Restoration era, as well as a 17th-century bedroom, and so on into later periods. In fact, for all their wealth, many burgesses lived surprisingly simply and owned comparatively little furniture. In some early 17th-century burgess houses there would have been one table, one sideboard, one bench or a couple of chairs, one or two beds with suitable sheets, one or two blanket or clothing chests, some cooking pots, a kettle and grill, basic cutlery (but forks were very rare), a few books, candlesticks, barrels for fish or ale, a chamber pot, perhaps a washing basin, and little else.

By the end of the century, those merchants who had not been ruined by war had begun to imitate the finer Dutch and Flemish-influenced oak and walnut furniture already adopted by the nobility — gate-leg tables, straight-backed split cane chairs, some leather upholstery, chests of drawers, the occasional mirror, and a preference for wood-panelled rooms and carved or plastered ceilings. Windows also tended to become larger and as the price of glass came within reach, the traditional wooden shutters began to disappear, making interiors generally brighter. Floors were still stone-flagged or wooden but an occasional oriental rug or carpet did sometimes give a warmer, more luxurious feel to the best room. There were no toilets and, like everyone else of every social rank, burgesses quite happily emptied their chamber pots into the streets outside.

So much for the homes of merchants. Some burgesses were of more modest shopkeeping rank, but their homes also survive here and there. Just as richer people usually lived near the top of the town, so it seems that poorer folk also tended to live in fairly well-defined areas or quarters. Butchers often lived around the flesh-market — smelly but generally less crowded than the poorest areas. Tanners often lived on the edge of town, close to a suitable water supply but also to keep the offensive smell of their work away from others. At Selkirk, for example, they worked around a stream at the Foulbridge Port, an aptly named entrance to the town. At Stirling the tanners were found at the very bottom of the castle hill, around the Dirt Row Port.

In small, less crowded, burghs these divisions were not so sharp

A tirlin' pin or risp, the old equivalent of a door knocker or bell. The ring was rattled up and down the notched door handle. An original 17th or early 18th-century risp can be seen at the Inverkeithing Museum. Modern copies are seen (and used) on houses at Culross, Falkland and elsewhere.

and a mixture of different occupations could be found throughout the town. Bessie Bar's Hall at Culross, end-on to the street and with a projecting outer stair (or forestair) to the first floor, was originally the home of a early 17th-century maltstress — the 'hall' below stairs was her malt house. Similarly, Snuff Cottage, built in 1673, was the modest home of a Culross snuff merchant. A stonework inscription round one window reads 'Wha wad ha' thocht it' — the first line of a snuff-maker's rhyme which went on, 'Noses wad ha' bought it' (originally on another snuffmakers's house in Edinburgh). In fact, given the smell of 17th-century streets and people alike, it is not surprising that snuffmakers were prosperous burgesses — anything which helped to mask unpleasant odours must have been a bestseller.

At Brechin, a series of six early 18th-century houses stand gable-end to the High Street; these once had shops on the ground floor

Culross is a village famed for the forestairs of its 16th—18th century houses. This example dates from the 17th century. *Photo*: Craig Mair.

with burgess houses above, and are a rare reminder of similar buildings which used to be typical and common in every burgh. Merchant goods were usually stored in the attic or in back rooms, which was both convenient and secure. By presenting gable-ends to the street, burgesses saved on paying local rates on long street frontages, and yet could extend back down the tofts if more space was required. Many craftsmen also had workshops in these backyards and urban archaeological digs often turn up evidence of metalworking hearths, tanning pits, leather off-cuts and pottery waste — sometimes even the remains of pottery kilns. Most evidence goes back to well before the 17th century and indicates how artisans long preferred to live sideways to the street, since this allowed workshop expansion into the burgess lands behind the street front.

Almost all the gable-ends at Montrose have now gone, but this early photograph shows the High Street about 1860. The gables first appeared about 1700 when merchants began to extend their houses forward into the market area. *Photo*: Angus District Libraries and Museums Service.

In 17th-century burghs, 'shops' as we think of them generally did not exist. Most selling occurred in the market place, at stalls and trestle tables set up and dismantled each day. An exception was Edinburgh, where the Luckenbooths near St. Giles Cathedral were permanent lock-up stalls in the High Street. Towards the end of the century, however, this absence of shops began to change. Some craftsmen, with stalls outside their own homes, began to extend their houses forward into the street to incorporate the stall into a more permanent 'foreshop'. Sometimes this was tucked away under an outside stair, but some stalls were the full width of the house itself. The next step was to extend the house itself out over the foreshop, creating a new room upstairs.

In most burghs strict regulations controlled the forward extension of houses. At Brechin, for example, it was completely forbidden, which explains why many gable-ended houses developed backwards instead. In 1614 Stirling's council decided that the burgh streets and lanes were becoming so narrow that all unauthorised building would henceforth be punished with a £100 fine, and that anyone complaining of this new regulation would be similarly fined. At

A series of fine gable-ends at Brechin, with narrow closes between. Backyard clearance has resulted in several car parks, so that the original reason for these alleys is now less obvious. *Photo*: Craig Mair.

Elgin in 1693 Thomas Watson was specifically granted leave to erect an outside stair for his house in School Wynd, on payment of two shillings Scots annually to the burgh — presumably a sort of rates increase for having improved his house. In many cases the width of forestairs was specified by the council, and burgh records are peppered with examples of burgesses being ordered to pull down unauthorised extensions, as still happens today. In some places the street width was preserved, but the first floors of many houses projected out instead.

Finally to poorer folks' housing. Although 'unfreemen' made up the greater part of any burgh population, their homes have proportionately survived least of all. This is not really surprising for the unfreemen of any burgh lived in the cheapest accommodation, often poorly built so that it did not last, and with no architectural merit to make it worth saving. There was a wide variety of cheap housing, ranging from the uniquely Scottish tenements of larger towns to the cottages and 'little houses' typical of smaller burghs. In many places folk lived crowded down narrow closes or pends — by 1850 over 250 people lived in Edinburgh's Bakehouse Close, for example, but even in the less-congested days of the 17th century this was the general trend. Elsewhere the grand houses of lairds and burgesses sometimes decayed and were turned into cheaper rooms for unskilled labourers — John Knox's house was already subdivided by the 16th century.

Examples of cheaper housing do still exist, but considering how much there must have been at one time, it is sad to think how little survives today. Edinburgh gives the best impression of high-rise 17th-century living, with people crammed into single rooms in the 'lands' owned by richer landlords. The cheapest tenement accommodation was either at street level, where the smells and sewage were overpowering, or in garrets at the highest levels, which were the most tiring to reach, especially when carrying buckets of water from the street wells. In fact, because of the great High Street fire of 1824 and later Victorian demolition, few present-day Edinburgh closes or tenements actually date from the 17th century, although the sites are very ancient. According to one estimate, two-thirds of Edinburgh's old housing was pulled down between 1860 and 1900, but the *impression* still lingers.

Some original buildings fortunately do still survive in old Edinburgh. Russell House near Holyrood Palace was a 17th-century tenement and is still occupied today. Also, towards the top end of the High Street the beautifully restored buildings of Milne's Court survives from the 1690s. Here and there the occasional narrow entrance leads to a tiny court and turnpike stair reminiscent of older days. But *the* best example by far lies hidden and unseen by people today, for it is Mary King's Close.

This was a bustling 17th-century alley which ran from an entrance gate on the High Street opposite St. Giles Cathedral to a point by the Nor' Loch where the Princes Street Gardens now lie. Four more closes ran parallel to this one and, with a warren of interconnecting houses and passages, formed a private world almost entirely hidden from the High Street. In 1645 the population was decimated by plague and the close was sealed up as a public health precaution. From then on it decayed into the haunt of vagrants until the buildings were converted to warehouses during the 18th century and then finally wrecked by fire in 1750. In 1753 the city fathers decided to erect the Royal Exchange on the same site, but instead of first demolishing the entire area, they simply dismantled the tenements to the level of the High Street and built their new

G

One of the commonest features of burgh housing was the turnpike or spiral stair tower. This example is in Stirling, but much the same scene survives in many older towns from Thurso to Jedburgh. *Photo*: Craig Mair.

building on the solid thick walls of the old houses. The original closes, however, ran downhill so that although the entrances and gates were lost, the buildings themselves survived like cellars under the Royal Exchange, forming a sloping street roofed over by the newer buildings above.

From then on little changed. The Royal Exchange became the City Chambers in 1811 and the houses of Mary King's Close became the convenient depositories of dusty old boxes and files. The construction of Cockburn Street carved through the lower end of the close in the 1850s but the upper part survived undamaged. During two world wars secretaries in the City Chambers took shelter there from air raids but no bombs fell to destroy the old street. And so it still remains today, virtually intact and unchanged since that plague in 1645.

Sometimes small groups are taken on a conducted tour, like an exploration of the *Marie Celeste*, for that is the strong feeling in such an empty street. Entry is through the now-District offices, down some obscure stairs as if to a basement. Then a door opens and there lies the narrow close, only seven feet wide and stretching downhill with buildings rising on each side. They stand only one storey high at the top end, but down beside Cockburn Street they rise to six floors and originally towered to eleven storeys in what must have been a dark and airless vennel teeming with humanity. Near the top end stands a wine shop, and a baker's shop complete with ovens. Across the street is a barrel-roofed butcher's shop, with meat hooks still fastened to the ceiling. And then begins the warren of housing, with the steps and doors and windows still untouched, and inside fireplaces and decorations changed only by the needs of storage space over the decades. But for the absence of people, Mary King's Close is like a time capsule preserved as if for ever. However, there are no signposts to this close, and there is no mention of it in guidebooks or histories of Edinburgh, for the District Council can hardly be happy at the idea of tourist trips trailing through their offices looking for that stairway to the basement. And so for the present Mary King's Close will remain inaccessible, but at least undamaged also by vandals and graffiti-writers.

Happily there are other closes which can be enjoyed. Mitchell's Close at Haddington has been well restored, and a number of craft enterprises also revive the feeling of 17th-century life. On the other hand, there are numerous alleys and closes in Dunbar or Stirling or Pittenweem which, by their very decayed appearance, perhaps offer a more realistic atmosphere. Likewise, the arched pends of Kirkcudbright, Elgin or St. Andrews offer glimpses into quieter burgh backwaters, and the opportunity for visitors with a little imagination to visualise them as they once were, away from the bustle of modern life.

In smaller burghs the forestair to a 'little house' was a more typical sign of poor housing. In many cases farm animals lived downstairs and were taken out to graze on the burgh pastures each day, a visible sign that most people in burghs were partly dependent on food or income from farming. The house above may well have been occupied by more than one family, often living in just one room, and probably enduring the miseries of a turf roof leaking brackish water every time it rained. On the other hand, most burgh houses had a proper chimney — a feature of everyday life which did not reach country people until very much later — so that warmth and the facility to cook were both available.

Four 17th-century burgh closes: top left at Dunbar, where the neglected appearance is probably more realistic than the prettier but sanitised restoration at Elgin, top right. In the Dunbar photo, there are seven doors, once those of houses, between the camera and the street. Lower left is at Pittenweem and is comparable with Mitchell's Close, a restored example at Haddington. *Photos*: Craig Mair.

Colourful, vernacular examples survive all over Scotland, but particularly in Fife where their crowstepped gables and pantiled roofs are very photogenic. Virtually every Fife seaport has a number of little houses, but the best are probably those at Culross and Crail. The old part of Culross is almost completely a 17th-century burgh, still intact with all the original features except for the shoreline which is now cut by a railway. Many little houses still stand, basically unchanged and still occupied, complete with forestairs and original marriage lintels. The oldest is dated 1577, but more typical is the butcher's house near the mercat cross — this has a stone-carved meat cleaver on the wall and a date of 1664.

At Crail the oldest houses are those in the Shoregate where No 13 is dated 1632, but there are more houses from the same period in the street known as Rumford. In fact, such is the impression of cottages and forestairs in Crail that it is a delight to stroll round any part of the burgh. Then, having learned from examples on the Fife coast, it becomes easier to find similar houses elsewhere, as at Falkland, Dunkeld, Haddington or Dunblane, where little houses (though sometimes altered) also survive. Indeed, such is the quaint and 'arty' impression of the Haining around Dunblane cathedral that the area has been called 'the Greenwich village of Perthshire'.

Most burgh buildings were first made of timber, but by the 17th century so many trees had been felled that this was no longer possible. Stonemasons began to appear in burgh records during the 17th century, indicating a change of emphasis. This was just as well, because fires took a regular toll of burghs (as already mentioned in Chapter 1). Crowded vennels and closes, and buildings roofed with thatch or heather, must have made many burghs highly combustible. As a result, council regulations began to appear, aimed at reducing the fire risk by avoiding too much congested housing and having ladders available for emergency rescues. In 1669, for example, Stirling's burgh council provided the town with 'twa dozen of leather buckets' and 'six double and six single ledders for the townes use, and not to lend them to any persone without fourtie shilling for ilk lend'. In 1674 the council also provided a number of hooks and ropes for dealing with fires. Dangerous occupations such as those involving kilns were also sited well away from buildings. Similarly, as at Banff in 1695, it was sometimes enacted 'that no person have within a house where fire is, heather, broom or lint drying'.

Housing at Culross from the 1590s — a patchwork of little windows, crowstepped gables and pantiled roofs typical of many smaller burghs three hundred years ago. *Photo*: Craig Mair.

Looking at any High Street today, it is difficult to imagine the much greater variety which that same scene must once have presented. In the 17th century only parts of the street or 'causey' would have been paved (usually with cobbles) — the rest would have been a rutted, earthen track. There were sometimes gutters; in some places, such as Peebles or Stirling, these were specifically built in an attempt to channel away the most noxious fluids, while elsewhere the road was simply cambered to allow liquids to run to the side, leaving the cobbled 'crown of the causeway' as a place for rich people to walk with less risk of spoiling their best shoes. Although there were no pavements, some towns such as Glasgow and Paisley enjoyed a limited cobbled area known as the plainstanes, where merchants often held open-air meetings and even council business was sometimes transacted. Wheeled transport hardly existed in Scotland, certainly not beyond the largest burghs. Captain Slezer, whose detailed prints of Scotland are an invaluable source of detail on burghs in the 1690s, included only two wheeled vehicles among the dozens of scenes which he recorded. The sedan chairs

An excellent example of a wall inscription from Falkland — this one clearly intended to flatter the king whose palace stood across the street. More modest inscriptions can be found on houses all over Scotland and pay their due to their former occupants.

associated with 18th-century Edinburgh confirm that wheels were still a handicap even a century later.

Similarly, the shops in any High Street today would then have been little more than booths, and most business would still have gone on around the mercat cross and tron. Houses would have pushed out into the street in a straggling, random manner — no street had anything like the clean lines of modern house or shop frontages. At Lanark, for example, the conversion of the High Street to its present appearance was very gradual; in 1787 one house was extended forward to align it with some neighbours, followed in 1825 by four more which were demolished and rebuilt in line, and then by a bank which encouraged three more property-owners to follow suit until, eventually, all the properties were standing in the neat line they show today.

Houses would also have looked more tumbledown than they do today, often with the remnants of plastered or limewashed walls, smeared and stained with dripping rainwater, patched and repaired, with crumbling chimneys and ragged thatched roofs. Some had additional storeys jerry-built above the ground floor, often sagging or lop-sided looking — indeed the general impression in most burghs seems to have been one of general decay and dilapidation, alleviated by the occasional fine houses of richer people. By the 1690s, for example, Tain's trade and prosperity had declined to the point where the burgh council could only report that 'a great part of the buildings of this poor place is waist and turned ruinous . . . the kirk steiple, councill and prison house of this burgh are so ruinous and demolished that they . . . cannot be made up in the same integrity as it was formerly without payment . . . which is a thing impossible . . . to do without the christian and charitable supply of weel affected neighbours'.

The sad state of Tain's buildings might just as easily have applied to any other burgh. A description of Glasgow in the 1730s, for example, praised the substantial houses of well-to-do citizens, with their quaint Flemish-styled architecture, crowstepped gables, flower gardens and beautiful orchards (which 'sent forth a pleasant, odoriferous smell'), but it also mentioned the 'mean, dirty, broken down hovels' in other streets, with their stinking middens and gutters 'against which the magistrates vainly objected'.

CHAPTER 13

Public Health

Surviving examples of 17th-century housing may look picturesque in today's tidier, more hygienic world, but three hundred years ago houses crawled with vermin and were little better than squalid hovels. Not surprisingly, in an unwashed world of outside privies, dungheaps in the street, and barely a water basin in any house, life expectancy was low — between thirty and forty years on average. Personal and public health was, quite simply, dreadful.

Evidence from skeletons unearthed during urban archaeological digs has shown that people were shorter than today; the average height of a man was around 5'6" (168 cm) compared to 5'8" (172 cm) today, while that of a female was 5'2" (160 cm) compared to about 5'5" (167 cm) nowadays. This is probably because children, in particular, suffered from more illnesses in the past, which stunted their growth. Food was also less plentiful and less hygienic — meat was butchered in public with no knowledge of germs, flour was often mixed with dust or dirt, oats and barley were full of grit from millstones, ale was impure, no-one washed their hands when handling food, and so on.

Dental evidence has shown that the absence of sugar and the sparing use of honey as a sweetener caused far fewer cavities, but the tops of teeth were regularly worn away by gritty food, while fruit seeds and the habit of holding everything from bowstrings to sewing needles between the teeth caused regular abcesses, which must have been a misery for high and low-born alike.

The most serious health hazard, however, was simply the widespread filth in every street. Many burghs, such as Edinburgh, Dunfermline, Aberdeen, Stirling, Glasgow, Brechin or Culross, were built on sloping sites which permitted some natural drainage of effluent. But this did not solve the problem of filth, for the poor people who usually lived at the bottom of any slope suffered a higher rate of illness. It is no coincidence that many a Rottenrow or Stinking Wynd stands at the foot of an incline, where the disadvantaged people lived.

It is obvious today that public dunghills were a lethal cause of disease, but this was not realised in the 17th century. Dunghills were seen as a valuable source of manure, and were actually sold or auctioned off for barrowing away to the fields. Complaints about dunghills tended to arise only because they blocked the street or because the stench became so offensive in warm weather that folk could stand it no longer (many dungheaps were covered with sand to deaden the smell). In 1659, for example, members of the Forres burgh council made a formal visit to David Brodie's house, because his midden blocked the King's High Gate — not because it was a health hazard.

As mentioned in Chapter 5, primitive attempts were made to organise street cleaning in some burghs, either by threatening to fine those who did not remove their middens when they grew too large, or by employing someone to cart them away. Many burghs actually confiscated offending dungheaps and then sold them to other folk for manure — an excellent example of the saying, 'where there's muck there's money'! However, the reasons for cleaning the streets did not usually include a concern for public health.

Although sickness was routine in every town, few doctors existed beyond the larger burghs. Some medical men did practise in 17th-century Edinburgh, where the Royal College of Physicians was established in 1681 and where there was even an Incorporated Guild of Surgeons (from which some members became burgesses). There was, therefore, some limited opportunity to study and practise as a physician, but generally in Edinburgh.

Apothecaries, on the other hand, were usually taught for five years as apprentices for a fee of around £50 — a less academic training, although some were undoubtedly learned and capable people. In Edinburgh, at least, there was a Fraternity of Apothecaries, and no-one could practise without being first admitted. Many styled themselves surgeon-apothecaries and acted as physicians, even surgeons, for the less affluent members of burgh society. This sometimes brought them into conflict with real physicians who felt that the variable standards of apothecaries gave the entire medical profession a bad name. At Stirling in 1609 the council suspended and discharged Alexander Sklaitter (Slater) from 'exercising the office and cure of a chirurgeon from hence forth until they be further testified of his knowledge and sufficiency, under the pain of banishment'. It is not clear, however, if this man was a proper physician or an apothecary.

Apothecaries were the equivalent of modern pharmacists or

A 16th-century surgeon at work. Since amputations and operations were performed without anaesthetic, patients usually went to the man who could cut or saw the fastest. A good surgeon could amputate a leg in less than one minute. Most patients nevertheless died of shock, loss of blood or infection.

chemists. As well as being unofficial doctors, they grew or imported the plants required for making their own drugs. Many plants known to the Romans were still commonly used by apothecaries in the 17th and 18th centuries. Some went to Hadrian's Wall on collecting trips, searching for herbs once cultivated especially for medical purposes and still growing wild after centuries. These were then prepared, either to the order of a physician's prescription, or for sale to the public. Some drugs seem to have been sub-standard, however, and physicians were supposed to inspect apothecaries' premises to destroy unsatisfactory medicines.

Lower still down the medical hierarchy came the barber-surgeons.

Inclusion of the word 'surgeon' gave the occupation a professional-sounding ring but, in fact, these people were little more than common barbers who did a bit of tooth-pulling and blood-letting on the side. The barber's red and white striped pole still signifies the bandages used in blood-letting from the arm. Since barber shops were generally unsavoury places of rough men, vulgar gossip and common music, barber-surgeons never quite achieved a position of social respectability. Nevertheless, they were the cheapest, sometimes the only, form of medical help available in most burghs and were fairly popular.

It is clear that most ordinary people simply tholed whatever ailments they had, or else fell back on handed-down knowledge of herbal cures. Every child knows even today that the antidote to a nettle sting is to rub the affected area with a dock leaf, but this sort of folk remedy was, for most people, the only thing they could turn to. The local spey wife or old crone with a long memory for ancient medicines was a valuable burgh citizen, though many were horribly persecuted as witches during the 16th and 17th centuries.

Folk remedies were used, not just because some actually worked, but because they were cheaper than doctors' fees. At Stirling in 1615 bailie John Cunningham was wounded and needed medical attention. The surgeon's fee was two hundred merks but since the wound was received during the execution of the bailie's duty, it was accepted that the burgh should meet the bill. The money was raised by diverting fees of £36 due to the provost, bailies, dean of guild, treasurer and clerk; by adding on £40 from fines charged in court; by asking the Kirk to pay £40 from its poor box; by taking £40 from the town's common good fund; by asking the guildry to 'give according to their good pleasure'; by asking for voluntary contributions from neighbours; and then by permitting the burgh treasurer to borrow the rest and agreeing to meet all interest charges and other expenses thus incurred — all to pay one surgeon's bill! Little wonder that most ordinary folk went to the barber-surgeon or did without.

What were the common illnesses of the 17th century? Many sprang naturally from unhygienic conditions, including food preparation and water supply. Typhus was a constant scourge which took a particularly heavy toll during times of famine when people were already weakened by hunger. One historian has described it as possibly the greatest killer of the 1640s, when hunger was widespread, and it did appear in another strong outbreak during the 1690s when famine again struck during the so-called 'Seven Ill Years'.

Malaria was another problem. 17th-century Scotland was a land of extensive marsh and boglands which offered fertile breeding grounds for malarial mosquitoes. Although not usually a fatal illness in itself, it weakened people, especially children, and made them prone to other killers instead.

As mentioned in Chapter 9, leprosy still existed in Scotland. This was the social outcast disease of its time and victims languished in leper colonies maintained by various religious orders beyond the walls of most burghs. Undoubtedly many people with other skin disorders were often assumed to be lepers and were also banished from towns. In some places such as Perth, lepers were allowed to come into markets during certain hours, but at Prestwick, for example, citizens were prohibited from any contact on pain of banishment. Many burghs kept lists of the names of lepers and their families, and checked them against those of strangers found in their street. Fortunately, leprosy seems to have died out in Scotland around 1600.

Smallpox, however, first appeared in Scotland around 1600 and then grew steadily into a very serious threat, with nationwide epidemics in 1639, and serious local outbreaks at Aberdeen in 1641 and Glasgow in 1672 (when at least 800 people died). In the 1750s a contemporary account reckoned that in good times smallpox accounted for about one in seven deaths, which rose to one in six during normal years and one in three or four during epidemics. A more recent study of Kilmarnock between 1728 and 1764 also showed that one in six people died of smallpox.

Other common illnesses included cholera and syphilis, both thought to have originated from the East, while the degenerated bones in some skeletons show that tuberculosis and other chronic diseases also existed (acute infections killed people too quickly to leave any tell-tale signs in their bones). Bone fractures were also common, especially broken wrists and ankles. Some may have been the result of battles or street fights, for broken ribs and bashed-in skulls were also prevalent. A surprising number of fractures did heal, but many others may have caused death; broken ribs could puncture the lungs, for example, while scalp wounds could easily become infected and cause meningitis.

The most terrifying 17th-century word, however, was plague. It may be that many contemporary references to plague or pestilence are inaccurate descriptions of other epidemic diseases, but the fact is that the very mention of the word was enough to cause panic. By the 17th century, the dreadful 14th and 15th-century outbreaks of bubonic plague or Black Death were generally over. There were further outbreaks in the Fife and Lothian areas during the 16th century, but these seem to have been confined to towns and did not spread throughout Scotland. Even these more limited epidemics were devastating; contemporary accounts claim that during the period 1584—1588 alone, plague killed 1400 people in Edinburgh, another 1400 in Perth, over 400 in St. Andrews, 300 in Kirkcaldy and hundreds more in other burghs — a swathe of death through towns whose small populations were decimated. Nevertheless, taking Scotland as a whole, the 16th century was a period of fewer plagues.

The respite ended in the 1590s when waves of pestilence swept over the whole country. By 1606 it had affected burghs as far apart as Dumfries, Glasgow, Edinburgh, Ayr, Perth, Stirling and Dundee, raging for an entire decade and sometimes also revisiting towns which had already been devastated and were only just beginning to recover. Further outbreaks occurred in 1624, and then again in 1644 when the manoeuvrings of the Covenanter and Royalist armies seem to have spread it to many parts of the country in an outbreak which lasted four years. It reached Aberdeen and killed a fifth of the people, and then Leith where half the burgh's population of 5000 perished — one account claims that the figure was nearer two-thirds of the people. A stone slab at Brechin cathedral records the death of six hundred plague victims in 1647 — half the town's inhabitants.

Word that plague was in the neighbourhood was the worst possible news for any burgh council. The first action was to prohibit contact with areas where the pest was said to be. Thus, in 1645 when Anstruther's burgh council was 'credibly informed that the neighbour burgh of Crail is infected with the pestilence, they ordain that all back gates and vennels of this burgh be closed, and the ports to be kept [guarded] both night and day, and none of the inhabitants of the burgh of Crail to be received within this burgh'. When plague threatened Falkirk that same year, similar precautions were taken. No-one was allowed to travel to Glasgow, and 'no shearers are to be hyred without ane pass'.

Glasgow responded likewise in 1588: 'This day the council and bailies having consideration of the present peril of pest now being in the town of Paisley, has statute and ordained that the bridge port be looked after by two honest men of the Bridgegait and the Town Officers are to warn them nightly'. The Stinking Vennel and Grey Friars ports were also locked, and the School Wynd was to be shut and patrolled daily by the schoolmaster. Anyone neglecting his guard duty, or failing to keep his fences mended (to keep out strangers), was to be heavily fined.

In 1665 during the famous plague of London (which then began to spread elsewhere in England), Peebles burgh council passed a regulation which prohibited trade with any English merchant for three months. It was also made illegal for any citizens to leave the shire without a local magistrate's testimonial, or to return to the shire without a paper from a similar authority stating that the area from which they came was free from plague. Finally it was made illegal, on pain of death and loss of all property, to offer lodgings to any stranger who did not possess a clean bill of health from the burgh where he had last been. Inhabitants were also placed on guard at the gates and ordered to patrol the streets as directed by the magistrates.

In every burgh, those who knew of someone with the plague were required to report this immediately — failure to do so generally meant execution, for with the very survival of the town at risk there was no room for sympathy. To make the same point at Aberdeen when plague threatened in 1585, a gibbet was erected at the mercat cross, another at the Brig of Dee, and another at the harbour mouth. In some burghs such as Edinburgh, victims who did not die were often branded on the cheek, having first been 'cleansed' on the burgh muir with some kind of disinfectant. Wealthy people meanwhile left town if they could, while those suspected of having had contact with victims were made to live in shanty huts beyond the town walls.

Stirling offers a particular study of the response to plague in 1645, for the burgh records contain a fair wealth of detail. Among the precautions taken, the burgh ports were, of course, locked and the bridge was closed but people were also told to stay in their own part of town and not to wander about. A town guard was appointed to watch between 5am and 9pm for strangers. The town's records and documents were also taken from the tolbooth and placed in coffers, which were presumably thought safer.

A group of buildings well outside the burgh and near the bridge was appropriated for housing plague victims — the owners were promised compensation, but it is unlikely that they would ever have wanted to return. A special burial ground was prepared, where all victims were ordered to be interred. (This strict rule was relaxed once when James Davis was allowed to bury his daughter in his own yard.) Several local people, women as well as men, were asked to help dig graves and carry corpses but this cannot have been enough, for later the council also asked Linlithgow for volunteer help.

Later, the guildry was asked to help the town raise charity money for survivors, and burgesses were taxed to cover the cost of cleansing the town and disinfecting houses. Guildry records are missing for this period, suggesting that its activities were suspended during the plague emergency. The plague period from 1644 to 1648, coming at the same time as the Covenanting wars, must have been really devastating for many burghs.

Finally there was the question of burial grounds. Edinburgh's victims were buried on the Burgh Muir near Bruntsfield; in just one year, over 2500 people died of plague and were mostly buried there. The precautions taken by Anstruther's burgh council did not avert the deaths of over seventy people. They were carted out to the Billowness and buried in mass graves with not even a coffin or shroud. At Falkirk the victims were buried on Graham's Muir, near the present-day Brockville football ground. The graves were marked by flat stones and the site was walled off in 1647. For many years locals avoided the place and it is said that if cattle ever wandered onto the Pest Graves their milk was thrown out for the next fortnight. This habit went on right into the 19th century, when the site was finally built over. As elsewhere, the legacy of the plague was a deep and terrible memory.

CHAPTER 14

Games and Recreation

It would be easy to imagine that the combination of war, famine and plague left little room for pleasures in life, but of course this was not so. There were many years, even some decades, when things were peaceful and trade was good. Then, when life was normal, fairs flourished, people danced at weddings, sports events were held and children played in the streets, for 17th-century Scotland was certainly not a dull place.

So deep-rooted was the desire for enjoyment that even the stricter discipline of the Reformation could not snuff it out. People were punished in droves for promiscuous dancing, the wearing of gaudy clothes, gluttony and over-indulgence, the excessive enjoyment of music, getting tipsy, excessive frivolity, playing games on Sundays, pre-marital sex, gambling and so on — punished in droves because they would not give up the ingrained habits and pleasures of generations. It was as if the need for enjoyment was an instinct. Whatever the Kirk said, people simply would not stop having fun.

Burgh records are dotted with references to sports and games especially. They were played by children in the streets, banned by councils from the kirkyards, encouraged by councils with prizes at fairs, and apparently enjoyed by all. Reference has already been made in Chapter 3 to archery, which was additionally a useful skill to acquire in an age of warfare and burgh defence, and one which could be adapted to shooting the odd duck or rabbit for the pot. In similar vein, the sport of hunting, popular with landed gentry and royalty, was not just the enjoyment of hawking or the chase, but also provided food for a variety of larger houses.

Games commonly found in burghs included chess, billiards, quoits, a kind of fives or 'hand squash', and an early form of croquet, played with mallets but only two hoops. Another favourite game was kiles, which involved lining nine skittles in a row, rather than in three rows as they are placed today, and knocking them over with a ball or stick. 'Playing at the kyles' became a pastime which the Kirk particularly frowned on, though it is hard to understand why. Bowls was also widely played; although bowling greens already existed before 1707, and a few still survive including those at Stirling and Dirleton, many participants simply played in the streets, as French boule players still do. In 1654, for example, Elgin's burgh council proclaimed by tuck of drum through the streets an Act on 'the playing of boulls or bullets that none cast either of them at the east port west of the sub-chantor's wynd and at the west port east of Thomas Anderson's house'. Bullets may well have been a form of marbles, for Scottish children still call them bools.

Tennis was also well known, but only to the rich. The game was very different from that played today and included the use of the walls and projecting roofs of the court, and a much slacker net which was actually only a cord with tassels hanging from it. One example of an original tennis court still survives at Falkland Palace — both James V and his daughter Mary Queen of Scots played there but it is now open for anyone to walk around and imagine the players in action. Fortunately a few enthusiasts still follow the ancient rules and so are preserving the game for the future.

The most popular sports in burghs, however, were those which still survive today. Golf was played by everyone from the king himself (accounts survive of James IV ordering clubs and balls in 1503) to the ordinary towndweller in a host of Scottish burghs (provost Duncan Paterson of Stirling was assaulted with a golf club in 1613 by Adam Donaldson, for example). Although regarded as a traditional Scottish game centred on Musselburgh and St. Andrews, golf seems to have come from Holland from where it was imported with the trade in luxuries for wealthy folk. Some Dutch even seem to have played it on ice, though what happened when they holed the ball is not clear. 17th-century golf balls were made of leather and stuffed with feathers; the Elgin court book records for 1649 mention a case in which a skinner called Alexander Geddes sued George Watson, a golfball maker who had not paid for leather hides or for work done on golf clubs (perhaps leather for the handles).

Golf seems to have been so popular that it was always under criticism. Throughout the 16th century laws were passed at regular intervals demanding that people practise more archery and desist from golf, but to no avail — the Scots never did become decent bowmen. Then during the 17th century the Kirk did its best to suppress the sport, which it seems to have viewed as a frivolous pastime. Sunday golf was a particularly heinous crime, as at Stirling

'Real' tennis — the court included the walls and roof, and the net was a rope with tassels, which a volunteer had to hold. The game is still played at Falkland and Troon. *Photo*: BBC Hulton Picture Library.

in 1621 where David Hairt was fined by the local kirk session for playing golf in the park on a Sabbath afternoon.

Matching golf for popularity was football, which was also enjoyed by everyone from royalty (James IV paid two shillings for footballs in 1491) to low-born (Forres burgh council ordered in 1586 that 'no person must play in the kirkyard at futt baw . . . under penalty of 10 shillings'). Rules were still very vague — in country areas the 'pitch' could be any size and the 'goals' could be miles apart, but the playing area seems to have been smaller in towns. In the early 1590s a dozen men of Perth admitted to their kirk session that 'on the Sunday of the Fast in time of preaching they had succumbed to play football in the Meadow Inch of the Muirton north of the city', while in 1682 the Banff burgh council passed an Act which threatened a fine of 40 shillings on 'players of football in the streets'.

There was also football violence. Traditional rivalries between clans or even burghs lay behind some of this trouble, but there were others who used the cover of a match, and the crowds attracted

Seventeenth-century golfers. The ball was made of leather and stuffed with feathers, while the clubs were made of wood. Drivers, wedges and putters had already appeared. The game quickly spread from Scotland to England after the Union of Crowns in 1603. *Photo*: Mary Evans Picture Library.

to a game, to commit robbery and even murder. One case was the death of Sir John Carmichael of that Ilk, Warden of the Middle Marches in the borders, who was murdered by a group of Armstrongs on his way home from a match in 1600. The game itself also seems to have been pretty rough; a poem by Sir Richard Maitland, written around 1550, mentions 'broken banes, strife, discord and waistit wanis [wounds]', although these were clearly not enough to dissuade young men from playing.

The game of Hand Ba' played for centuries at Kirkwall, but especially in border towns such as Jedburgh, Hawick, Duns and

Melrose may have originated from the same roots as football. All that was needed was a ball and two teams — the 'uppies and doonies', married men and bachelors, those from either side of a river, or anything else which identified two sides of roughly equivalent size — so that a match could be held through the streets. The game itself was more like rugby with no rules, and to outsiders must often have resembled an enormous heaving scrum from which someone occasionally broke free with the ball (often an inflated cow's bladder), to be hotly pursued by the others until caught and a new scrum formed.

As with golf, Scotland's other traditional game, curling, seems to have come from the Low Countries, perhaps brought by 15th and 16th-century traders or craftsmen. The very word *bonspiel* (a curling contest) has a Flemish ring to it, sounding rather like a mixture of French and Dutch or German. The oldest curling club seems to have been formed at Kilsyth around 1510, and stones from 1511 survive at Stirling, but the earliest written account of the 'roaring game' seems to have been that of Henry Adamson, a Perth poet who mentioned it in 1638. Skating on ice was also known, but in the 17th century a sharpened branch was used like a punting pole to push the skater along; it was held between the legs like a witch sitting on a broomstick.

Gambling was also popular. Cockfighting, dice and card-playing were all common, and were all vigorously attacked by the Kirk and burgh councils alike, generally to no avail. People seem to have had an irrepressible compulsion to gamble since time immemorial; during excavations at the Roman town of Vindolanda near Hadrian's Wall a loaded dice was found which, when tested, threw a six more often than any other number — about six times out of ten.

On fair days, already described in Chapter 7, amusements of all kinds were part of the attraction. Pipers, jugglers, dancing bears, acrobats, fiddlers, fire-eaters and other entertainers helped to bring in the crowds and make the day a great success. People could try to enter various sporting contests. The Festival of Popinjay, for example, included competitions for shooting, and was still held into the late 19th century at Maybole and Kilwinning. Peebles burgh council offered a silver arrow for archery, while at Stirling the prize varied between a silver arrow or a silver goblet (both, however, worth £24 Scots).

The greatest attraction at fairs were undoubtedly the races. Most burgh councils seem to have decided that the cost of donating prizes was justified by the publicity it gave the town and the crowds who came to spectate at such events (Peebles burgh council paid 14 shillings to two boys for going to Selkirk in 1660 to proclaim the fair and races). Banff offered a silver cup for its horse race, which was won by Lord Huntly in 1684 — an event noted in the burgh records because he generously returned it to the town and so saved them the cost of another the following year. At Lanark the most notable prize was the famous silver bell, which seems to have dated from around 1600 and was competed for until recent times when the local race course closed.

Races seem to have been graded for different categories of citizens. At Lanark, the silver bell was for 'the horses of a person of qualitie and of a neighbouring gentleman'. At Stirling they held goose races to be ridden for by the maltmen (a goose was the prize, but where maltmen got horses from is not clear, for many would not have owned one themselves). In some burghs there were also foot races for ordinary people. At Stirling the prize for the 1706 foot race was a pair of new stockings, a pair of new shoes and a blue bonnet — which immediately prohibited burgesses from taking part, since they were expected to wear proper hats and not common blue bonnets. At Peebles there was a race for boys round the limits of the marches for which the prize was some sheets of paper — undoubtedly a valuable possession for any child at that time, and a race which had the additional purpose of helping children to learn the burgh's grazing boundaries.

One Stirling horse race was held from the burgh gate to William Shirra's house at Cambusbarron and back — a distance of two or three miles. This nevertheless required the streets to be emptied and obstacles to be cleared away so that the horses could turn at a special post specially erected for the occasion — a vision of tight turns, hay bales and horses clattering through the streets reminiscent of something from the Monaco grand prix motor race. It must have been a colourful and exciting occasion.

Some public amusements had nothing to do with fairs or even sports. In pre-Reformation times especially festivals and religious plays (described in Chapter 9) were very popular. Mystery and Mummer plays and pageants, presided over by the Abbot of Unreason or Lord of Misrule (some local worthy disguised and dressed up for the occasion), were usually performed in the streets by strolling players. Some plays actually poked fun at the Roman Catholic church itself, with a host of stock characters as well-known and regularly-repeated as those in any Punch and Judy show. The Church seems to have tolerated this teasing, even when donkeys were dressed as clergymen and indecent parodies of hymns were sung, but this quickly disappeared with the Reformation.

Although the Reformation began during the 1550s, and criticism of plays began soon after, the Kirk did not quickly break the public's enjoyment of theatre. In some burghs there were even riots against the suppression of plays, most notably at Edinburgh in 1561 when the provost and council, who had banned a production of Robin Hood, had to take refuge in the tolbooth from an angry mob. The crowd then smashed in the tolbooth doors and threw stones through its windows, while both the Constable of the Castle and the Deacons of the Incorporation refused to intervene, presumably not wishing the townspeople to turn on them for being killjoys as well. The matter was eventually resolved by a public retraction by the council at the mercat cross; the people had made their point.

Nevertheless, the suppression of public entertainments did gain ground. Secular plays, most notably the *Satire of the Three Estates* but even comedies and tragedies, were criticised by the Kirk and went out of circulation for years. The performing of virtually any play on a Sunday, especially those based 'upon authentic parts of the Scripture', was totally banned by the General Assembly in 1575, while at Aberdeen the local presbytery commanded in 1599 that 'there be nae play-Sundays hereafter under all highest pain'. Even the portrayal of biblical figures by mere mortals was considered a profanity or, as was said a few decades later in Edinburgh, in some plays 'they have the boldness to act some of the most awful and terrible works of God, such as thunder and lightning etc, which is too daring for creatures to imitate'. The very actors themselves were denounced in a special proclamation from every pulpit in 1599 as 'unruly and immodest', while those who attended the theatre were 'irreligious and indiscreet' — a description which did not please King James VI, under whose patronage William Shakespeare later worked.

The pleasures of the theatre were not the only victims of suppression. The Kirk also tried to stamp out the observance of Christmas, widely regarded as a popish or episcopal practice. In

1575 the St. Andrews kirk session carpeted James Clunie, a cutler, and Walter Younger for 'violating the Sabbath Day by superstitious keeping of the Yule Day holy-day and abstaining from their work and labour that day'. Similarly during the 1690s the Kincardine kirk session accused Edward Bruce of attending a Christmas dinner at the Laird of Clackmannan's house.

Even gypsy dancers were branded as wanton harlots and hounded out of town. In 1555 an Act of Parliament forbade the choosing of May Queens and warned that 'if any women or others by singing about the summer trees and making perturbation through the burghs and other landward towns, the women pestering others for money shall be taken, handled and put upon the Cuckstools of every Burgh or Town'. A local statute at Banff also criticised Hallow'een guizers 'mascarading' through the burgh, and another in 1709 said that guizers were simply idlers and therefore could be press-ganged (into the army or navy).

But of course pleasures and entertainments carried on. Morris dancers wearing 'fantastic dress' leapt and danced in the streets. Tightrope walkers and jugglers sometimes performed in burgh streets. In 1561 an Englishman brought a chestnut coloured horse called Marocco to Edinburgh where he 'made the horse do many rare and uncouth tricks, such as never horse was observed to do the like before in this land'. In 1680 someone brought an elephant to Glasgow and caused a public sensation. At Aberdeen in 1628, Janet Smith dressed herself up as a man, and with John Horne dressed as a woman, 'sported and danced through the town' — fitting proof that the urge to have fun and pleasure could never be wholly suppressed.

CHAPTER 15

Recognising Newer Towns

As must be obvious from the preceding chapters of this book, Scotland has many old burghs with plenty of interest to offer. Some, such as Lanark or Dumbarton, may not immediately look ancient or be bursting with historic buildings but the clues *are* there. As already explained, the street layout, at least in the town centre, may be original. Closes, pends, wynds or house plots and backyards may all indicate some aspect of the burgh's history. The kirk may be important, even if the surviving tombstones are all Victorian. Street names, even modern names such as 'The Mercat Cross Chip Shop', may reveal *something* — the mercat cross may no longer exist, but its memory lives on.

There may also be useful plaques, perhaps erected by the local authority or even some antiquarian body, offering snippets of history to anyone with a keen enough eye to spot them (it is surprising how many plaques or street cobble markings are difficult to spot, as if designed not to be conspicuous — why?). Some plaques can be especially baffling; one at Stirling points out brass studs in the street which show the location of the old Barras Yett, the main burgh gateway — except that the brass plates have been covered with tar for years!

Some burghs are so full of history and character that little effort is needed to appreciate the past. Among the smaller burghs, Crail and Culross are surely outstanding, though rather picture-postcardy. A stroll through old Culross *reeks* of history; only a philistine could not visualise the cobbled streets full of bustle and life, or the pretty, gleaming white houses draped with washing and swarming with ragged children. A visit out of season, preferably on a Sunday morning when traffic is light and streets are empty, is well worth the effort.

Of the medium-sized burghs, Linlithgow, Elgin, Haddington, Dumfries, St. Andrews and perhaps Kirkwall are among the most rewarding. The west port at St. Andrews is the only surviving burgh gate in Scotland, while the long, straggling High Street at Linlithgow preserves the flavour of the old medieval Hiegait in many towns. The well-preserved closes in Haddington similarly

convey an impression of vibrant life thriving just off the main
streets, almost lost in a different world, while the collection of 17th-
century High Street buildings at Elgin must surely be the best in
any comparable town. But the very best medium-sized burgh is
probably Stirling; it has no gates or any obvious old High Street,
but its unique walls and bastions, the feel of Broad Street with its

THE HAWICK MERCAT CROSS
WAS SITUATED IN THE
ROADWAY 9 FEET FROM
THIS SPOT ⊗ THE CROSS AND
THE ADJOINING FLESH MERCAT
WERE TAKEN DOWN IN 1762

THIS PLAQUE WAS ERECTED BY THE HAWICK
CALLANTS CLUB BY PERMISSION OF THE TOWN
COUNCIL MAY 1950

THESE PREMISES
RESTORED 1983
ARE HELD TO HAVE BEEN
THE PISTOL FACTORY
OF THE RENOWNED
THOMAS CADDELL
WHO FOUNDED THE
CRAFT IN DOUNE
IN 1645

CUSTOM STONE OF HADDINGTON
THIS ANCIENT STONE WAS FOR
CENTURIES THE SEAT OF THE TACKSMAN
WHEN PETTY CUSTOMS WERE LEVIED
IN THE BURGH

A selection of wall plaques — they can be found in burghs all over Scotland and are often very interesting and useful. Unfortunately they are not always easy to spot — perhaps the fun is in looking for them.

tolbooth and mercat cross, the burgess tenements and grand nobles' houses at the top of the town, the great castle and ancient Kirk of the Holy Rude, all combine to keep a sense of the past very much alive today. Even medieval markets are held in summer.

Edinburgh is the only larger town or city where history still hangs heavy in the atmosphere. Industry and commerce have rubbed away the past in most towns so that Glasgow cathedral, for example, now stands in a city of Victorian tenements, modern high-rise blocks and public parks. Glasgow's High Street still survives but it does not excite the senses as Edinburgh's Royal Mile does, with its scores of narrow closes and names from the past, like the Old Fishmarket Close.

Edinburgh is fortunate because the old burgh's heart remains relatively intact, preserved from the ravages of industrialisation by a lack of local water and coal power; the city's main industrial areas developed further off nearer the Water of Leith, well away from the Old Town with its colleges, banking houses and churches. The town centre has also survived (so far) road and railway planners so that today no motorways or bypasses plough through the historic parts of the city. Even shopping centres and multi-storey car-parks have been kept reasonably at bay. As a result, the High Street and the Grassmarket areas retain many old houses or housing plots, and a great many features of burgh life ranging from the mercat cross and marked-out site of the tolbooth to the principal kirks, burgh ports, fragments of town wall, and plaques recalling long-lost taverns or markets.

It is, of course, best to discover in person the delights of Scotland's old burghs. Nothing can beat the fun of exploring, preferably with a little prior reading (even if only a local guidebook) and a bit of imagination. The burghs mentioned here are by no means the only places to see. Atmospheric corners await the visitor in a host of places — the old harbour part of Stonehaven, the centre of Dunbar, the cathedral area at Dunblane, the old university part of Aberdeen, old Dunkeld, the tolbooth area at Inverkeithing, central Jedburgh, most of Whithorn, most of Falkland, the High Street at Lanark, the abbey corner of Dunfermline, old Eyemouth, and so on.

There is no reason why a visit to *any* 17th-century burgh should not be rewarding. With experience, an awareness of clues and signs can be developed, and then any older town can change from just a high street with shops into a place with roots. Take a stroll through Peebles, or Falkirk, or Ayr. Have a closer look at Dundee or Dumfries, Biggar or Banff, Perth or Pittenweem, Kirkcudbright or

Kirkintilloch. Remnants of the past are all around — notice the back lanes, the long burgage plots, the closes, the street names (they're not all called after trees or local councillors!). Keep your eyes open in Brechin, Selkirk, Inverness, Dumbarton, Queensferry, Tain, Prestonpans, Forres and most other towns already mentioned in this book, for the clues *are* there.

It is true that many old burghs have grown so large that their historic centres are now lost in a sea of Victorian tenements or suburban bungalows. Fortunately it is easy to spot the difference, for there is a pattern to 17th-century streets which varies from that of later periods. For example, there are no avenues or crescents in an old burgh. Even town squares are unusual, except where the market area has been so renamed. 17th-century house plots also have no front gardens, and generally are terraced rather than detached.

The houses themselves are also easy to differentiate. In Edinburgh the first real housing changes came with the Georgian period. Although some buildings within the old burgh area were modified or rebuilt in a Classical or Georgian style, these were only a few, whereas beyond the city's heart entire streets of Georgian development sprang up. Gone were the tall, narrow 'lands' with their little windows, street-facing gable ends and dark closes. Now there were lower buildings, usually three stories high, facing the street, with tall, airy windows and hints of ancient classical architecture such as columns or porticos — very easy to spot. Edinburgh's Heriot Row or Drummond Place could never be mistaken for the Old Town!

Then came the Victorians with their solid suburban houses, set in gardens and looking every bit the residences of prosperous middle-class citizens. Or the endless streets of tenements typical of large sections of many towns, not least Glasgow and Edinburgh. As with tenement housing of the 17th century, they may have closes and stand in terraced ranks, but there the similarity ends. The difference between the houses in Edinburgh's High Street and those in, say, Gorgie or Dalry Road, is very clear and, once noticed, is not easily forgotten. The same can also be said of Glasgow, Aberdeen, Falkirk, Leith, Kirkintilloch, Perth, Hamilton and so on.

If anything, the even more solid Edwardian houses found in many suburbs are even easier to identify. They stand isolated in their own grounds, hidden behind shrubs and gates, proclaiming the doctors and lawyers and successful businessmen who once lived there. There is absolutely no similarity with any of the larger houses in 17th-century burghs — no marriage lintels, no turnpike stairs or dormer windows or crowstepped gables or coats of arms. Stirling's old town may lie only a stone's throw from the prosperous houses of the Edwardian suburbs, but the difference is plain as a pikestaff.

Of course, some towns eventually spread into industrial districts. Nowadays old Dunfermline merges into the area later built up by the spread of linen mills, but the street names change and the difference is clear. Indeed it is usually very obvious in an industrial town — the rows of Victorian back-to-back workers' houses or four-storeyed tenements, the railways or canals, names like Union Street, Railway Bar or Mill Road. The signs are usually quite plentiful, certainly enough to indicate that this is no longer the older part of a burgh.

There are some towns which have little to offer because they do not date back far enough. Whereas burghs such as Perth or Dundee or Aberdeen have changed a lot, there are nevertheless many signs of the past, but some towns do not have much of a history and they are worth mentioning, if only as a warning checklist. Most tend to be in the industrialised central part of Scotland.

The most obvious recent towns appeared during the industrial revolution of the later 18th and 19th centuries when many tiny villages became sprawling manufacturing towns. Airdrie and Coatbridge grew largely out of the 19th-century iron industry and the opening of the Monkland Canal which linked to Glasgow and the River Clyde. From that successful and thriving start much of Lanarkshire followed suit, until towns such as Motherwell and Wishaw appeared and grew into the large industrial towns they are today.

Among the easiest to spot are the mining towns — places like Newtongrange, Bonnyrigg, New Cumnock, Cowdenbeath or Glenboig — where remaining slag heaps and decaying coal pits give a clue, reinforced by the regular rows of miners' houses. The shale mining towns of West Lothian, such as Armadale, Whitburn, Midcalder or Winchburgh have a similar feel, except that the bings (remnants of the shale oil industry) are gradually being removed and landscaped; if the process is ever completed, a useful clue to the area's once-thriving past will have disappeared. Lead mining in the Lowther Hills seems to have gone on for centuries and doubtless mining communities existed from early times. The present villages of Leadhills and Wanlockhead are largely 18th and 19th-century creations, however, with the same miners' rows as elsewhere.

The textile industry has also produced quite a few comparatively recent towns, from cotton centres such as Gatehouse of Fleet, Catrine, New Lanark, Johnstone, Balfron, Fintry or Blantyre in the south and west, to the woollen towns of Alva and Tillicoultry along the 'hillfoots' of the Ochils. The great rectangular mill buildings, usually three to five storeys high, are an obvious sign of the past, but many street names are also helpful — David Livingstone, for example, was born at a house in Shuttle Row, Blantyre. It should be remembered, however, that several well-established old burghs also grew into textile towns, not least Forfar, Montrose and the other linen-making towns of Angus. The woollen mills at Stirling and Bannockburn made most of Scotland's Victorian tartan, while the border woollen towns of Galashiels and Hawick, the city of Paisley which became world-famous for its patterned cotton shawls, and Aberdeen, where there were also cotton mills, are further examples.

At the same time as the rise of industrial towns, there was much development of Scottish transport. The opening of the Forth and Clyde canal saw the birth of Grangemouth and the slow demise of Bo'ness as a seaport. Further down the Forth estuary Limekilns and Charlestown also developed as harbours. On the west coast, Oban grew into a fishing port and harbour serving the outer isles. Buckie was one of several ports in the north-east planned to exploit the North Sea fishing grounds. On the Clyde, the need for an outlet for Glasgow saw the establishment of Port Glasgow, which thrived until the Clyde was later deepened and vessels could sail further upstream. As a result, Clydebank then became an important shipbuilding town (as did the older burgh of Dumbarton). Other towns which appeared largely because of shipping include Helensburgh and Troon on the Clyde, Invergordon on the Moray Firth, Cairnryan in the south-west and Stromness in Orkney.

The agricultural improvements of the 18th and 19th centuries also saw the creation of several planned market communities, or towns with local industries based on farming products. The Square in Callander is a clue to one such town, but even more striking examples include Dufftown, Laurencekirk and Fochabers in the north-east, Castle Douglas in the south-west, Bowmore on Islay and Ormiston in East Lothian. Many were laid out in a gridiron pattern, with straight, regular streets quite different from the more straggling streets and wynds of older burghs.

The Victorian period also saw the expansion of tourism in Scotland and the development of new towns as resorts. The fashion for spas saw the particular growth of watering places and hydropathic hotels, though less so than in England where Harrogate or Cheltenham and many other places completely outshine anything north of the border. Nevertheless, towns such as Pitlochry, Moffat, Bridge of Allan, Ballater and Strathpeffer all developed around local mineral springs and a Victorian belief in 'taking the waters' — the sickly Robert Louis Stevenson was a regular visitor to Bridge of Allan, for example. The hydro hotels still seen at towns such as Peebles, Crieff or Dunblane were similar establishments but in well-rooted older burghs.

Finally there are Scotland's 'New Towns', namely East Kilbride founded in 1947, Glenrothes (1948), Cumbernauld (1955), Livingston (1962) and Irvine (1966). Plans for two others at Stonehouse in Lanarkshire and Tweedbank in the borders were shelved and now seem to have faded away. In some cases these towns have sprung from earlier villages, as at Cumbernauld where the older houses of Condorrat lie incongruously beside the concrete boxes of the newer town, or at Glenrothes where the older burghs of Leslie and Markinch have been absorbed into one larger town. There is no danger of mistaking any of the new towns (except Irvine which *was* a royal burgh) for something older — the planners have seen to that, with their regular streets, high-rise blocks, industrial estates, ring roads and pedestrianised town centres.

Three hundred years is a very long time for a burgh to survive unchanged, but most towns have at least retained the flavour of their history while some have hung on to a great deal more. The preservation of heritage has often depended in the past on the energies and interests of only a few people. Fortunately that may now be changing — the signs are that an awareness of the need to protect what remains is spreading to local authorities, thanks to the efforts of environmental groups, the individual restoration of buildings by private owners or sensitive architects, the publicity and interest-fostering work of local history groups, the excellent restoration work of the National Trust for Scotland (which also encourages people to *live* in renovated properties), local studies teaching in schools, and the commercial pressures of tourism. As a result, there are stricter planning controls and, hopefully, more appreciative planners. Almost every old burgh now has a conservation area of some kind and a start has been made to keeping whatever has survived this far. New roads bypass historic burgh centres — as at Forfar or Elgin. Urban archaeology (still too little of it) throws new light on long-buried remains. Perhaps the picture really is improving.

It would be nice to think that in ages to come, people will look back to the people of later 20th-century Scotland and thank them for preserving their history. In an age of growing mobility and rootlessness, there will surely be a desire to wonder how things used to be. With a bit of luck and effort, the wealth of burgh history under our noses today will still be there for others to learn from and enjoy later. But only if we can enjoy it now, and come to believe that it is worth keeping.

APPENDIX 1

Is your town here?

Royal burghs

This is a list of all royal burghs created up to 1707, except for a few such as Roxburgh, Rattray and Tarbert in Knapdale, which no longer exist as towns. It should be remembered that some towns, such as St. Andrews or Brechin, were burghs of barony before they became royal burghs. Others did not always remain royal burghs. In the case of some early burghs, the precise date of granting the charter is uncertain. This is shown by giving the nearest known dates within which the charter must have been written.

Aberdeen 1124—53
Airth c1195—1203
Annan 1532
Anstruther Easter 1583
        Wester 1587
Arbroath 1599
Auchterarder 1246
Auchtermuchty 1517
Auldearn 1179—82
Ayr 1203—06
Banff 1189—98
Berwick on Tweed 1119—24
Brechin 1641
Burntisland 1541
Campbeltown 1700
Clackmannan 1153—64?
Crail 1150—52
Cromarty 1264
Cullen 1189—98
Culross 1592
Cupar 1327
Dingwall 1227
Dornoch 1628
Dumbarton 1222
Dumfries 1186
Dunbar 1445
Dundee 1191—95
Dunfermline 1124—27
Dunkeld 1704

Dysart 1594
Earlsferry 1589
Edinburgh 1124—27
Elgin c1136
Falkland 1458
Forfar 1184
Forres 1130—53
Fortrose (and Rosemarkie) 1590
Fyvie 1264
Glasgow 1611
Haddington 1124—53
Hamilton 1549
Inveraray 1648
Inverbervie 1321
Inverkeithing 1153—62
Inverness 1153—65
Inverurie 1195
Irvine 1372
Jedburgh 1124—53
Kilrenny 1592
Kinghorn 1165—72
Kintore 1187—1200
Kirkcaldy 1644
Kirkcudbright 1330
Kirkwall 1486
Lanark 1153—59
Lauder 1313—28
Linlithgow c1138
Lochmaben 1440

218

Montrose 1124—53
Nairn c1190
Newburgh 1631
New Galloway 1630
North Berwick 1425
Peebles 1152—53
Perth 1124—27
Pittenweem 1541
Queensferry (South) 1636
Renfrew 1124—47
Rosemarkie and Fortrose 1590

Rothesay 1401
Rutherglen 1179—89
St. Andrews 1620
Sanquhar 1598
Selkirk 1328
Stirling 1124—27
Stranraer 1617
Tain 1439
Whithorn 1511
Wick 1589
Wigtown 1292

Burghs of Barony

This is a list of some better-known burghs of barony, created up to 1707. It does not differentiate between those, like Dunblane or Kelso, which were under church control, and the majority which were under feudal barons. Towns which subsequently became royal burghs have not been included even if, like Glasgow, they were originally burghs of barony. Some towns used to have different names; Leadhills was once called Hopetoun, Carluke used to be Kirkstyle, and so on. They are listed here under the names by which they are known today.

Aberdour 1500—01
Abernethy 1458—59
Aboyne 1676
Alford 1594—95
Alloa 1497
Auchinleck 1507
Bathgate 1663
Biggar 1451
Blackford 1706
Blairgowrie 1634
Blantyre 1598—99
Bo'ness 1668
Bothwell 1602
Buchlyvie 1672
Canongate 1587
Carluke 1662
Carnwath 1451
Ceres 1620
Coldingham 1638
Coupar Angus 1607
Crawford 1242—49

Crieff 1672
Cumnock 1509
Dalkeith 1401
Dalmeny 1616
Dollar 1702
Doune 1611
Dunblane 13th—14th cent.
Dunning 1511
Duns 1489—90
Elie 1598—99
Ellon 1707
Eyemouth 1597—98
Falkirk 1600
Fettercairn 1504
Fraserburgh 1546
Galashiels 1599
Gargunnock 1677
Girvan 1668
Glamis 1491
Gourock 1694
Grantown-on-Spey 1694

Greenock 1638
Hawick 1511
Houston 1671
Kelso 1237, 1614
Kilbarchan 1704
Killin 1694
Kilmarnock 1591—92
Kilmaurs 1527
Kilsyth 1620
Kincardine-on-Forth 1663
Kingussie 1464
Kinross 1540—41
Kirkintilloch 1211—14
Kirriemuir 1457—58
Langholm 1621
Largo 1513
Largs 1629
Leadhills 1661
Leith 1636
Lesmahagow 1668
Leven 1609
Mauchline 1510
Melrose 1605

Methil 1662
Moffat 1648
Moniaive 1363
Musselburgh 1315—28
Newton Mearns 1621
Newton Stewart 1677
Paisley 1488
Pencaitland 1505
Peterhead 1587
Polmont 1611
Port Glasgow 1668
Portpatrick 1620
Prestonpans 1552
Prestwick 1165—74
St. Monans 1596
Saltcoats 1528—29
Stonehaven 1587
Stornoway 1607
Thurso 1633
Tillicoultry 1634
Tranent 1541
Turriff 1511
Wemyss 1511

Reference tables

Coinage:

Scottish coins were worth only one-twelfth of the English equivalent. For example, £1 Scots was worth only 1s 8d Sterling (8½p) and a Scots farthing was one-twelfth of an English farthing — hardly worth anything at all. Clerks and treasurers distinguished the two by using 'Scots' (e.g. 'Twa pund Scots') and either 'Sterling' or 'Money' if the sum was calculated in English values (as often happened — the two currencies could even appear freely intermixed). The variety of coins was bewildering, but commonly used currency included:

Ryal	=	a French silver coin worth 60s Scots, later devalued to 36s 9d. Sometimes the name for a silver penny.
Merk	=	a silver coin worth 13s 4d or 1s 1⅓d Sterling (6p). Also half and quarter merks. Rarely seen as a coin but often used for reckoning.
Testoon	=	a silver coin worth 7s 4d Scots.
Dollar	=	5 shilling piece (25p).
Groat	=	a coin, originally silver, worth 4d Scots.
Bawbee	=	originally a silver coin worth 3d Scots, but more famous as a halfpenny.
Plack	=	originally worth 8d Scots, but later a copper quarter-penny.
Bodle	=	sometimes called a Hard-head and made of copper. Worth 2d Scots.

Weights:

See also Chapter 7.

The Lanark Stone	=	16 lbs.
One lb	=	2 marks or 16 ounces.
One mark	=	½ lb.
One ounce	=	16 drops.
One drop	=	36 grains of corn.

N.b. Kirkwall had its own peculiar weights, including pundlars and bismars, and also a unique method of weighting.

Liquid measures:

See also Chapter 7.

1 Scots gallon	=	8 Stirling pints or 24 Imperial pints.
1 Stirling pint	=	3 Imperial (or English) pints (said to have been 3 lbs 7 oz of 'clear running water of the Water of Leith').
1 choppin	=	½ Scots pint.
1 mutchkin	=	½ choppin.
1 jowcatt	=	¼ mutchkin.

Grain measures:

See also Chapter 7. These were used for wheat, barley etc but also for flour. The measure was not by weight but by volume — how much was needed to fill a particular container. Post-1707 Imperial firlot or bushel containers can be seen in many museums, but older ones are quite rare.

1 chalder	=	16 bolls.
1 boll	=	4 firlots.
1 firlot (or bushel)	=	4 pecks.
1 peck	=	2 gallons (loaves were often measured in gallons).

Measures of length:

See also Chapter 7.

1 ell	=	37.2 inches.
1 rood	=	1440 square ells (about one-third of an acre).

N.b. The 'Dumfries foot' was used in that town to sell cloth. Its inches seem to have been of varying length. There is an example in the local museum.

Kings and Queens:

The dates are those of *reigns*, although some monarchs, including Mary Queen of Scots and James VI were infants when they inherited the throne.

Robert I (the Bruce)	1306 – 29
David II	1329 – 71
Robert II	1371 – 90
Robert III	1390 – 1406
James I	1406 – 37
James II	1437 – 60
James III	1460 – 88
James IV	1488 – 1513
James V	1513 – 42
Mary I (Queen of Scots)	1542 – 67

James VI	1567 — 1625 (James I of England
	from 1603)
Charles I	1625 — 49
Charles II	1649 — 85 (exiled 1651 — 60, during
	Cromwell's Commonwealth)
James VII	1685 — 89
William and Mary II	1689 — 1702 (Mary died 1694)
Anne	1702 — 14 (Scotland united with England 1707)

How to find out more

Exploring an old burgh on foot can reveal much and give great pleasure, but eventually the desire to dig deeper may develop. That's when this list may be helpful. It is arranged in order of likely use.

Tourist information offices:

These can be quite useful places, provided the person at the counter has learned a few helpful facts. They may not be able to tell you how old the local castle is, but should at least be able to give you a suitable booklet or map. They will also be able to tell you what is open or closed and how much entry costs are. Some will also lay on local guided walks in the summer season. Look out for the 'Caddies' in the Royal Mile.

Local guide books and pamphlets:

Almost every old burgh now has its local guidebook or pamphlet, usually obtainable at the library, museum, tourist information office or from bookshops. Some are very much better than others; there may be a map or route to follow, or illustrations. The Angus burghs have a good series of pamphlets, as do the border towns around Hawick and Melrose. Bo'ness and Falkirk have handy little guided walk maps, as do Inverness, Elgin, Forres and Kirkwall, while Edinburgh has a host of excellent publications to help visitors explore every nook and cranny of the Royal Mile. A useful guide to Kirkcudbright has been produced by the local school, and there is also a helpful town trail for Biggar. These are, of course, just a sample available at the time of writing.

Local history booklets:

These concentrate more on burgh history, and range from the simple typed sheets left inside many old kirks to really useful, but nevertheless affordable, booklets such as *Old Thurso* by Donald Grant, *Lochmaben: its historic past* by John Wilson, *Auld Anster* by Alison Thirkell, *Selkirk 1714* by Walter Elliott or *Discover Dumfries* by James A. Harkness. Aberdeen's past is explained in a series of good booklets produced by the Friends of St. Machar's Cathedral, while the Linlithgow Civic Trust have written a useful architectural and historical guide. One of many interesting booklets on St. Andrews is an updated reprint of Dr Hay Fleming's 19th-century guide, while *The Haven under the Hill* by Elizabeth Christie gives a simple outline of Stonehaven's past. The *Exploring Scotland's Heritage* series produced by HMSO covers all parts of Scotland and offers an excellent introduction to burgh, village and rural history and the buildings and monuments which can still be seen today. Again, these are just a few of the many helpful booklets easily available in old burghs.

Local museums:

Few visitors who are really interested in burgh history will want to miss the local museum. Indeed there seem to be more museums and more visitors than ever nowadays — a very healthy picture. Many excellent museums do tend to concentrate on 18th and 19th-century history, perhaps because exhibits are easier to find, but most include enough earlier objects or explanations to make them worth visiting nevertheless. Some interesting museums are part of the local library (as at Forfar, Brechin, Huntly or Dumbarton), or art gallery, as at Stirling or Inverness. Others are larger and offer a wider selection of exhibits; those with collections of historic burgh items include Dumfries, Kirkcudbright, Hawick, Selkirk, Dingwall, Elgin, Aberdeen, Glasgow, Crail, St. Andrews, Inverkeithing, Dunfermline, Dundee, Montrose, Arbroath, Bo'ness, Edinburgh and *many* others. In addition, there are specialist museums such as the Fisheries Museum at Anstruther, the folk museums at Ceres and Glamis (among others), the weaver's house at Kilbarchan or the cathedral museums at Dunblane and St. Andrews. Don't forget that some museums, such as those at Banff or Stonehaven, are only open seasonally.

Libraries:

Once you move on to libraries, you have become a more serious explorer, for here begins the wealth of heavier reading which any historian must eventually tackle. First there are the innumerable local histories written by antiquarians and some excellent historians over the past two centuries — those dusty Victorian books with titles like *Reminiscences of old . . .* or *Traditions of . . .* They may look old-fashioned now, but many are well worth dipping into, and even reading. Some local histories, such as *A thousand years of Aberdeen* by Alexander Keith are more recent, with a more readable style. One which, from its title, might be overlooked is *Thomas Buchanan, minister of Tulliallan 1692 – 1710*, by the Rev. W. Meiklejohn, which paints an excellent and scholarly picture of the Kirk and everyday life in the burgh of Kincardine. There are also useful reference books on all sorts of specialist burgh topics, such as crafts and trade, harbours, education, domestic life, the persecution of witches, gravestones, churches and, of course, many on architecture.

Archives:

This is where *real* history begins, either in the handful of regional archive centres or at Register House in Edinburgh. Here is where you have a chance to dig into burgh, guildry, court and kirk records. Fortunately, many burgh records and accounts have been printed, which makes them easier to read, although the language still has to be understood.

As a simple guide, the language of old records is basically that which parents and teachers all over Scotland have been earnestly knocking out of children for generations — fortunately with only limited success — spelled much as it is said: 'The magistrats and counsell ordains the haill inhabitants to meit at the mercat croce the morne betuixt aucht and nyn houris in the fornoon' (Banff burgh records) or 'The baillies and counsell heirby grantes libertie to Richard Gillone, deane of gild, to build up the sessioun house with ane stair aff the streitt . . .' (Lanark burgh records) or 'The counsell ordines the thesaurare to by and furnes to the foure officiares and to the drummer and pyper, ilk ane of thame, ane garment of rid Ingleshe kaser [cashmere], viz., coit, breikis, and shankes, with whyte knettingis, wrocht in gude fassoun' (Stirling burgh records). One word of warning: *quh* sounds like *wh*, as in quha (who), umquhile (once-while, or erstwhile), or quhinger (whinger or short sword). Fortunately most printed records include a glossary.

Having familiarised yourself with the language of printed burgh records, the next step is to tackle something in the original handwritten form. This takes practice, but once breakthrough is achieved the rest is simple. Kirk records are perhaps easiest to start on, for they are often reasonably well written and spelled, and cover predictable topics, which makes indecipherable words easier to guess. From there, the world of archive documents lies before you!

Local history groups:

These are the keenest local historians, who usually know their own patch best of all. Many a learned academic has been helped along by the local knowledge of amateur historians who, year in and year out, attend lectures on local subjects, or plod along on rainy field trips, or dig up and preserve local remains. The Nithsdale local history group have already done much to preserve and restore an 18th-century lade system, for example, while the Kincardine local history group have rescued an old kirkyard from dense undergrowth, even to the point of excavating and re-erecting long-lost tombstones. Such groups thrive all over Scotland, in Ayrshire and the West of Scotland, in the Forth Valley and elsewhere. Many publish reports or helpful booklets, and most are happy to conduct visitors around on guided walks. Why not join, or if necessary form, a group yourself?

Index

abbeys: 7, 19, 20, 61, 137-8, 139
Aberdeen: 7, 11, 14, 16, 19, 20, 22, 25, 38, 45, 50, 62, 78, 83, 85, 88, 89, 98, 105, 106, 112, 113, 118, 130, 139, 140, 143, 144, 153, 155, 193, 197, 199, 207, 208, 212, 213, 214, 215; records 49, 95-6, 97, 147-8, 148, 150; buildings 74, 98, 138, 170, 174, 176, 179, 180; cathedral 137, 139, 140, 150; in wars 110, 159, 160, 161, 163, 168
Abernethy: 16, 146
Aboyne: 14, 18
Airdrie: 214
Airth: 41-2, 55, 58, 59
Alloa: 16, 22, 51, 114, 131, 132, 146
almshouses (see also individual burghs): 28, 150
Alva: 132, 215
Annan: 111, 139
Anstruther: 91, 110, 111, 158, 159, 164, 171, 198, 200
apothecaries: 194-5
apprentices: 77-8, 129-30
Arbroath: 37, 38, 105, 137, 139
Ardrossan: 44
Armadale: 214
Auchtermuchty: 5, 13, 37, 169
Ayr: 8, 10, 11, 14, 15, 20, 22, 32, 38, 52, 62, 88, 117, 164, 169, 176, 198, 212; records 85, 97

bailies: 84, 148; water bailies 88
Balfron: 215
Ballater: 216
Banff: 8, 19, 51, 212; records 3-4, 73, 82, 86, 87, 95, 102, 115, 116, 119, 120, 123, 124, 157, 176, 189, 206, 208; fairs and markets 118, 120; tolls 120; punishments 4, 99, 100, 115, 127
Bannockburn: 215
barber-surgeons: 195-6
beggars: 102-3, 112, 150-2
beheading: 98-9
bellman: 88
Berwick-upon-Tweed: 7, 8, 11, 19-20, 34, 120, 164

Biggar: 14, 41, 65, 212
Blair Atholl: 18
Blantyre: 215
Bo'ness: 15, 23, 114, 133, 155, 170, 175, 215
Bonnyrigg: 214
bowls: 201-2
Bowmore: 216
branks: 101
Brechin: 17, 36, 40, 45, 57, 60, 61, 139, 152, 181-2, 184, 193, 198, 213
Bridge of Allan: 216
bridges: 8, 12, 32, 45, 86
Bruce, Sir George: 104, 109
Buckie: 215
burgesses: honorary 75-6; power of 81, 84, 85, 92; privileges 104; taxation of 72-3; obligations of 72-3, 156, 216; housing 174-5
Burghead: 42
burghs: 5-7, 8; councils 47, 78, 82-8, 92-4, 95-8; charters 10-12, 29, 48, 69, 78, 82; royal burghs 12, 15, 16, 69, 104; of barony 14, 15, 16, 17; sources of income 85
Burntisland: 12, 21, 84, 141
butts (bow): 64

Cairnryan: 215
Callander: 215
Cambuslang: 139
Campbeltown: 17
Canongate: 47, 170
Carluke: 102
Castle Douglas: 216
castles: 9-10, 45, 157
Catrine: 215
Ceres: 60, 83, 101
Chanonry: 11
Charlestown: 215
charters: see burgh charters
Clackmannan: 12, 45, 48, 49, 51, 52, 132
Clerk (burgh official): 86, 92
clocks: 48, 49, 88, 130
closes: see streets
Clydebank: 215

coal trade: 16, 22, 104
Coatbridge: 214
coinage: 26, 221
Coldstream: 37, 65
common good fund: 85, 88
commons (grazing land etc.): 42-4, 71, 87-8, 92, 97, 119
Convention of Royal Burghs: 13, 14, 76, 85, 110
Covenanters: 13, 31, 110, 136-7, 157, 160, 161, 163, 165-6
Cowane, John: 77, 89, 104
Cowdenbeath: 214
crafts and trades: general 17, 26, 80, 89, 114, 126-7, 131-5; bakers 114, 116, 130; bonnetmakers 79; butchers 80, 87, 114, 117, 119, 127; hammermen 126, 130; maltmen 74, 80; pistolmakers 130; shoemakers 79, 80, 130; snuff-makers 181; tailors 80; tanners 180
Crail: 2, 8, 19, 20, 31, 37, 40, 45, 64, 65, 67, 105, 198, 209; tolbooth 48, 50; mercat cross 51, 52; housing 189
Cromarty: 11
Cromwell, Oliver: 13, 105, 110, 159, 164, 165
cross: see mercat cross
Cullen: 57
Culross: 2, 21, 22, 31, 36, 46, 62, 114, 131, 165, 175, 181, 182, 189, 190, 193, 209; harbour 45, 63; mercat cross 51, 53; palace 75, 109, 170, 174; tolbooth 50, 51, 58; trade 104, 105
Cumnock: 38, 52, 64, 65, 214
Cupar: 46, 170
curling: 205

Dalkeith: 47
Dalmeny: 127
Dalry: 18, 61
Darien Scheme: 112-13
Dean of Guild: 86, 92, 119, 123, 124
diet: 193
Dingwall: 11, 45, 155
Dirleton: 202
disease and illness (see also plague): 140, 196-7
doctors: see physicians, surgeons, apothecaries or barber-surgeons
doocots: see dovecots
Dornoch: 11, 19, 124
Doune: 56, 211
dovecots (doocots): 67, 172

drummer (burgh): 88-9, 90, 93
Dufftown: 215
Dumbarton: 8, 10, 111, 154, 170, 209, 213, 215
Dumfries: 8, 14, 26, 38, 40, 50, 61, 124, 138, 152, 165-6, 198, 212; defences 31, 35, 158-9, 164-5; witches 155
Dunbar: 14, 21, 22, 40, 46, 50, 139, 153, 187, 188, 212
Dunblane: 45, 60, 134, 136, 137, 139, 140, 142, 189, 210, 212, 216
Dundee: 8, 14, 17, 19, 31, 34, 37, 38, 40, 53, 57, 65, 78, 103, 105, 114, 130, 131, 138, 139, 140, 142, 144, 152, 155, 198, 212, 214; in wars 110, 159, 160, 165
Dunfermline: 7, 38, 45, 63, 65, 130, 139, 144, 170, 193, 210, 212, 214
Dunkeld: 14, 45, 60, 122, 136, 139, 159-60, 189, 212
Duns: 204
Dysart: 14, 110, 175; tolbooth 48, 50, 93

East Kilbride: 216
Edinburgh: 2, 7, 14, 23, 25, 29, 31, 45, 48, 61, 62, 65, 74, 76, 78, 83-4, 108, 111, 113, 114, 119, 120, 130, 140, 146, 148, 166, 181, 193, 198, 200, 208, 212; records 4, 74, 75, 115; population 25; Netherbow Port 35, 65, 66; layout 37, 38-9, 40, 43, 63, 64; fire in 1824 27; housing 27, 170, 178-9, 185-8, 213; mercat cross 52, 54, 207; cathedral 60; punishments at 98, 100, 155; merchants 104-5, 183; council 115, 207; medical training at 194
Elgin: 8, 10, 19, 25, 26, 31, 34, 35, 36, 37, 40, 41, 42, 45, 50, 60, 61, 64, 78, 125, 138, 140, 209, 210, 217; records 49, 54, 55, 71, 73, 86, 88, 89, 94, 97, 99, 114-15, 123, 128, 147, 162, 202; markets 52, 118, 120; school 63; crafts 126, 133; housing 177, 178, 184, 187, 188; punishments at 127, 128; cathedral 139
Elie: 35, 175
ell: 121, 122, 124, 125, 222
executions: 88, 98
Eyemouth: 22, 212

fairs: 12, 15, 43, 91, 117-20, 141-2, 205-7
Falkirk: 14, 31, 36, 40, 43, 48, 59, 64, 65, 160, 168, 198-9, 200, 212, 213
Falkland: 13, 45, 69, 170, 181, 189, 202, 212

famine: 87, 111-12, 151, 167, 197
Fettercairn: 57, 124
fines: 99, 127, 128, 146
Fintry: 215
fires: 26-7, 98, 185, 189
firlot: 121, 222
fiscal (burgh official): 86
Fochabers: 42, 215
football: 203-4
forestalling: 120, 127-8
Forfar: 34, 38, 79, 124, 155, 215, 217
Forres: 5, 8, 19, 26, 36, 41, 42, 45, 57, 62, 73, 92, 93, 116, 117, 153, 213; records 97, 99, 162, 167, 194, 203
Fortrose: 11, 119, 142; punishments 99-100
Fraserburgh: 16
friaries: see monasteries
furniture: 172-4, 180
Fyvie: 13

gaberlunzie: 102-3
Gairloch: 17
Galashiels: 14, 170, 173, 215
gambling: 205
games: (see also individual sports) 201
Gargunnock: 141
Gatehouse-of-Fleet: 215
gates, burgh: 29, 33-5, 38, 199, 209
Gifford: 51
Glasgow: 8, 14, 15, 17, 27, 31, 36, 38, 40, 42, 57, 61, 67, 88, 106, 111, 113, 123, 139, 140, 151, 190, 192, 193, 197, 198, 208, 213; records 97, 199; layout 42, 43, 45, 58, 65, 212; population 25; tolbooth 48; industries 108; destruction by fire 26
glebe: 64
Glenboig: 214
Glenrothes: 216
golf: 202-3, 204
Grangemouth: 215
Grantown-on-Spey: 42
gravestones: explanation of 131-5, 142
graveyards: see kirkyards
grazing lands: see commons
guilds: crafts or trade 79-80, 129-30, 142, 143; merchant 78, 141; function of 80-1, 92, 116
guillotine: 98

Haddington: 8, 10, 13, 14, 32, 40, 51, 57, 61, 67, 110, 140, 170, 187, 188, 189, 209, 211; school 62-3
Hamilton: 8, 36, 42, 88, 108, 123, 166, 213
handba': 204-5
Hanse: 19
harbours: description 106-7
Hawick: 16, 34, 43, 45, 57, 60, 99, 204, 211, 215; records 67, 98
Helensburgh: 215
herds (burgh): 91-2
heritors: 70-1, 72
Holyrood: 7, 139
hospitals (for aged): 88, 139
housing: general 2, 27-8, 38, 169, 191-2; before 1550 25-6; of wealthy folk 170-4; of merchants 174-5, 176-80; shop-keepers 180-4; of poor folk 184-9; 19th-century 213-14
Huntly: 45

Inchcolm: 9
industry: 108
Innergelly: 172
Inveraray: 42
Invergordon: 215
Inverkeithing: 8, 10, 25, 31, 34, 46, 51, 57, 61, 62, 85, 96, 121, 131, 170, 175, 176, 181, 212
Inverlochy: 164
Inverness: 8, 11, 17, 19, 25, 26, 38, 45, 113, 118, 129, 130, 164, 170, 213
Inveruchill: 18
Ireland: 20, 22
Irvine: 10, 15, 36, 40, 61, 88, 89, 110, 216

Jacobites: 158-9, 161-2, 164, 168
Jedburgh: 7, 8, 43, 57, 61, 64, 139, 170, 204, 212
Johnstone: 215
jougs: 54-5, 98, 101, 146

Keith: 86, 103, 124
Kelso: 7, 16, 138
Kennoway: 18
Kilbarchan: 90, 131
Kilbucho: 18
Kilmarnock: 14, 79, 148, 153, 197; records 150, 151-2, 154
Kilmaurs: 25, 50, 52
Kilsyth: 205; Battle of 110, 159
Kilwinning: 205

Kincardine-on-Forth: 17, 18, 51, 65, 131, 133, 134, 141, 147, 148-9, 150, 154, 175; records 145, 147, 154
Kinross: 51
Kippen: 131
Kirk (as an institution): and personal behaviour 95, 144, 145, 146, 147-9, 201, 202-3, 205, 207-8; and education 144, 152-4; and poverty 144, 150-2
kirk buildings (see also under individual burghs): 2, 45, 59-62, 141, 146, 164
Kirkcaldy: 21, 40, 105, 110, 152, 175, 198
Kirkcudbright: 36, 40, 58, 147, 152, 188, 212
Kirkintilloch: 15, 213
kirk sessions: 144, 207
Kirkwall: 6, 152, 204, 209
kirkyards: 2, 3, 62, 63, 64, 114, 131-2, 141-2, 175-6, 201
Kirriemuir: 14, 42, 63, 141

Lanark: 8, 10, 25, 42, 44, 45, 46, 57, 59, 62, 65, 67, 75, 76, 92, 99, 113, 120, 121, 123, 126, 129, 155, 169, 209, 212; records 73, 102, 127-8, 162, 163, 167, 168, 206; layout 34, 36, 40, 41, 64; defences 31, 34; militia 156, 167; burgh council 83, 84, 86, 87, 88, 92, 98, 99, 116; tolbooth 46, 47, 167; fairs 118, 206; shops 117; weights 123, 124; craftsmen 79, 80, 126-7; housing 169, 170, 191; school 62; Corpus Christi procession 142-3
lanes: see streets
Langholm: 43
Larbert: 79
Largs: 118-19
Lauder: 36, 42, 50, 60, 65, 111, 141
Laurencekirk: 215
law and order (in burghs): 87
Leadhills: 215
Leith: 14, 16, 19, 20, 22, 37, 45, 105, 107, 108, 112, 152, 164, 176, 198, 213; wine trade 106-7
Leslie: 216
liberty lands: 11
licensing hours: 116
Limekilns: 215
Linlithgow: 5, 8, 14, 31, 34, 35, 38, 40, 44, 45, 50, 60, 65, 69, 70, 84, 89, 117, 121, 136, 139, 140, 164, 165, 177, 209; guilds 79-80, 97; trade at 117
Livingston: 216

Lochmaben: 159
Lockerbie: 43
Longforgan: 57

marches: see riding the marches
markets: 12, 52-3, 97-8, 119-20; regulations 120
Markinch: 216
Master of Works (burgh official): 86
Maybole: 40, 48, 170, 205
Melrose: 7, 8, 35, 45, 52, 101, 205
mercat crosses (see also under individual burghs): 2, 50-5, 125
merchants (see also housing): 13, 71, 72, 80, 84, 92, 104-5, 113; social position 107-8
Methil: 23
Midcalder: 214
mills: 66-7
Milntoun of Ore: 18
Minto: 18
minstrel, burgh: 88
Moffat: 216
monasteries: 7, 8, 19
Monck, General: 110, 136, 159, 160
Moniaive: 52
Montrose: 8, 17, 19, 23, 36, 40, 57, 78, 105, 149, 152, 183, 215
Montrose, Duke of: 110, 159, 160, 163, 165
Motherwell: 214
museums (see also under individual towns): 1, 2, 89, 123, 130, 225
Musselburgh: 48, 51, 202

Nairn: 8, 10, 19, 118
New Lanark: 215
Newtongrange: 214
North Berwick: 61, 115

Oban: 215
Ormiston: 51, 216

packmen: 11, 81, 104, 113-14, 119
Paisley: 4, 87-8, 91-2, 113, 139, 155, 190, 198, 215
Peebles: 8, 36, 44, 57, 99, 111, 114, 138, 139, 140, 152, 167, 190, 212, 216; records 56, 58, 93-4, 97, 108, 117, 152, 156, 162, 163, 167, 199; defences 31, 32, 156; burgh council 82-3, 88, 92, 93, 97, 206; heritors 71-2; fairs 12, 118, 205; punishments 128

pends: see streets
penny weddings: 147
Perth: 7, 8, 10, 14, 19, 20, 25, 26, 31, 35, 37, 45, 57, 61, 78, 105, 111, 114, 131, 152, 155, 164, 197, 198, 203, 212, 213, 214
Peterhead: 22
physicians: 194
pipers, burgh: 76, 88, 89-91, 93
Pitlochry: 216
Pittenweem: 21, 37, 40, 59, 155, 170, 172, 174, 187, 188, 212
plague: 23, 198-200
Pleasance: 64-5
poinder (burgh official): 87-8
police: see law and order
population distribution: 23, 24, 38
Port Glasgow: 215
Portpatrick: 67
Portree: 18
Port Seton: 23
poverty: 102-3
Prestonpans: 51, 52, 54, 67, 78, 141, 177, 213
Prestwick: 52, 197
provost (burgh official): 82-4, 92
punishments (see also jougs, stocks, tolbooths etc.): 3, 54, 88, 98-102, 115-16, 129, 146, 148; burgess ticket destroyed 73, 93; stool of repentance 146, 149, 208

Queensferry (South): 48, 118, 170, 213

races: 206
regrating: 128
Renfrew: 7, 15, 110
riding the marches: 43, 53-4, 87
Rob the Ranter: 91
Rosemarkie: 11, 141-2
Rossie: 57
Roxburgh: 7, 13, 120
Rutherglen: 7

St. Andrews: 3, 7, 14, 25, 26, 31, 32, 34, 35, 37, 40, 45, 57, 61, 64, 76, 83, 98, 110, 113, 131, 142, 146, 155, 188, 198, 202, 209; records 208; cathedral 136
Saltcoats: 23, 44
salt trade: 22, 108
schools: (see also individual burghs, and under Kirk) 28, 45, 62-3, 74, 152-4
Scone: 9

Selkirk: 7, 12, 31, 35, 37, 42, 83, 87, 111, 113, 126, 154, 155, 165, 180, 213; population 24, 75, 76, 79, 129; mercat cross 52; water supply 97; fairs 117
sexual offences: 146-7, 148
shops: 47, 114, 117, 183
ships: 19, 22, 105-6, 111, 191
Simpson, Habbie: 90, 91
skating: 205
smuggling: 128-9
Solway Firth: 21
stallingers: 76, 119
Stenton: 58-9
Stirling: 2, 3, 7, 8, 10, 12, 14, 20, 25, 36, 45, 61, 69, 77, 88, 98, 104, 105, 108, 114, 120, 121, 122, 128, 129, 131, 140, 156, 162, 190, 193, 198, 202, 205, 209, 215; records 76, 81, 95, 116-17, 123, 145, 162, 163, 166-7, 189, 194, 196, 205; population 25; layout 37, 40, 64, 210-12; defences 31, 32-3, 34, 35, 157, 158, 161-2; council 92, 95, 116, 165, 189; tolbooth 50; mercat cross 51, 52, 54, 56; housing 72, 95, 128, 170, 171, 177-8, 180, 183, 186, 188, 214; fairs and markets 120, 205; crafts and trades 128, 132; guildry 78, 81, 88, 116, 130, 141, 200; punishments 100, 116; Holy Rude Kirk 60, 136, 138, 141, 150-1; plague 199-200; bridge 12, 13, 47, 120, 159; school 63, 152, 153, 154; drummer 89
Stobo Kirk: 146
stocks (see also under individual burghs): 3, 55-6, 98-9
Stonehaven: 22, 38, 110, 137, 160, 210, 212
Stornoway: 17
Stranraer: 25, 36, 81
Strathpeffer: 216
streets: general 2, 33, 63-4, 65, 190-1, 209, 213; layout 26, 29, 30, 36-41, 59, 68, 183-4, 216; filth and cleaning 85, 97, 169, 193-4
Stromness: 215
surgeons: 194-5, 196

Tain: 11, 14, 25, 36, 44, 48, 60, 67, 97, 192, 213
Tarbat: 18
Tarland: 18
tennis: 202-3
theatre: 206-7

Thurso: 6, 17, 52-3, 118
Tillicoultry: 215
tolbooths (see also under individual
    burghs): 2, 28, 45, 46, 85, 94, 98;
    explanation of 46-51
tolls: 47, 104, 120
town crier: see bellman
town guard: 53
trade (foreign): 11, 12-13, 15, 16-17, 18,
    85, 104, 168; in 13th century 18-21, 26;
    in 16th century 21-3; in 17th century
    104-7, 109-10, 112-14, 126
treasurer (burgh official): 85, 92
tron (weighbeam): 45, 57-9
Troon: 215
Tulliallan: see Kincardine-on-Forth
Tullibody: 64

unfreemen: 76, 77
Union of the Crowns (1603): 2, 69, 109
Union of the Parliaments (1707): 2, 22,
    109, 123
universities: 45, 63, 130, 153, 154

vennels: see streets

walls, of burghs: 29-33, 157
Wanlockhead: 22, 215
waupenschaws: 156-7
weights and measures (see also tron): 58,
    86, 120-5, 221
wells: 65, 97
Wemyss: 48, 130
Westquarter doocot: 67
Whitburn: 214
Whithorn: 6, 8, 36, 60, 140, 212
Wick: 11
Wigtown: 37
Winchburgh: 214
Wishaw: 214
witches: 155
women: 74-5, 76, 101
wynds: see streets